ORGY PLANNER WANTED

ORGY PLANNER WANTED

❖ ❖ ❖ ❖ ❖

ODD JOBS AND CURIOUS CAREERS
IN THE ANCIENT WORLD

VICKI LEÓN

Quercus

First published in Great Britain in 2007 by

Quercus
21 Bloomsbury Square
London
WC1A 2NS

Originally published in the United States
as *Working IX to V* by Walker & Company, New York

A CIP catalogue record for this book is available from the British Library

ISBN 1 84724 096 8
ISBN-13 978 1 84724 096 5

Printed and bound in Great Britain by Clays Ltd, St Ives plc.

10 9 8 7 6 5 4 3 2 1

A NOTE ON THE AUTHOR

Author of thirty nonfiction books, including the popular Uppity Women series, Vicki León wanders widely but calls California home. In her travels, she's worked at a variety of bizarre jobs, from egg polisher on an Israeli kibbutz to film extra in Greece, a CV that gives her added empathy for her subject matter. León delights in historical research, calling it "the most satisfying form of time travel."

By the Same Author
Uppity Women of Ancient Times
Uppity Women of Medieval Times
Uppity Women of the New World
Uppity Women of the Renaissance

CONTENTS

TEN DOOMED CAREERS & DEATHLESS PURSUITS

ACKNOWLEDGMENTS

A book like this is a mosaic, painstakingly assembled with the knowledge and help of countless people along the way, from coin experts, archaeologists, and historians to local sources in Italy, Greece, Turkey, Israel, Spain, and elsewhere.

My special thanks and everlasting gratitude also go out to the following people and places:

❖ my agent David Forrer; co-director of subsidiary rights Susan Hobson; and the stellar staff at InkWell Management;

❖ my editor, Michele Amundsen, and George Gibson of Walker & Company, who believed in me from the beginning;

❖ my excellent copy editor, Phil Gaskill, and Walker & Company's managing editor, Michael O'Connor;

❖ Julian Alexander at LAW Ltd, Anthony Cheetham of Quercus Publishing, and RCS Libri Sonzogno of Italy, who also believed;

❖ the Morro Bay library staff and their amazing ways of retrieving obscure reference works for me;

❖ and Stan Thompson, whose patience, photographic genius, and tolerance for oversized tomes taking over his living space are exemplary.

MONEY MATTERS IN THE ANCIENT WORLD

The Greeks and Romans lacked paper currency, but had quite a lineup of coinage and an array of mysterious abbreviations for them. Fortunately, this book will not subject you to their intricacies. Frequently mentioned mediums of exchange and their approximate buying power:

GREEK
THE OBOL: smallest silver coin; six obols = one drachma
THE DRACHMA: roughly equivalent to the Roman denarius
THE TALENT: not a coin but a large sum represented by its weight in gold or silver; six thousand drachmas = one talent

ROMAN
THE SESTERCE: a bronze coin; four sesterces = one denarius
THE DENARIUS (PLURAL DENARII): a silver coin
THE AUREUS (PLURAL AUREI): a gold coin; twenty-five denarii = one aureus

As you'll see throughout this book, daily wages often fell in the one- to three-drachma (or the equivalent in denarii) range—or less. Countless jobs also paid by piecework, from the Acropolis sculptures to brickmaking. The lack of records, along with inflation and coinage debasement, make it difficult to assess buying power over centuries. It's safe to say that a tiny percentage had obscene wealth, while most workers scraped by, aided by a few social programs. For instance, a baker or a carpenter might earn fifty denarii a day, then spend twenty-four denarii to buy two pounds of pork to feed their family.

Annual pay for legionary soldiers went from 112 denarii in the second century B.C. to 300 denarii per year in A.D. 83. But their daily bread and other expenses were deducted from that sum.

On Emperor Diocletian's list of wage and price ceilings of A.D. 301, a bushel of wheat or beans cost one hundred denarii and a gallon of the cheapest wine, sixty-four denarii. It would take a teacher with four pupils a month to earn that sum.

At the other end of the scale: in the first century A.D., a man needed a net worth of one million sesterces to qualify for Roman senatorship.

INTRODUCTION

Two thousand years ago, a world uncannily like ours moved at a hustle, its people working a jaw-dropping assortment of jobs to earn their daily bread. Instead of going on a Mediterranean diet, they ate one. Their traders made a killing, traveling on business. So did their food products and manufactured wares, sailing in superfreighters or moving around an intercontinental highway system fifty-three thousand miles long.

That world, spreading like an anaconda around the Mediterranean and Black seas and into the Atlantic, we now call the Roman Empire. A deceptive tag, since its political expansion began around 220 B.C. when Rome was still a republic. Like the anaconda, the republic-turned-empire swallowed cultures whole to get to its size. It didn't digest them, however. Instead, its new subjects were free to swear in their native languages and worship their own gods.

The head honchos had an ingenious corporate policy: rather than force those they conquered to assimilate, they adopted the best-loved customs, festivals, and deities of their new subjects, a neat trick called syncretism. Being rather intimidated by Greek culture, they stole it wholesale, lifting great chunks of science and the arts, giving new names to ancient deities.

The Roman Empire was all about business. To conduct it, everyone used two lingua francas, Latin and Greek. People shared the same laws, calendar, and currencies. The ease of buying and selling, safeguarded by a standing army of peacekeepers, made this early version of the European Union boom.

Across this world, workers put in their eight hours between dawn and 3 P.M. Weekends off? The concept didn't exist yet. Instead, there were growing numbers of festivals, emperors' birthdays, theater-bloodsport-and-racing days, and evil-omen dates on which no work could be done. In A.D. 165, Emperor Aurelius froze the runaway holiday calendar to 135 days a year. However, by A.D. 354, it had risen to 177 days of leisure—or its possibility. (Like our official holidays, many people had to work while others played.)

On the job, employees gossiped about their superiors and jockeyed for perks. When management took a long lunch, they checked their horoscopes. They made bets on favorite teams while snacking at fast-food joints. They met for drinks at the end of the workday. From CEOs to entry-level employees, everyone griped about taxation on almost everything. Everyone, that is, except the gainfully employed legions of bean-counters and papyrus-shufflers who collected taxes.

Some job-holders had nest eggs; a great many more had crushing debts. Most socialized at work-related associations, which helped them squirrel away money for a decent burial. Certain workers, notably the military, got lump-sum pensions upon retirement. Others spent their later years in retirement colonies. Most civilians, however, got nothing. For health care, they sought help at holistic centers like the sanctuaries of Asclepius, god of healing.

Even their growth industries anticipated ours. Government bureaucracy and the military were big business. Likewise entertainment and spectator sports, from musical theater to celebrity-studded chariot racing. Construction for new colonies, new ports, grander temples, and second villas for senators kept carpenters, plumbers, crane operators, hydraulic engineers, salvage divers, and surveyors busy. Agribusiness, especially wheat, wine, and olive oil, was huge, supplying the staff of life to three continents. Much of it was shipped and stored in clay amphorae, the cheap, recyclable packaging of the day—itself a moneymaker for manufacturers.

Small businesses thrived everywhere. Fast-food outlets, wine shops, and service jobs like signwriters, town criers, anointers, tattoo removers, and armpit pluckers kept the economy rolling. There were less respectable operations, most of them infamous but perfectly legitimate: auctioneer, gladiator trainer, and the informer or accusation specialist. Posts of more prestige included an alphabet soup of priests, entrail readers, and oracle utterers.

At mid-sized enterprises, workers built ships, fashioned chariot wheels, made bricks, sculpted bronze. The biggest civilian employer? A glossy, full-service version of the spa industry: the public baths, thousands of them, employing workforces in every town and city from Spain to Syria, Gaul to the Black Sea.

But the Roman Empire, this Greco-Roman fusion of labor and energy, was also a world unlike ours. The biggest difference? Their tools. Instead of relying on combustion engines and high technology, they used living tools: millions of human beings, male and female, young and old. Owners called their tools *servus* (source of our word "servant"); we'd call them slaves.

In their minds, widespread slavery was normal and justifiable. Their warfare had no prisoner exchange, no POW camps. Instead of killing all opponents and civilian bystanders, they opted to enslave most of them, often selling to middlemen like pirates. Slavery engulfed people in other ways: if you were a debtor, criminal, abandoned baby, or child of a slave, you could find yourself in human bondage.

Religious beliefs gave slavery a tenuous moral underpinning, since the gods decreed the star you were born under, your status. You might also become a slave due to some disaster, a word that literally meant "bad star." There was wiggle room for upward mobility, too. For instance, during one thirty-year period B.C., records show that over half a million men and women were emancipated, most going on to more prosperous lives.

These factors made the labor force a mix of slaves, freedmen, and freeborn. Enterprises from bakeries to funeral homes had workers from all classes, side by side. The exacting art of exquisite Greek temples, the construction of the noblest buildings in Athens and Antioch and Alexandria were done by teams of subcontractors, slave and free, often paid the same daily rates.

Over the centuries, regardless of who happened to be in power—king, tyrant, citizen assembly, senators, emperor—a class and gender system tried to keep people in their fate-designated seats. That effort was often unsuccessful. Women, for example, sashayed their way into all sorts of jobs and "inappropriate" activities, from philanthropy to freelance gladiating. Further social mobility came from the Roman patron-client system, a more benign forerunner of the godfather syndrome.

Nevertheless, a fraction of one percent held staggering wealth. Roman fat cats accumulated assets in the hundreds of millions of sesterces; they could buy their own armies—and some did. They could pay the yearly budget of the entire military if they chose. (Though they never did.) One filthy-rich Greek city-state even passed a law giving women advance notice for celebrations so they'd have a full year to shop for the glitziest clothing and jewelry. That state was Sybaris, the source of our term "sybaritic."

A much fatter percentage of the populace lived on the razor edge of beggary. Even the most hardworking could be poor. In the peacefully prosperous reign of Augustus, a Roman schoolteacher made the same pitiful amount per month as a mule-driver.

Beyond uncovering the parallels and contrasts of our working world and theirs, these pages brush away the dust of centuries to reveal the human faces of long ago, telling the unsung stories of wage slaves and big shots, giving new meaning to ancient battles through the woes of soldiers and generals.

As historian Professor Brian Fagan once put it, "People, in all their diversity and quirkiness, not sites and artifacts, are what drove history and human societies."

Through these working lives and personal moments, you'll glimpse the bedrock of ideas and ideals on which our own lives are lived. Our notions of law, science, sexuality, and psychology are Greek and Roman. Our language is riddled with words and concepts they invented. Without their cultural DNA, we can't even discuss politics or philosophy or architecture.

Understanding where we came from and what our long-ago ancestors did for a living has an added bonus. Examining the past, getting insights from it, may give us a better handle on how our own societies work—or could work better.

The "nothing new under the sun" learning process began for me aged ten, a bookwormish enthusiast of the ancient world. Once a young woman, circumstances gave me the chance to live and work in the sunny, thyme-scented lands around the Mediterranean for years—a stroke of good fortune that also let me study Romance languages and other tongues.

During my wanderlust years in seven countries, I saw first-hand the artifacts used by ancient working people, from bakers' ovens to gladiators' helmets; read hundreds of inscriptions left by them or their co-workers about their jobs and civic honors; admired countless tombstones, monuments, and mausoleums on which were artfully depicted the working lives of plumbers, butchers, authors, legionaries, cooks, contractors, and more, ad infinitum.

By degrees, I came to understand the enormous Greco-Roman pride in work, their deep longing to be remembered as individuals of the community. Not just as a family man, but as the town's best baker. Not just as a wife and mother, but as a talented jeweler.

Unlike Julius Caesar, as I came and saw, I myself was conquered by the workaday worlds that slowly opened their doors to me. More intensive study allowed me to glean from an amazing breadth of primary source materials, including archaeological digs that uncovered worksites from barber shops to roadside inns. Other excavations, like Egypt's Kellis, called the "desert Pompeii," showed me how far-flung cities gained fame for their workmanship. The recent work done in underwater archaeology continues to confirm ancient writings, revealing the robust nature of a long-ago economy and the global reach of its goods.

Research also helped me smoke out fond clichés and Hollywood-inspired myths. On these pages, you'll get the lowdown on galley slaves, gladiator lifespans, the secret business life of Vestal Virgins, and even the real nature of ancient orgies.

In the end, I was thunderstruck to realize that my own astonishment and fascination came from a language that was far from dead: Latin. "Astonish" from *attonare*, to be struck by lightning, a bolt from the blue. "Fascination" from *fascinum,* the all-purpose phallic symbol that the Greeks and Romans carried to ward off bad luck so that good luck might find its way.

My enthusiasm for this work also came as a gift from the ancients. For the Greeks, *enthusiasmos* meant an ecstatic state: being god-possessed, at least momentarily.

Like Studs Terkel, Barbara Tuchman, and other historians I admire, this book talks about people and livelihoods you won't hear about in other books or films or television miniseries. These ordinary people and the jobs they did, the interests they had, the struggles they endured, are only "ancient" in chronological time, in artificial constructs like B.C. and A.D. Their deeds, their heroics, even their skullduggeries are timeless; they are a mirror in which you and I can more clearly see ourselves.

Vade mecum—come with me. And prepare to be thunderstruck.

ONE

MY BOSS IS A REAL SLAVE-DRIVER

❖ PIRATE ❖

FLESH-PEDDLERS ON THE BOUNDING MAIN

Pirates wouldn't turn down a cask of pearls or a hold filled with wine, but frankly, they preferred flesh-and-blood merchandise: passengers and crews, ideally on a nice fat grain-ship that might carry up to a thousand souls.

Two thousand years ago, demand for slave labor was like the California real estate market: everyone said it couldn't keep going up, but it did. Pirates were its major suppliers.

After a hard day's attack, these professional abductors delivered their terrified live goods to one of several wholesale outlets. The Greek islands of Crete, Delos, and Chios were superstores of slavery, along with several commercial ports in Asia Minor (present-day Turkey). According to the Greek historian Strabo, Delos alone could process ten thousand slaves in a day. Their motto? "Sail in and unload—everything's as good as sold!"

How did pirates manage to abduct with such ease? They used ships that were swifter and more maneuverable than the ones they chased; hot-looking vessels too, adorned with gilded sails and purple awnings. When such a rig came over the horizon, the sight must have frozen the blood of sea voyagers.

Giving chase was fun, but pirates weren't too proud to take advantage of a shipwreck or a vessel in trouble. Your average pirate had no qualms about kidnap or extortion on dry land, either. Over the years, pirates squeezed tribute out of more than four hundred cities and towns around the Mediterranean and Black seas. At its peak, the outlawry business fielded over nine hundred pirate vessels.

Not every pirate toed the line; a few rogues even went quasi-legitimate. City-states like Sparta hired them to harry its Athenian enemies. Rulers like Mithridates, king of Pontus, employed them and even joined their raids at times.

While at work, pirates occasionally captured someone of importance and put in a ransom demand, but it wasn't good business practice. Poor cash flow, for one thing. For another, demands could backfire. Take the misguided Julius Caesar abduction. Snagged by a band of Cilician buccaneers and ransomed for twenty-five silver talents, the ungrateful ransomee promptly returned to their lair and had his troops crucify everyone.

Homicide was a job-related risk, occasionally reducing pirate numbers. But the rewards of sea-going roguery had great appeal to unemployed workers—mercenaries, for instance. Warring nations regularly paid mercenaries to fight; but once the conflict was over, downsizing took its toll.

By the first century B.C., the employment numbers for pirates began to look bleak. Word came down that piratical workers had been *too* successful at meeting their goals. They'd knocked off one too many superfreighters, putting the food supply of Rome itself in jeopardy. It was time for a hostile takeover. With unlimited resources behind him, Roman general Pompey roared into action, driving most flesh-peddling pirates out of business.

A mere handful of survivors ran for the lawless waters of the Black Sea, where they plundered in relative safety for a century until the Romans made another sweep. Although a few aging buccaneers limped along, plying their noxious trade, their golden age of full employment was over, not to be revived until the 1500s.

❖ MANGON ❖

MIDDLEMAN OF THE SLAVE TRADE

Slavery was pervasive in ancient times. Even the most enlightened believed it to be the natural order of things. Given that circumstances from war to shipwreck to piracy often turned lives upside-down, this belief system had a lot of holes in it. One of the few Greek voices to question slavery was the playwright Euripedes.

Slavers, or *mangones*, the dirtiest link in the chain of human trafficking, were a scummy lot, probably laughing all the way to their treasure chests. Mangones like Thoranius, an infamous flesh-peddler during the reign of Emperor Augustus, were shamefully wealthy. They led busy lives, often following armies into battle—at a safe distance, of course. Once the fighting was over, instead of housing and feeding inconveniently huge numbers of prisoners of war, the victors sold the losers to the slave dealers for a pittance. Warfare also involved the capture of villages and noncombatants; in this fashion, the slavers snapped up women and children as well.

When hostilities were slow, slavers found prey in other places. Children abandoned by their parents and left at temples were fair game. So were unwanted infants of prostitutes and paupers. Most frequently, slavers bought their raw material from pirates, reselling them on the retail market.

Major auction venues existed on the three aforementioned Greek islands and on the mainland of Asia Minor at Side, Ephesus, and Sardis. Athens and Rome had secondary markets. At these markets, human misery from all races and creeds was amply represented: Alexandrians to Sarmatians, Persians to Gauls, Jews to Ethiopians.

At auction, the slaver prodded the item for sale onto a raised platform. He or she typically stood naked with a scroll tied around his or her neck. The scroll spelled out the slave's health, nation, and age, and warranted that the item had no tendencies toward thievery, suicide, or epilepsy. This guarantee came with a six-month return policy; slaves sold without a warranty wore special caps. Fancy goods, such as Greek doctors, actors, eunuchs, and beautiful boys, brought the highest prices and were often sold to purchasers in private.

Slave traders occasionally came to bad ends, killed by irate gladiator slaves or poisoned by rivals. But perhaps the most gruesome fate was the one that befell Panionios, a slaver from Chios. He specialized in buying good-looking boys, removing their testicles, then selling the ones who survived for big money to Eastern potentates.

One of his victims was Hermotimus, who ended up as the favorite eunuch in the service of Persian king Xerxes. Much later in life, Hermotimus ran into Panionios, pretended to befriend him, and got the unsuspecting slaver in his power. He forced Panionios to castrate his own four sons—then compelled the sons to do the same to their father! This grisly but apparently true story of revenge came from the historian Herodotus, who lived and wrote in that era.

It's easy for modern readers to be appalled at the bloody, hard-hearted realities of long ago. But perhaps we should aim our outrage at today's heartless trafficking of countless children and adults from Latin America, Asia, and other regions into the rich countries of the West, where the sellers find a ready market. Modern slavers and an ancient evil are still with us.

❖ CLOCK-WATCHER ❖
GOT THE TIME? MY SUNDIAL'S STOPPED

Clock-watching tends to be frowned on today—not so in the Athens of long ago. When courts were in session, a specialist riveted his gaze on the clock as the day's cases were argued before one of those big fat Greek juries of 201 (or more) male citizens.

The clock watched by the clock-watcher slave was a *clepsydra*, which the Greeks called a "water-thief."

The device positioned two clay or bronze pots, one sitting above the other. After the top pot was filled, a standardized hole at its bottom let the water stealthily escape into the lower pot. The clepsydra held enough liquid to fill a regular six-gallon amphora. Besides announcing when it had emptied, the clock-watcher had to "stop the clock" with a wax plug from time to time while documents were being read aloud in court. Water-thieves came in different sizes. Smaller clepsydrae held about six minutes' worth of water, so the clock-watcher had to be on his toes.

The Greeks and later the Romans never did settle on a standard sixty-minute hour and twenty-four-hour day. Instead, for their version of daylight saving, they made summer "hours" gradually expand up to seventy-five minutes on June 21, and winter "hours" gradually shrink to a modest forty-five minutes on December 21.

Since hours varied by season, the loquacious Greeks opted to prioritize. A major criminal trial would be given a certain number of amphorae of water, while minor disputes, like a right of inheritance case, got less. The accused, who often defended himself in that largely lawyer-free era, got more time than the accuser.

Roman courts also used water-thieves to time all parties. They alternated, giving the accuser two amphorae's worth of time and the accused, three amphorae—all of these intervals verbally announced by a court-appointed clock-watcher.

Greeks and Romans sometimes clock-watched at home, using smaller glass clepsydrae. The army also put military clock-watchers and water-thieves to good use at night, for the accurate changing of sentries.

Water-clocks were old news, developed by cultures in China and Egypt. The Greeks probably borrowed theirs from the temple priests of the Nile, who used the timepiece to carry out their nightly religious rituals.

Although sundials couldn't perform at night or in weather where no shadow was cast, Greeks and Romans were fond of putting them in public places. During republican times, victorious Roman troops hauled an oversized example called the Great Sundial of Catania into the Forum; since it was set for the latitude of southern Italy, however, the time it kept was decidedly off. That matter was remedied a mere ninety-nine years later, when Roman officials erected a new sundial calibrated for local time.

Sundials aside, Rome kept its citizens up to the minute in a vocal way. At midday, a time-keeper slave would shout out the hour as the sun moved between two celebrated buildings in the Forum. Thanks to the writings left by their contemporaries, we get glimpses of these men who were literally slaves to the clock and the time-honored job they did.

❖ HOPLITE SLAVE ❖
PERSONAL ASSISTANT TO AN ARMORED WARRIOR

Much has been made of the glorious hoplite, the middle-class Greek citizen who answered his city-state's call to war as an unpaid volunteer. Named for the *hoplon*, the three-foot circular shield of wood and bronze he carried, the citizen-warrior set out nearly every summer to defend the homeland. With him on this mighty quest went seventy pounds of bronze shin-guards, chest armor, and helmet, plus a shield, a sword, and an eight-foot lance.

Each man paid thirty drachmas (the going rate for six good oxen) for his gear. In Athens, males from eighteen to sixty years old had to serve in the military, so more than a few of these hoplites were gray-haired and creaky. (Philosopher Socrates was a senior hoplite.)

Greece being an agricultural society and fond of tradition, Greeks fought each other in ritualized ways. Invariably in the summer (when males on both sides had fewer chores), usually on flat areas, they held one brief battle of brute strength, shield to shield. As infantrymen, hoplites fought in a close-massed rectangular formation called the phalanx, five to eight men deep, using their bodies to push and their javelins to thrust. Once one side broke the other's formation, the hoplites usually dropped their shields and took off running. That was when most casualties occurred, rather than during the battle itself, as archers and cavalry troops picked off the fugitives.

Before you pity the hapless hoplite, take a look at who actually did most of the heavy lifting. The unsung heroes of Greek combat were actually the personal slaves. Each hoplite had his own guy who toted all the gear and dressed his owner in battle armor.

29

After each battle, the slave cleaned the gore off the equipment and his owner, served him wine, then got cracking on the evening meal—usually a mix of barley groats and cheese, heavy on the onions.

Very occasionally, the Greeks and later the Romans saw fit to allow male slaves to fight wars or defend the homeland. It wasn't necessarily their homeland to begin with, of course. Most slaves weren't born slaves. A large percentage of them got that way by being on the losing side somewhere else: captured as prisoners of war and promptly sold.

❖ SILVER MINER ❖
TALK ABOUT A DEAD-END JOB

The Greeks never did manage to organize themselves into a nation. Instead, for five hundred years or more, their city-states fought almost nonstop—making and unmaking alliances to crush the other guy. As a result of that warfare, victors tended to kill or sell male losers, and enslave females and younger civilians. Women served several purposes and, moreover, could make new slaves. Children were even easier to train and discipline. Besides, they ate less and had a longer life ahead. Well, some did.

During the golden age of Athens, its public projects, from the temples on the Acropolis to its works of art, were largely financed by the rich silver mines it owned at Laurium. To exploit them, upper-crust Athenians operated a rent-a-slave program.

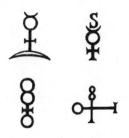

People once believed that spirits resided in everything. They used these symbols to depict the spirits of silver, mercury, copper, and tin.

According to the writings of Xenophon and other historians, citizens like General Nicias leased a thousand of his slaves to the mine concessionaires, earning an obol a day on each. Other owners leased hundreds of their own slaves in the same fashion. Over the decades, hundreds of thousands of men slaved in horrendous conditions at Laurium. The grimmest abuse? Child miners, young boys of ten or so. Their small bodies were ideal for work in the claustrophobically tight quarters of the hot underground shafts.

A typical day for a silver miner was spent flat on his back in a coffin-sized hole, digging out ore with a bronze pick by torchlight. After collecting ore in baskets, he passed it, fireman fashion, to the next wretched slave and so on. There were two thousand mine shafts at Laurium, accessed by crude pegs of wood pounded into the dirt; some went as deep as 390 feet.

When darkness fell, there was no respite; slaves big and small were fed poorly. Many were kept in shackles. On the surface next to the mine shafts, charcoal fires constantly burned, smelting the ore and filling the air with poisonous fumes.

No attempt was made to make life more humane for the mining slaves— they were foreigners, prisoners of war, even the boys. As they became injured or died, they were replaced by new captives. Laurium was notorious for its evil conditions, but other mining operations were little better.

For centuries, Rome derived much of its silver and gold from Egypt and Spain. In the second century B.C., forty thousand slaves, male and female, worked the silver mines near Cartagena, Spain. Life expectancy? Three months. During Vespasian's ten-year emperorship, captive labor clawed the equivalent of nearly 450 million dollars in gold out of Spanish mines. Rome invaded Britain largely to exploit its resources of tin, lead, and silver. Two years after the invasion, two-hundred-pound lead ingots were coming from the island, extracted by enslaved workers.

Did mining slaves ever escape their harsh bondage? Rarely. Archaeologists estimate that in one century, up to thirty thousand men and boys may have sweated and died in the silver mines of Laurium, Athens's sad and dirty secret behind its shining coins and temple.

❖ ❖ ❖ ❖ **TIRO** ❖ ❖ ❖ ❖

Fastest scribbler in Rome

The boy was born a slave on a farm owned by M. T. Cicero, known then and now as one of Rome's greatest orator-authors. Early on, Cicero noticed the child's intelligence and had him educated. Nicknamed Tiro or "beginner," he wasn't for long.

In due course, Tiro became Cicero's personal scribe, a far from easy job. While a skilled scribe could take down 35 words per minute, an orator could orate 150 words per minute, with gusts up to 180. To keep up, the young slave developed a speed-writing system. After Tiro used it to capture Cicero's furious oration debates in the Roman Senate, every senatorial slaveowner wanted his words immortalized, Tironian style.

Tiro taught other slaves his system, a forerunner of shorthand, which included at least one symbol we still use: the ampersand. Versatile Tiro shouldered other tasks, from keeping accounts to managing Cicero's country estates. As loyal confidant, editor, and bookkeeper, he became indispensable—giving the orator ample time to pursue a political career that won him a consulship in 63 B.C.

A man of monstrous conceit, Cicero fancied himself a fond master, often praising Tiro by throwing out mentions of manumission. He also had other feelings for the boy, and very probably used him sexually—another reason for not freeing him. (It was perfectly legal for Romans to bonk their male slaves—but hands off free males or someone else's slave.)

As the years wore on, the older man's blather about freedom remained idle talk. By his forties, Tiro was a nervous wreck. If Cicero fell into debt or died, he could be sold to a crueller owner. His master had political enemies. If he ended up in court, Tiro as a slave could be legally tortured as a witness.

While the two were traveling in Greece, Tiro fell feverishly ill and was thought near death—a state of affairs that finally shamed his master into setting a date to free him. Tiro was nursed by a new friend of Cicero's who gained the orator as a patron—a satisfactory outcome all round.

As a *libertus* or freedman, Tiro continued to travel with Cicero and carry out his literary labors. The novelty of being paid for his work let him salt away money; at length he bought a small farm in Campania, becoming a landowner like his former master. Well, not quite; Cicero, thanks to his wife's dowry, was known as one of Rome's most infamous slum landlords. His tenement highrises regularly collapsed.

Even after Cicero's political star sank below the horizon and he retired to write, Tiro remained his ally, cataloguing and wearily publishing every one of the statesman's writings. In 43 B.C., Cicero openly backed the wrong political horse and found himself on Mark Antony's "to do in" list.

After a short interval to mourn the beheading of his former master, Tiro sat down and wrote Cicero's biography. Sweetness and light, it wasn't. In his books, Cicero had advocated high-minded morality and ethics, but

Tiro had seen first-hand how his master "solved" problems. Cicero, who never felt he had quite enough money, divorced his blameless first wife to marry a young heiress, then dumped her for wife number three.

After setting the record straight with his warts-and-all book, a newly vitalized Tiro enjoyed life as a freedman for a surprising number of decades.

As soon as super-scribe Tiro filled a book's worth of scrolls, he stored them in a leather box called a capsa.

❖ GLADIATOR SLAVE ❖
OBLIGED TO ENTER THE ARENA

Romans, like the Etruscans before them, felt duty-bound to honor dead big shots. Since a mere funeral didn't seem enough of a sendoff, one thrillseeker suggested some fighting to the death to enliven the event. Soon the idea was refined to guest warriors going at it with the *gladius*, the short sword used by the military.

From gladius came gladiator and ultimately a whole teeming industry built on blood, sand, and entrance fees.

Most candidates for gladiator had their jobs chosen for them, being slaves, prisoners of war, or condemned criminals. As raw material, they were bought by a trainer who put them through lengthy training before renting them out to fight.

Gladiatorial schools or *ludi* were staffed with specialists, including physicians. By A.D. 80 Rome had three ludi, one of them connected by an underground tunnel to the Colosseum. The word also referred to the games themselves and to other festivals.

Once training began, there were those who didn't make the grade. Failures didn't get to slink home, either. Instead, they might train as *bestiarii* or hunters of wild beasts in lesser events. Most of the criminals became "arena fodder," thrown to the aforementioned beasts or killed in some unspeakable way.

The remaining men, closely guarded in barracks and locked up at night, ate well by Roman standards, slurping down a high-protein diet of barley grains, beans, oatmeal, and ash, thought to add fat and slow down bleeding.

A gladiator-in-the-making trained with a wooden sword, later graduating to straw-dummy attacks and mock battles with fellow students. Larger schools had practice arenas. The trainer (often an ex-gladiator) taught footwork, sword moves, and human anatomy—such as how to find major arteries with a dagger thrust.

Once through basic, novice gladiators were assessed for speed, strength, size, and skill, then allocated one of five classic styles: Thracian, Samnite, *retarius, murmillo*, or *secutor*. There were other, weirder fighting modes, such as the *andabatus,* who wore a helmet with no eyeholes—but most fans came to see skill rather than novelty. Gladiators were carefully paired up to make fights fair—and interesting.

It used to be thought that every bout ended in one gladiator's death, a belief given color by the often-repeated but never-accurate use of the melodramatic "thumbs down" and "We who are about to die salute you!" in books and films. Owners had substantial investments in these men and wanted their careers to be long and profitable. Like pro boxing, matches weren't frequent. Trainers toured their fighters to outlying arenas. Gladiators were ranked, and trainers could charge accordingly. When a gladiator did die in combat, the trainer billed the game sponsor one hundred times what the man had cost.

Even as slaves, gladiators could win freedom. Some became trainers at the schools. Others retired on their winnings, which, with gifts from fans, could be substantial. One fighter called Felix made it to age forty-five with glory, gold, and the unusual gift of Roman citizenship.

Despite our modern difficulties understanding this, some pros clearly enjoyed their work. A respected secutor gladiator named Flamma won twenty-one victories. His reputation grew even further when he was offered retirement and turned it down—four separate times.

❖ NOMENCLATOR ❖

THE FORERUNNER OF THE BLACKBERRY

Aristocratic movers and shakers in Rome not only had myriad friends, enemies, clients, family members, business associates, voters, and peers, they actually interacted with them frequently. Being seen at the Forum was big; being recognized was even bigger.

How could a fat Roman cat with a creaky memory cope? By utilizing a kind of personal assistant known as a *nomenclator*. This slave, selected for his ability to call up a name with a face (plus flattering personal details if it were someone really important), stuck by the side of his master like a remora on a shark.

Being politicians, Roman senators all had first- and second-string nomen-clators on tap, since they were expected to greet everyone like a long-lost friend. Like other figures in the limelight, each senator held a daily open house. As the senator sat in splendor, welcoming a long line of clients and constituents, the nomenclator would whisper the next person's name, number of children, and services rendered in the past, including delicate matters such as any loans outstanding.

Now and then, an oddball with a photographic memory came along. The Emperor Hadrian was one such. Everyone got thoroughly sick of hearing him boast that he had a staff of nomenclators but no need for them whatsoever. Even if true, it was so...ordinary, moving through one's day without that confidential murmur in one's aristocratic ear.

From the first century A.D. on, as the Roman republic morphed into an empire, the wealthy and powerful collected slaves as they did jewelry: for ostentation. The epitome of pretension? The bigwig who had a specialized nomenclator just to identify his own enormous staff of slaves.

❖ SCRIBE ❖

LOVE TRIANGLE OMENS: READ ALL ABOUT IT!

There were some mighty fast writers in ancient times, the speediest being the Greeks, who were centuries ahead of the Romans in terms of literacy. Happily for the Romans, after they had subjugated the Greeks and everyone else, they found themselves with a plethora of educated men now available to them as slaves.

These *librarii,* as they were called, did a huge array of jobs. They worked as private secretaries to important men and women. They acted as editors and librarians, making extracts of books and organizing private libraries. They labored as copyists, transcribing books being read to them onto papyrus. They even did scroll repair.

Some librarii were public slaves, owned by the Roman state, who tackled the endless correspondence generated by bureaucrats and officials in faraway provinces.

One particular group of librarii who excelled at shorthand or speed-writing worked on the *Acta Diurna* or Daily Record, the Roman equivalent of the newspaper. Initially begun in Julius Caesar's day, its pronouncements were at first written on large whitewashed bulletin boards. Later, as the *Acta* grew more complex, it was recorded on tablets, then posted in the Roman Forum.

A great many citizens sent their own slave scribes to make copies. Others bought hard copies on papyrus, made by an on-the-spot scribe. Each day, the prior day's *Acta* was deposited in the library, forming a permanent record.

The news-gathering for the paper, overseen by magistrates, was carried out by lightning-handed reporters or *notarii* who covered the courts, the temples, and the Senate. From descriptions left by Tacitus, Juvenal, Petronius, and others, we get a good idea about the contents of this grand-daddy to *The Times.*

Headliner items reported on the latest festivals, chariot-race wins, and juicier trials, including who was acquitted and who was for the chop. Besides edicts from magistrates, decrees of the Roman Senate, and honors lavished on the current emperor, there were wills of the prominent and carefully censored tidbits about any war Rome was waging.

Another section covered births, deaths, and divorces. The business section gave updates on the all-important wheat supply, plus a tally of the tribute flowing into the state treasury from subject provinces.

The most addictive part of the *Acta*, however, was its mix of astrology, scandal, and news of the odd, an eerie preview of what newspapers would offer two thousand years later. The birth of a hermaphrodite or a three-headed chicken; a shower of frogs in Capua; an ominous portent in Britain; the spicy details of a love triangle involving a society dame, a senator, and a gladiator, right down to the names, deeds, and places—you could read it all in the *Daily Record*.

Begun around 50 B.C. and published until Rome lost its power to Constantinople, this periodical had a run of nearly five hundred years—not half bad for a paperless newspaper without photos, political cartoons, or advertising.

❖ ORNATRIX ❖

A HARROWING CLIENTELE

Although a talented Roman *ornatrix* might reach the heights of hairdresser to the stars, her working conditions were unenviable. More often than not, she was a female slave in a well-to-do household.

Whether vainly trying to hide the scalp of an aging empress or seeking a look that flattered an imperial daughter-in-law, we are talking pressure, pressure, pressure. Roman matrons, most of them bored out of their well-coiffed skulls, were exacting customers. Most demanded raven-black hair—or a mane of blonde locks. Neither was that easy to achieve. Hair-dye ingredients included walnuts, cuttlefish ink, and gall. To get a really dark, sultry mane, most ornatrices swore by decomposed leeches.

Bleaching was far trickier; the ornatrix mixed up a mess of pigeon dung and ashes, following it with a urine rinse to condition the hair. Problems

with dandruff or thinning? Another generous application of dung did the job—or so the Romans thought. (No surprise that it took potent perfumes to mask these eye-watering treatments.)

In addition to dyeing or bleaching hair, the ornatrix could weave in braids taken from female captives of colder climes, or ease on a full-coverage blonde wig. This could be a godsend. On days where nothing went right, the evil potions used to change hair color sometimes led to temporary baldness.

Once the dye took and the follicles stayed put, the ornatrix set to work to demonstrate her crowning-glory skills. The towering hairdos of patrician women during the imperial centuries took hours to prepare with pins and curling irons. All those cornrow braids, curls, twists, and gewgaws were woven onto a scaffolding. Deft fingers, patience, and a gift for light-hearted patter to appease the mistress were key. If madam were unhappy with the final look, the ornatrix slave could look forward to slaps, pinches, or even a whipping instead of a tip.

Some ornatrices worked with female counterparts in beauty shops around the city. While more independent, they labored as hard as slaves. The ornatrix had to placate sniffy wives and fussy courtesans who craved imperial hairdos at knock-down prices.

38

A hairdresser's life hadn't always been this difficult. For centuries, Greek and Roman women were content to wear simpler fashions: hair tied in a knot or pinned atop the crown of the head, or as long tresses pulled back in a bun or braids. But about the time that Emperor Claudius became defunct, so did the classic, part-in-the-middle Joni Mitchell look.

Women had tried alternative hairwear, such as caps or coifs that covered most of the head, at times with a ponytail pertly sticking through it. High-rolling matrons bought caps made of fine gold mesh; poor women and slaves used animal bladders for their bad-hair days. Wide bands of brightly colored cloth were also sought after.

But these simple solutions to bad-hair days didn't suffice, and thus the job market for ornatrices grew to imperial extremes.

❖ ❖ ❖ ❖ **CLESSIPUS** ❖ ❖ ❖ ❖

Chandelier with a silver lining

Clessipus might have been a slave, but that wasn't the bad news: he was also born into poverty, a hunchback, and ugly to boot.

Growing up, he found work as a fuller, one of the fellows who cleaned togas and other garments. Each day at his place of employment, he danced for hours on the dirty clothes, splashing in a mixture of stale urine and sulfur fumes. There were worse jobs; he didn't complain.

One day an auctioneer named Theon showed up. While waiting for his drycleaning, Theon caught sight of Clessipus sloshing around in the fuller's vats and thought of an outrageous ploy to draw bidders. Upper-class Romans were fond of collecting human oddities. Since there was a lively market in the sale of the disabled and deformed, the auctioneer decided to use the slave as a value-added gimmick for a fancy Corinthian chandelier he planned to auction off the following day.

At the sale, Theon talked up the bronze chandelier, then pointed to Clessipus and declared, "Make the winning bid for the lamp, and I'll throw in this hideous rascal for free, the perfect ornament for your next dinner party!"

After excited bidding, a rich Roman widow named Gegania took home the chandelier and the add-on for a mere fifty thousand sesterces. Off the odd couple went and Gegania duly began arranging her next dinner party. After some thought, she decided to make her "centerpiece" appear in the nude. The sight of Clessipus in the buff did amuse the other guests; but something untoward happened. Gegania herself fell prey to a genuine passion for the man she'd bought.

In no time, he was sharing her bed. After an unknown number of years together, Clessipus inherited more than the bed. When Gegania died, he got most of her wealth—and his freedom.

The hunchback was evidently a simple man, one who shared the religious beliefs of his time. He became convinced that he owed his good fortune, not to his own qualities or the generosity of his deceased partner, but to some divine essence in the Corinthian chandelier. From that time forward, he worshipped the chandelier as a deity. The bronze lamp became his own little cult. Other credulous souls, it was said, even joined him in lampstand idolatry.

When his days on earth were nearly over, Clessipus did what all Romans dreamed of doing: he set up a huge and noble tomb for himself on the Appian Way. On the stone edifice, he engraved the story of Gegania, the magic chandelier, and his own rags-to-riches life—an inscription made in the first century A.D. that continues to amaze.

❖ SLAVE ROUNDUP ❖
RUNNING WITH SCISSORS & OTHER PLUM JOBS

In the unfree workplace, there were certain positions that most slaves would fight to get.

The dream job for a female house slave was that of *sandaligerula*, a post that took more time to spell than to do. High-born Romans and Greeks engaged in shoe rituals with rigid standards as to where they could be worn. A man who wore a toga with sandals, for instance, would be laughed out of the Senate.

To guarantee that her mistress was properly shod at all times, the sandaligerula accompanied her mistress to dinner parties. Once there, the sandal-slave took off her owner's street shoes and replaced them with party slippers. Removing one's own footgear was so declassé that even the humblest guest brought along a sandal-slave. After the partygoers went in to dinner, the shoe-girls enjoyed a little downtime until the event broke up. At deluxe events, guests got their feet bathed as they reposed on dining couches; this job, however, was carried out by the host's special toe-cleaning, oil-'em-down slaves.

Another hankered-after position that younger slaves lobbied for was *flabellifer*. Open to males or females, it involved carrying a fan for the mistress, flapping it on command. During the dog days of August, slaves might be in for some marathon fanning; most of the time, however, flabellifers were there for show, and knew it.

Seasoned slaves with good memories and diction became *salutigeruli*. They spent their days carrying complimentary messages from their owners to friends, acquaintances, and those on the "need to be flattered" list.

Musically inclined slaves nabbed the coveted *fistulator* positions, available only to those whose owners were public speakers. Fistulators carried a reed pitchpipe. To start, the fistulator gave a subtle tootle or two so that the great man could proceed to orate at just the correct pitch. Gracchus, famed orator in republican times, was said to have been the first to flaunt a fistulator.

Upper-class foodies had a problem: how to dine with elegance while lolling on a couch? Then some bright guy invented a labor-saving device called the scissors, a word that meant both the cutting instrument and a slave of the same name. Any household of consequence assigned a scissors slave to attend each dinner guest. A fellow of steady hands and good hygiene, the human scissors used his bronze instrument to cut up his guest's meat and other messy items.

Most slaves could only fantasize about working part-time. The most brilliant part-time job? Triumph slave. Whenever a victorious Roman general killed five thousand of the enemy in a single battle, he earned a triumph, a massive musical celebration with oxen sacrifices, booty distributions, and a huge parade, complete with cringing captives in golden chains.

The slave stood behind the triumphant general in his chariot, holding a heavy, jewel-laden gold crown over the man's head. His other task was much trickier. As the procession moved along amid cheers, the slave whispered wet-blanket remarks into the general's ear: "You're not that great. Look around you and remember you're only a man."

When it came to averting bad luck—or military megalomania—the Romans thought of everything.

❖ SLAVE ROUNDUP ❖
LOO DUTY & OTHER DIRE ASSIGNMENTS

It's unlikely that slaves in the vast Greco-Roman captive workforce relished their jobs. Most were fatalistic, thanking the gods that they didn't have one of the truly appalling employments.

Whether in Greece or Rome, *carnifex* or executioner was a gruesome career. The job-holder, a public slave, worked on his own. So odious was his position that he was forbidden to live around others; instead, he occupied a hovel outside the city walls in a filthy locale used for the punishment of slaves. Due to the fact that the gallows had not yet been invented, the carnifex had to manually strangle his victims with a rope. The carnifex also had the task of administering torture, mainly scourging or whipping. His "clients" were other slaves and foreigners, that is, non-Greeks or non-Romans who'd committed crimes.

Being employed as a mithraeum cleaner was stomach-turning in a different way. Mithras worship was a males-only cult popular among Romans, especially military men. To initiate new members, adherents slaughtered a bull over a pit and gave the initiate a bull's-blood shower. Such ceremonies left the mithraeum, the underground chamber where such sanguinary activity took place, a real mess.

Speaking of unspeakable messes: the loo attendant slave faced them daily. Throughout the Roman Empire, cities had unisex public latrines— 144 in Rome alone. In them, customers sat side by side upon stone thrones, below which water ran continuously. In front of the sitters was a trough of running water filled with sticks. The business end of the stick (i.e., a sponge) was for wiping: a cheap, workable amenity in an era before toilet paper. On occasion, when a late-night reveler hit the place or someone happened to grab the wrong end of the stick, the results were predictably unfastidious. Such mishaps represented more work for the loo attendant—who could, however, expect tips now and then.

The gladiatorial games employed huge slave crews, many with jobs nearly as grim as the gladiators. Certain slaves worked full-time in semi-darkness, beneath the amphitheater. To send great numbers of caged wild animals (and prisoners) to their deaths, these slaves used a manual system of cranks and hoists to raise the subterranean cages up to arena level. In the nastiest sense of the word, they were the world's first elevator operators.

Other slaves working below the arena were scenery changers. For the easily bored audiences of the games, spectacles had to be ever more spectacular. One crowd-pleaser was to convert the sands of the arena into a forest, complete with full-grown trees. This scene change was accomplished by slave manpower, muscling it all into place between acts with professional skill that the crew at Cirque du Soleil would admire.

In the average Roman home, the most hated job (and job-holder) was the *silentiarius*. A minor management figure in the household, the silentiarius carried a wicked whip or rod. His sole purpose was to keep the entire staff of slaves from making a peep whenever the master or mistress were present. Even a sneeze or a cough might provoke a whipping, which seems counterproductive, given the amount of noise that would generate. The silentiarius job was self-selecting, probably going to the most loathsome finagler and fawner on the staff.

❖ VICARIUS ❖

BODY DOUBLE

Back in B.C., slave-drivers were literal, and vicarious thrills weren't. *Vicarius* meant a deputy or stand-in. This job title represented employment mobility, an opportunity for one slave to buy another slave to "stand in" and do his work. A chance, praise Apollo, to delegate.

Historical researchers have found a variety of vicarius purchase agreements, usually involving a slave with middle-management duties. Even as slaves, some civil servants made enough money to buy a vicarius—or twenty. For example, in Emperor Tiberius's time, an imperial slave named Musicus had a staff of sixteen vicarii. The guy was merely a low-level bureaucrat in the provinces, but he owned three secretaries, two footmen, two cooks, two chamberlains, a purchasing agent, and a doctor!

So where did a slave, imperial or not, find the loot to go shopping at the slave markets? Most often from the *peculium*, a peculiar but common form of nest egg or assets portfolio. Such a nest egg belonged to the slave's owner and might consist of real estate, equipment, shops, other slaves, or cash. If he chose, the master could let a trusted slave manage his portfolio up to its full value—with the option to withdraw permission at any time. The slave made regular financial reports on the peculium, and got to keep all or part of the profits. Since it operated a bit like an employer's pension scheme, the slave might contribute to it in another way—through additional income generated when his master rented him out for special skills he possessed.

This system made reliable slaves into entrepreneurs, with the peculium as a long-term credit instrument and the master as a silent partner. Once the slave turned thirty, he or she could use the profits to buy his or her freedom. Or to buy a vicarius or two.

Now things really get complicated. Once our entrepreneurial slave bought a vicarius at the slave market, and the six-month period for returns of defective merchandise had passed, the new vicarius also had access to a peculium. Eventually the new vicarius could buy his or her own vicarius! A primary source document found in Roman Britain confirms that such slave-owning daisy-chains did occur.

In later centuries, the term *vicarius* came to refer to the jobs of various nonslave officials; still later, it became the root of the English word *vicar*. Thus the pope bears the title *Vicarius Christi*, the vicar or representative of Christ on earth.

❖ ❖ ❖ ❖ **VALERIAN** ❖ ❖ ❖ ❖

A back-breaking career arc

As the military might of the Roman Empire began to sag in the third century A.D., emperors came and went as often as the plague.

There was, however, a break from this downward spiral in 253, when Valerian was chosen for the imperial purple. From a distinguished family, he was an intelligent fellow whose CV included superior military service and all the high offices. Everyone, from Roman senators to the ordinary guy in the street, was dead chuffed, especially after such a string of losers.

With his son Gallienus, Valerian began mopping up the empire's borders, which had been sadly frayed by Persians, Germans, and other aggressors. Soon Valerian's victories gained him several shiny new titles, including "Restorer of the Human Race."

But the brutally indefatigable Persians kept coming back for more; in the summer of 260, Valerian had to put on his field armor again. Besides being hit by enemy arrows, his Roman troops got hit with another round of plague, which thinned the emperor's army terribly.

Assuming that he was dealing with human beings, the sixty-something emperor went to negotiate with the enemy—only to find himself made a slave.

Those early Persians played hardball. No ransom, no plush quarters, not even extra rations for a fellow monarch. Whenever Persia's strongman, a tough potentate called Shapur the First, wanted to mount his horse, poor Valerian was put to use as a stool.

Valerian's back eventually gave out and he expired, whereupon Shapur had the emperor flayed and his skin dyed scarlet. That blood-red imperial Roman hide occupied a prominent place in one of the Persian temples, where it terrified visitors for generations.

TWO

PROFESSIONAL VIRGINS & MORE PROFANE CALLINGS

❖ PRIEST ROUNDUP ❖

A CULT FOR EVERY TASTE

When the Greek philosopher Thales discovered a magnetic rock, he exclaimed, "All things are full of gods!" That sentiment drove ancient belief for a thousand years. Since all objects harbored deities, better safe than sorry. Build a temple, perform a ritual, keep those offerings flowing.

Greco-Roman cultures became polytheistic candy stores, where spiritual seekers could find any flavor. The Greeks worshiped tangled dynasties of Olympian gods and goddesses, but the Romans soon outstripped them in the diety stakes in terms of numbers and variety.

To protect Roman doorways, it took four gods (including one for hinges). Interested in an afterlife? Join a mystery religion, from Isis worship to the gory, males-only Mithras cult.

This plethora meant countless jobs for priests and priestesses. Originally laypersons, selected by their communities on a part-time basis, the calling became more professional by the first century B.C. Priests and priestesses had no services to hold, no parishioners to attend to. Tasks revolved around one thing: keep that deity happy. As temples got grander and membership grew, so did caretaking duties. Priests had to guard temple treasures and safe-deposit boxes, including a jaw-dropping amount of excess coinage belonging to rich people, stored in temple cellars.

Call-of-the-wild fans joined the *luperci,* the wolf priesthood. Each February, nearly naked young men (including Mark Antony at one point) ran amok in the streets at the wolf festival, whipping women with goatskin thongs to make them fertile. Longing for meaningful masochism? The Galli priests of the Cybele cult welcomed new members, as long as you agreed to emasculate yourself in public at their March bloodfest.

Rome alone had four major colleges of priests. Pontiffs were the heavyweights, deciding on holy days, handling administrative matters, advising the Senate. Augurs inaugurated things and made sure signs were auspicious. They read omens in a variety of media, including bird flight, bird dung, animal livers, and lightning strikes. Lightning priests, a job with high appeal to risk-takers, sacrificed two-year-old sheep at a temple to Jupiter called a bidental, erected where a bolt had struck.

A post that any greedyguts would kill for was that of *epulon* priest or feast organizer. These weren't your ordinary nibbles: on special occasions of national rejoicing (mission accomplished!) or calamity (barbarians at the gate!), seven epulones put together a luxurious sit-down dinner for thirteen major gods. After placing deity images before tables laden with food, the epulones said a prayer, then dug in—consuming the entire banquet themselves.

After Rome had got into the swing of having an emperor, and people had almost run out of ideas for new cults, some fawning creep cooed, "Why

don't we worship dead emperors?" That created a temple-
building boom and an imperial cult that spread empire-wide,
with high-status jobs galore. Pretty soon the franchise
expanded to deify living emperors and their families.

Although people were free to worship any god (or none),
lip service to the imperial cult eventually became a loyalty
test—and the defining issue for the Jewish nation and The
Way, a tiny sect later known as Christianity. No matter how
persuasive a pagan priest might be, when followers of
Judaism or Jesus refused to pay homage to the emperor, conflict with Roman
authorities was inevitable.

❖ PROSTITUTE ❖

A CAREER LADDER WITH MANY RUNGS

Greeks of both genders were businesslike about sexual services and the
women who provided them. (There were male providers, too, whose jobs
are described in the entry on rent boys.) The sex industry offered job choices
as clearly defined as rungs on a ladder, from no-frills budget babes to pricey
companions.

In 594 B.C., civic reformer Solon, famous for laying down the law in
Athens, established an economy-class brothel program to pacify the randy
youth of the city. He established city-wide outlets where the price list for
intimate female services began at one obol. Solon's other bright idea was
to motivate customers and providers alike by funneling profits into a flashy
temple to Aphrodite Pandemos, "the people's Venus." Some eighteen million
obols later, Athens had a new temple and streetwalkers had a place to relax
off the job.

But Solon's cut-rate brothels were up against stiff competition from
other indecorous entertainment emporia, identified by oil lamps over their
doors. Along roads, at festivals, in towns, these multipurpose businesses
delivered food, drink, gambling, and beds that came with or without
wenches.

Further up the industry career ladder were the pricier, sex-optional
workers called *auletrides* or female pipes players. The auletrides, trained as

dancers and musicians and dressed in shimmering see-through gowns of Coan silk, were paid to entertain (and/or put out) at male drinking parties.

Affluent customers had more options. They could hire executive-package, full-service call girls known as *hetaerae* or "companions." Some of these glamorous, well-educated women worked through an agent, i.e. a pimp; many others operated independently, choosing or refusing assignations. Unlike other sex workers, hetaerae were usually freeborn; many came to Athens from points east, such as Ionia, and paid extra for their resident-alien status.

Whether you were an executive model with erotic bells and whistles or a bargain tart, it was hard work. Greek prostitutes shelled out surprising amounts for taxes. Those blonde wigs, platform shoes, and see-through gowns didn't come cheap, either. (Still, conditions were less bizarre than in Rome, where streetwalkers wore wool togas to announce their availability and paid rent to fornicate under fornix arches.)

Pregnancy and STDs were everyday perils. Sex workers knew more about birth control than wives did, often using cedar oil or frankincense in olive oil as spermicides. In a pinch, they applied vinegar to customers' organs—a douche in reverse! Abortion was a legal remedy, not a crime.

"Browsing," as hookers called the life, didn't wear a cloak of shame. Prostitution was legal and its workers had certain protections. Hookers could get out if they chose, going into business or training on the job to become brothel madams.

Sex workers formed a tightly knit community, with favorite places to socialize and worship. Most hookers were also regulars at the temple of Aphrodite Callipygiea or "Venus of the great ass." Their festivals rocked; one, called the Aphrodisia, was celebrated throughout Greece and with even greater enthusiasm at Corinth and on the island of Aegina.

Unlike Greek wives, sex workers had freedom of movement, in the community and in the bedroom. An astonishing number of *hetaerae* won imperishable places in history as the most talked-about, written-about, memorable females of their day.

❖ SOUL CONDUCTOR ❖

WHO YOU GONNA CALL?

Judging by ancient accounts, the Greeks had serious problems with the supernatural, often needing the help of a professional. Ancient psychics being fond of dignified titles, a Greek ghostbuster preferred to be called a *psychopompus* or soul conductor.

The most famous case of ghost-vanquishing started with a vainglorious Spartan general named Pausanias, who in 479 B.C. had just finished whipping some Persian invaders. While resting on his laurels at his base camp, he fell in lust with a chaste young thing named Cleonice. Successful on the battlefield but evidently no smoothie in love matters, he shunned the dating game, instead telling his guards, "Bring her to my room late tonight." In one of those madcap nocturnal mixups, the girl stumbled over an oil lamp in the dark, the insecure general grabbed for his bedside sword instead of the kama sutra oil, and—whoops—one very dead virgin.

Pausanias was already suffering from post-traumatic stress syndrome, and the virginocide incident unnerved him further. He headed for the nearest bureau for paranormal affairs, the Oracle of the Dead on the Black Sea coast. Cleonice's ghost was quickly summoned. She told him, "You think you've got problems? You want peace of mind, go home."

A relieved Pausanias headed back to Sparta, where he was immediately accused of treason, hauled off to Athens, and bricked up to die in the temple of Athena. Case closed, ghost satisfied, one would think.

But no. The Athenians, miffed because their goddess wasn't getting the attention she needed, demanded that the Spartans consult another oracle, the surefire one at Delphi. This oracle announced, "Bring in the pros." Two soul conductors arose to the challenge, ridding Athena's temple of Pausanias's ghost. They even took care of that awful smell.

Putting restless ghosts to bed was all in a day's work for soul conductors. They also carried out more queasy jobs, including one requiring tremendous poise, since it took place in the very public arena, in both senses of the word, of the Roman amphitheater.

As gladiators fought in one-on-one duels, a psychopompus representing the Etruscan, Greek, and Roman versions of the god Mercury, in his aspect as conductor of souls to the underworld, stood by. Dressed in black, he carried a bronze *caduceus*, a snaky staff that symbolized Mercury.[*]

His job was to make sure that the souls he conducted were genuinely dead. To do so, that metal caduceus was kept red-hot. When a fighter fell, the soul conductor conducted an antifakery test by zapping the luckless gladiator with his scalding serpentine staff.

The second soul conductor in the arena was dressed as Rhadamanthus, Judge of the Underworld. Wearing tall dark boots and tunic and a baleful raven's mask, he wielded a long-handled Etruscan mallet, with which he tapped the officially defunct gladiators to claim their souls for Hades.

Gruesome as their actions may sound, these two men brought an eerie closure to each duel—and a moment of religious respect for the passage of another human being from the land of the living.

❖ DREAM INCUBATOR ❖
HEAL WHILE YOU SNOOZE

The woman went blind. The philosopher suffered from chronic dyspepsia. The soldier had an arrow in his chest that had been draining pus for two years. Who did they (and thousands more) turn to?

Dream incubators, that's who. These were the skilled worker-priests at the sanctuaries of Asclepius, Greek god of healing, the last resort for people with chronic afflictions and mysterious illnesses. Epidaurus, the flagship sanctuary, was founded in the fifth century B.C.; its popularity encouraged new sites from Sparta to Syria, Athens to Tiber Island in Rome, African Cyrene to Albania.

When a patient arrived, he underwent a three-day ritual cleansing—sex, roasted goat, and cheese were all taboo. He

---

[*] Mercury (Greek Hermes) was the messenger god of commerce and the conductor of the dead. His caduceus, or winged staff, had two snakes intertwined. Asclepius, Greek god of healing, carried a wooden staff with one coiled serpent, signifying renewal. Ancient healers reverenced the Asclepius symbol, as you'll learn in the dream incubator entry. Over time, the significant differences between the symbols blurred; thus modern medicine unwittingly uses both.

made an offering of cakes and garlands, after which a dream incubator gave him an intake interview. That night, wearing a laurel wreath, the patient slept on a pallet in the abaton chamber. Sacred dogs wandered about; the dream incubator sat by the patient's side for a time, setting the stage for a hoped-for visit by the god. In most cases, the patient had vivid dreams—which the dream incubator took down when the patient awoke. Sometimes the patient dreamed his own cure.

Sounds wacky, but it's hard to argue with a millennium of documentary evidence. Many thousands of sufferers found relief and sometimes complete cures at the sanctuaries. These tranquil, wooded places combined the belief elements of a Lourdes with the comfort and care of a hospice. Plus a little supernatural razzamatazz: the god Asclepius often made an appearance in the form of a sacred snake.

Nonpoisonous house snakes were welcomed rather than shunned by the Greeks and Romans. Asclepius himself had said that serpents cast off old age just as he banished disease, and he carried a staff to which a snake clung. Greek physicians prayed to Asclepius for guidance, adopting the staff and snake as a symbol of their profession.

On a pragmatic level, sanctuaries were havens of rest, offering therapeutic equipment from running tracks to a variety of baths. Dream incubators practiced holistic medicine, urging healthful diet and offering sports options and other exercise to their patients. They believed in the healing power of music and poetry; for that reason, Epidaurus and other sites had marvelous outdoor theaters. (The fifty-five-tier facility at Epidaurus is still in use.)

The most poignant testaments to dream incubation were carved in stone at the sanctuaries. Others were recorded on monuments and in books by writers of the times, such as Aristides, a Greek orator who suffered from a variety of chronic ailments. He spent many months at Epidaurus.

Among the thank-you votives left was this testimonial from a military man: "The god advised Valerius Aper, a blind soldier, to take the blood of a white rooster along with honey and to blend them into a salve and to apply this to his eyes for three days. He saw again and went on his way and offered thanks to the god publicly."

What about that first soldier with the pus problem? When he awoke in Epidaurus, he found an arrow point resting in his hands. Out he walked, a well man.

❖ RENT BOY ❖

EQUAL-OPPORTUNITY SEX WORKER

A lustful male in ancient Greece had more sexual options than the Internet: classy hetaerae, no-frills sex in state brothels, marriageable women (once wed to them), and perform-on-demand slaves of either gender. At times, a libido-filled Greek sought a deeper relationship with a younger male of good family. From his standpoint, the critical issue wasn't gender or even social status. What counted in his world was who got to penetrate whom.

Aristocrats with their eyes on a male prize looked for young and beautiful. By beauty, they meant a youth with big shoulders, tiny waist, good muscle tone, and protruding buttocks. His nose should be straight, his lower lip Elvis-like, his hair a flowing mane. And he had to have dainty genitals, this being one society where size really didn't matter. Finally! An answer to the enigma of poorly endowed Greek statues.

According to his philosophy students, Socrates was boy-crazy, a man who felt overcome with divine madness in the company of good-looking adolescents. Most of the time, however, he sublimated his passions by teaching them moral philosophy instead of bedding them.

Since randy Athenian males on the prowl outnumbered beautiful freeborn twelve- to eighteen-year-olds with small penises, a service industry of boy hookers sprang up, if you will, to fill this need.

Most of these rent boys were eighteen or under. By selling their bodies in the short term, these boys forfeited their rights to citizenship in later life. Selling yourself for money wasn't the crime—being penetrated was.[*]

In Athens, rent boys worked the same areas of the city as female prostitutes did: Lycabettos Hill and the Ceramicus, the district where all of the pottery (and many of the illicit assignations) were made. Some of the more enterprising lads used

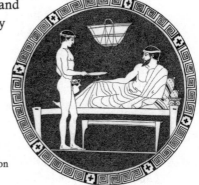

---

[*] Penetrated parties in Athens were punished by the application of a backdoors poke with a large radish; the sting of public humiliation, to say nothing of the way those radishes smarted, was deemed castigation enough. Amazing how Aristophanes' comedies get more understandable when the radish/penetration paradigm is understood.

the headstones and benches of the cemetery as chalkboards to advertise—and as informal working areas on occasion.

In contrast, Romans were unenthusiastic about the Greek ideal of high-minded mentor-adolescent relationships between male citizens. Various laws prohibited such behavior. On the other hand, they expected to penetrate their male slaves any time they chose, and they weren't averse to rent boys, either.

Like their female counterparts, rent boys in Rome were often managed by a *leno* or pimp. In Latin, they were known as *pueri lenoni* or "pimps' boys." Rent boys had higher status—and much higher prices—than their Greek counterparts. The Roman calendar even included an official festival each April 25, just for them.

Wherever they plied their trade, these boys ran continued risks of abuse and venereal disease. Although they didn't have to contend with pregnancy or abortion, young male hookers dreaded the onset of full puberty, when their beards would grow, their boyish looks would go, and their line of eager clients would shrink. Even a leno would admit this wasn't a career of longevity—or even much satisfaction.

❖ ❖ ❖ ❖ **SPURRINA** ❖ ❖ ❖ ❖

Seer to the rich & assassinated

As any examiner of entrails worth his salt knew, the soothsaying biz depended on word of mouth—no such thing as bad publicity. When a client heeded a warning about dire events ahead, a soothsayer's reputation was made. When clients ignored a warning, even better.

Take the career of one such soothsayer, Vestricius Spurrina. Although he lived in Rome at a time when street gangs roamed, jobs were scarce, and food shortages were frequent, he struck lucky, reading entrails for an up-and-coming dictator.

Spurrina had two problems with his client, a fellow by the name of Julius Caesar. Likeable, yes, but the man was notorious for leaving his bills unpaid. Even when he did cough up, Julius scoffed at some of Spurrina's best readings, declaring that prophesies were poppycock and he, Julius, refused to worry about plots in the real world or omens in the next.

On one embarrassing occasion, after Spurrina unzipped a sacrificial animal and found its heart missing, Caesar smirked and said, "No big deal. I need a favorable reading. You need to keep your job. Open another animal and keep gazing at the guts until we get good news."

Spurrina fumed; his client's attitude was enough to make a soothsayer turn atheist.

In 44 B.C., as the month of Mars, god of war, rolled around, Spurrina carried out his normal first-of-the-month entrail reading at Julius's house. The animal's liver simply screamed: "Danger ahead! Mid-month looks grim!" Spurrina had no option but to warn Julius, who of course laughed in his face.

On the fifteenth, more humiliation. Julius Caesar planned to address the Senate and, as he arrived, naturally he stopped at the curbside altar so Spurrina could do an official reading. When Spurrina got a nasty omen from the first sacrifice, Julius made him do another. Then he ridiculed the ominous portents—as though Spurrina had made them up!

Worst of all, right in front of the crowd, Julius cast aspersions on his soothsayer cred, saying, "You're a false prophet—look—the Ides of March are here and no harm has come to me."

As Caesar strode off, Spurrina lost his cool and barked out a mean-spirited retort: "The Ides have come, all right, but they're not over yet!"

Spurrina had barely cleared away the blood and carcasses from his readings when he heard an uproar. Looking up, he saw men in stained togas scuttling away from the building. The news was soon on everyone's lips: Julius Caesar, Rome's self-proclaimed dictator for life, had just been assassinated, stabbed more than twenty times by a bunch of conspirators.

Vestricius Spurrina watched sadly as the bloody body of his client was loaded onto a litter, to be carried home by the slaves. He didn't need to gaze at a single gut to know that he would now soothsay for a growing clientele of A-list celebs. But by Aplu and Jupiter, what a way to be proven right.

❖ AMULET MAKER ❖

FASCINATING MERCHANDISE

Life was uncertain; the gods were unpredictable; who knew when a comet might send things into chaos? It didn't do to walk through life unprotected.

From the cradle onward, even the most devil-may-care Greek or Roman wore an amulet, carried a charm, or fondled a *fascinum*.

Instead of a rabbit's foot, the classic good-luck charm worn by nearly everyone was a phallus, called a fascinum—the source of our word "fascination." From infancy on, one dangled from the chubby neck of each child. Amulet merchants and fascinum makers had a built-in market.

In Greece and Italy, phalluses were also painted over doorways, carved into walls and onto paving stones, and, er, erected as statues in gardens and at crossroads. Passers-by touched these hermae or herm statues for luck; residents regularly cleaned off bird droppings. Phallic symbols served as protective devices against bad luck and the evil eye, sometimes accompanied by the words *"Hic vivet felicitas*—here lives happiness."*

Modern tour guide patter at Pompeii and other sites notwithstanding, phalluses weren't always there to point the way to commercialized sex.

In ancient times, it was much more important to guard against bad luck, such as sickness, natural calamities, poisoning, difficulties in childbirth, and the omnipresent menace of the envious evil eye, than it was to court good luck. For protection, ordinary people wore amulets and rings. Some amulets were made of plant material or cloth in symbolic shapes, such as beetles, eyes, or totem animals, and sewn onto garments. The Greeks favored grasshopper shapes and hung a large one in front of the Acropolis to protect its temples. Rings often bore the image of Hercules, since one of his titles was "Averter of Evil."

The entrepreneurs who made and sold amulets often had a profitable sideline as herbalists. Like the popular healing crystals of our time, amulets of yesteryear were considered problem-specific. The amulet merchant examined her customer, then devised a talisman to cure or alleviate. A bit of cyclamen plant would prevent balding; bells warded off evil and made childbirth easier. An amulet with a peony on it helped wounds heal faster, while a bee brought good luck. Newborns, of course, had to be bathed in urine or wine before getting amulet protection.

Today's reader might release an incredulous snort at these beliefs. But the Greeks, who invented the concept of a panacea or cure-all, and the Romans, who similarly dreamed up the placebo, had psychosomatic wisdom on their sides. Given their deeply rooted belief system, amulets probably did as much good as (and less harm than!) most of the so-called medicines of the times, whose ingredients often included dung and other noxious substances.

❖ VESTAL VIRGIN ❖

YOU TOO COULD BECOME A MAXIMUM VIRGIN

The Vestal Virgin business kicked off in the eighth century B.C., when Rome was run by a king of sorts. Vesta, goddess of the hearth, soon came to signify the mother city.

To keep the fire burning on Vesta's sacred hearth, six girls were selected from twenty candidates. Qualifications weren't a problem—as long as you were Italian, not missing any limbs, and had freeborn parents who steered clear of seedy occupations like auctioneering. During the first centuries, vacancies for the thirty-year positions were largely filled from noble families.

Once they'd said their goodbyes to their parents, the girls lived together in spacious quarters and spent a decade learning their secret duties, the next decade performing them, and the third teaching them. After thirty years, a Vestal Virgin could lunge into lewdness—but few did. Rather than marry

or make merry, most aging ex-Vestals stayed put, reminiscing about past virginal triumphs.

Unlike most Roman females who spent lifetimes under male thumbs, with meager opportunities to move about, socialize, or exercise their brains, Vestals got to do it all. The more-driven girls could aspire to become head Vestal, known as Virgo Maxima or Maximum Virgin.

Vestals had the power to intercede on behalf of people in difficulties. That role came in handy about 60 B.C. when young Julius Caesar found himself on the most-wanted list of dictator Sulla. The Vestals begged for clemency, saving his life. Needless to say, the Vestals' quarters soon underwent an extreme makeover, courtesy of Julius.

Six months before his assassination, Caesar gave his will to the Maximum Virgin for safekeeping. She hung onto it for dear life—and no wonder. It contained a clause that would eventually turn Rome into an empire, making Caesar's nephew Octavian into his adopted son and heir.

After Octavian (dubbed "Augustus"—i.e. "reverend"—by the Senate) became top dog, he too showered appreciative gestures on the Vestals and amped up their privileges, from choice seats at entertainment venues to deluxe transport and matching sets of lictors or high-status bodyguards.

Each day, Vestals made Rome safe by purifying the hearth, monitoring the fire, and peeking at the secret jar of sacred relics (most suspected it held a clay phallus to honor the god Fascinus). They threw together a fresh batch of salt cakes (ten-minute recipe, same as Roman wedding cakes) for ceremonial use. If it were June, they opened the inner sanctum for a gals' ritual. June 15 was especially busy, with a sacred cleanup of the temple, after which the Vestals could return to mucky mode for another twelve months.

Ritual duties over, they embarked on their secular chores: acting as official safeguards, witnesses, and notaries; witnessing wills and treaties; giving evidence in court; and pardoning the occasional criminal they ran across.

Thanks to will-witnessing, the Vestals often got named as beneficiaries. After those souls shuffled off to the underworld, a Vestal could end up with a tidy equity in property and cash; this became her sole property, to do with as she saw fit. In turn, she could bequeath her assets to anyone, even a non-Vestal female. Some Vestals amassed fortunes.

Despite the rare chastity lapse (likely to result in burial alive) among Vestals, the institution held firm until A.D. 394, when Christians ordered it to disband. Vestals ignored the order. Six years later, the last crusty old Vestal caught a Christian noblewoman stealing the necklace off the Vesta statue and cursed her for profaning the sanctuary. Vestal curses still had hex power: a few years later, the light-fingered aristo and her family were executed by rivals.

❖ ❖ ❖ ❖ LYCORIS ❖ ❖ ❖ ❖

The queen of chironomia

Even as a youngster, Lycoris danced like Madonna, sang like Maria Callas, and carried herself like Katharine Hepburn. Such talents belonged in the earthy art form called mime theater. Seeing the monetary possibilities, her owner sent her to mime community college, where she took the stage name Cytheris.

Mime in Lycoris's day was far from silent. It didn't resemble ancient pantomime, either, which presented a ballet-like performance where a single actor silently mimed all the roles.

Instead, this purely Roman entertainment resembled British pantomime. It captivated audiences with musical improvisation and farcical plot twists. Its bawdy story was told through gestures, facial expressions, and dance by the chief mime, male or female. (Italians still converse with the help of *chironomia*, the eloquent art of gesticulation: just think Joey Tribbiani in *Friends*.)

As a mime, Lycoris performed barefoot, without masks or elaborate costumes. A narrator recited the lines and jokes, which sound vulgar enough to be modern, e.g., "Come into the bath with me and I'll give you a taste of the Cynics' doctrine."

After the curtain fell, Lycoris had another acting job: eye-candy "date" for her owner's powerful friends. Most of the money she earned went to him; eventually she won freedwoman status. Roman society had an intricate system of patronage; although freed, Lycoris remained a client of her ex-master, obliged to render services from courtesaning to mime performances at dinner parties.

When this gifted actress reached twenty-one, she and Mark Antony became lovers. Julius Caesar's number-one drinking pal at the time, this career soldier loved to party with disreputable characters. Riding next to Lycoris in a luxurious litter for two, Antony conducted business on the move, accompanied by an entourage of pimps, performers—and his mom.

This perversion of the natural order did not go down well with many, including local authorities who had to lodge them and treat Lycoris with the deference due a respectable matron.

Whatever his faults, Antony was no snob; he loved Lycoris and treated her with dignity. That behavior offended his soldiers as well, especially after he gave Lycoris a chunk of farmland.

In 47 B.C., Caesar intervened. Lycoris probably saw the break coming. For years afterward, people still called Mark Antony "Cytherius," meaning Cytheris's boyfriend (after Lycoris's stage name), which seriously disgruntled Antony's collection of wives and lovers, including Cleopatra.

Lycoris turned to her career for consolation. Her singing performance of Vergil's classic verses moved everyone, even snotty rich people who wrote poisonous things about her. Her personal life continued messy. Another patrician, Marcus Brutus, fell for her but became even more infamous than Lycoris after he helped to bump off Caesar.

Lycoris survived that scandal too, keeping her title as Rome's most popular mime actress. She went on to inspire feverish love and some decent verse from the poet Gallus, then followed her own heart for a change and disappeared from public view, seeking happiness with a mere army officer.

For centuries after, female mimes took the stage names Lycoris and Cytheris in her honor.

❖ PULLARIUS ❖

CHICKEN RUN, THE PREQUEL

The Roman army had spiritual specialists, but their holy men didn't hold services or try to boost morale among the GIs. They were augurs who read auspices (the word means "bird observation") to make sure that all was hunky-dory (or auspicious, as Romans would say) with the gods. On military campaigns, the troops didn't move an inch until the augurs had gotten the all-clear from Jupiter et al.

The most nitpicky specialist was the *pullarius,* who interpreted the movements of the *pulli* or sacred military chickens. Most of the time, pullarius duty was dull, dull, dull.

At key moments, however, especially when the high command was about to begin a battle, the chicken expert went into action. All the big brass gathered around the cage where the pullarius kept the sacred chickens. At a signal, the pullarius threw dried corn and a soft cake called pulse onto the ground and opened the cage door.

Then the fun began. As he and the anxious commanders watched, the chickens emerged and began to eat. All sorts of things could be learned from the manner in which the fowl feasted—or failed to. If the sacred birds ate greedily, that was a good omen. If some kernels or crumbs fell from their mouths and hit the ground, that was clearly a great omen. The pullarius would proudly yell "*Tripudium solistimum*—the corn danced!" and everyone would slap the B.C. version of high-fives.

If, however, those wretched chooks ignored the food and started flapping or squawking, as chickens have a tendency to do, the signs from the gods were clearly stormy. Whatever military maneuver was about to begin, was called off.

Only a suicidal pullarius would deliberately misread his flock. In 293 B.C., a pullarius, impatient with birds that wouldn't eat, told his superior officer that the corn danced when it didn't. In the ensuing battle, the Romans won, but the prevaricator was struck dead with a random javelin.

If the recalcitrant chickabiddies totally refused to emerge from the cage, that was a mean mother of an omen—one that no Roman military leader would ever ignore. Well, almost ever. During the First Punic War, a fleet commander had his pullarius check the chickens while sailing into battle. When the birds, who understandably hadn't found their sea legs yet, refused to come out or nibble, the commander shouted, "If they won't eat, let them drink!" and tossed the sacred fowl overboard. Almost immediately he lost the battle and was roundly condemned by Romans for his impiety.

No matter which birdbrain they were advising, those chickens weren't as stupid as they looked; on January 1, A.D. 69, when brand-new emperor Servius Galba was taking the auspices, they refused to have anything to do with the old geezer—and flew away. Two weeks later, Galba was stabbed in the neck, the first of three quickie emperors in the year of the revolving-door Imperium.

Other birds, from swifts to owls, were also Jupiter's messengers, their actions closely examined by augurs. But in its wisdom, the Roman army chose to base its decisions on the ordinary chicken.

In Rome, civilians could also vie for the post of pullarius, caring for the city's official sacred chickens in a revered place of augury on Capitoline Hill. As befitted Roman bureaucracy, the pullarius was overseen by a Procurator of Sacred Poultry.

❖ VICTIMARIUS, POPA, CULTRARIUS ❖
NOW HIRING: STRONG ARMS,
STRONGER STOMACHS

Say the word "victim" and we think of human beings in desperate straits, needing our compassion—and our cash. *Victim* used to have a much different meaning. Victims weren't human—they weren't even primates.

Instead, that word referred to domestic animals, birds, and other species singled out to be sacrificed as thank-you offerings by the Greeks, Romans, and other ancient cultures. When the goal was to avert the wrath of the gods, humans carried out the same sort of slaughter but called the critters *hostia*.

Who did the dirty deeds, and how? A proper sacrifice required a staff. This consisted of the augur or soothsayer to read the entrail secrets of the victim, musicians to accompany the procession, and a trio of assistants to wrangle and dispatch the animals: the *victimarius,* the *cultrarius,* and the *popa.* On the column of Trajan, one of Rome's most famous monuments, these workers can still be seen as they lined up for a sacrifice to Mars, the god of war.

Wearing a laurel wreath, what looked like a beach-towel wrap, and not much else, the muscular bare-chested victimarius led his dolled-up victim to its fate. Spectators watched the animal closely; if the victimarius kept the rope slack and the animal appeared to have no clue, that was a good omen. Most sacrifices were straightforward one-animal affairs. Should the authorities want to throw a sacrifice that really grabbed the attention of the gods in question, a *suovetaurilia* or bull-ram-boar combo went up in smoke.

Once the procession reached the altar, the victimarius kindled the fire, set out the salt, wine, and mola cakes, and arranged the knives and other instruments. Then, with gentle hands and consummate care, he got the animal into place and held it. For larger beasts, such as bulls, he had to persuade them to kneel—a dicey task, since it needed to be accomplished in silence.

After the augur sprinkled ritual foodstuffs on the animal's head, another highly buffed, half-naked lad called the popa stepped up. His job: to stun the animal with a heavy mallet or the blunt side of an ax he carried. Once finished, he was swiftly followed by the knife-wielding cultrarius, the specialist who dispatched each victim, then opened the carcass with a large cleaver so that the liver and other internal organs could be accessed by the entrail reader, the augur.

The next act had high disaster potential. The men had to catch all that red-hot gore in bronze bowls, then pour the blood over the altar, while the augur stepped lively to avoid another expensive trip to the drycleaners.

These solemn events were no sloppy, noisy, ramshackle slaughters. Sacrifices had to be perfect in every particular. If any of the animals (or humans) cried out or shivered, these bad omens would nullify the entrail reading and it would have to be done anew. Such ritual tasks took a trio of men with a tender touch and a thorough knowledge of animal handling so that the victims went without fear or knowledge to their deaths.

A lot rode on the work of these three assistants. They had to be deft at their jobs or they would become another sort of victim: the unemployed.

❖ AUGUR ❖

BEGINOPHOBIA

Although Rome had a weather goddess called Tempestates, jobs for weather forecasters were nil. Locals didn't care that much about road conditions on the Appian Way, either. What the average Roman wanted to know was how the gods felt about his upcoming trip or marriage. Senators and generals were just as spooked about beginnings. How did the gods view their next term in office, for instance? And just how kosher was that pre-emptive war with Parthia they were itching to launch...

A gamut of specialists worked full-time to tell them.

Augurs shied away from words like "predict"—they sought divine affirmation of a planned action. In their view, deities preferred to communicate via signs, the weirder the better.

Sneezes, for instance. Many a battle was postponed because someone sneezed to the left during a ritual. Some diviners used mirrors; others specialized in hydromancy or water readings. An even larger group practiced cleromancy or the casting of lots, using props like dice or dried beans. (Julius Caesar, no slouch at forecasts himself, used cleromancy at the Rubicon River when he made his famous "The die is cast" remark.)

The most ancient branch was augury or bird reading. This didn't refer to avian literacy, which even then was looked on as a lost cause, but rather to the interpretation of bird flight and calls. Certain birds were good news or bad, depending on context. A vulture sighting was ominous—except for fans of Zeus, whose birds were the eagle and the vulture. The flight of the first bird seen on January 1 each year carried especially weighty significance.

Hieromancy or entrail reading got an even higher approval rating. These augurs, also called haruspices, dated to pre-Roman times, when Etruscans were the first to gaze into animal guts. The job required special qualities: mastery of the esoterica of organ reading; ability to wrap one's mouth around the names of Etruscan gods like Fufluns; a strong gag reflex to endure the sight and smell of animal vivisection; and clawlike dexterity to hold onto hot, bloody, slippery entrails without dropping them.

Clad in goofy hats and saffron-colored gowns with fringed mantles, augurs deciphered a given deity's feelings by examining the imperfections of animal livers and gall bladders.

A missing liver lobe? Disaster. Double lobes? Great omen. To learn his craft, a haruspex in training worked with a bronze replica of a bull's liver upon which the forty gods and the sixteen sectors of the heavens were delineated.

A practicing haruspex had a sliding fee, depending on the animal being sacrificed. Pigeons and chickens were bargain-bin; rabbits, more pricey; lambs, pigs, and cows, top-of-the-line sacrifices.

When a gut-gazing ritual was over, what happened to all that freshly dead meat? Once the gods' portion had been duly burned on the altar, participants at the sacrifice got to eat the balance as barbecue. Leftovers—if any—were doggie-bag perks for the haruspex.

❖ ASTROLOGER ❖
READING STAR PERSONALITIES
FOR FUN & PROFIT

The great thing about being an astrologer two thousand years ago was that almost everybody bought into the concept from birth, since babies had their horoscopes cast in the delivery room. Star readers got respect— well, most of the time. Poets, comics, and skeptics sometimes sniggered at astrologers, casting doubt on their methods. In earlier times too, the city-states of Greece and its colonies were often astrology-free zones.

Throughout the centuries of Roman rule, though, the workings of astrology chimed well with prevailing religious beliefs. If the stars foretell it, the gods must will it, was the general idea. The acceptance of one's fate was a common factor in the worship of most gods and cults.

Besides, everyone loved the twelve houses of the zodiac and the movements of the seven planets and stars, which each night provided a soothing alternative to prime-time TV.

The symbols fit nicely on bracelets and amulets, giving cheap 24/7 protection against malign fate. Less costly than animal sacrifice, less messy than divination using chickens, astrology gave the stars and planets personality: each had its own name, color, plant, and favorite animal. (Onions and donkeys belonged to Saturn.)

Astrologers, known as "mathematicians" in the parlance of the time, were wonders with numbers and sky observations. The horoscopes they

cast came from the Greek words "I observe the hour." Not surprisingly, they were asked for predictions of human futures as well as celestial forecasts of eclipses and other phenomena.

Periodically the poll numbers of astrologers would fall, generated by a nervous emperor or some ghastly portent— amazing how even a shower of blood or the birth of triplets would set people off. The official reaction that ensued would force all astral practitioners to make themselves scarce until the whole scare had died away.

Emperors felt especially vulnerable. It was thought that astrologers would make predictions and, human nature being what it was, opponents would see to it that they were fulfilled, especially in times of crisis. In A.D. 11, a better-safe-than-sorry Augustus passed a law that prohibited anyone, astrologers included, from possessing an emperor's natal horoscope.

There were several orange alerts during the reigns of Tiberius and Claudius. In July of A.D. 52, an astrologer friend of Emperor Claudius leaked to the press that a lunar eclipse would occur on the emperor's birthday, August 1. He made the announcement to mitigate the bad omen of an eclipse. Imagine his disgust when, later that year, fearful Claudius banished every astrologer from Rome.

The popularity of astrology peaked in the reign of Emperor Hadrian, himself an accomplished astrologer and the sole emperor whose own horoscope has survived. Another high point was the reign of Septimus Severus, who established sun worship as Rome's official religion in A.D. 190, in which astrology played a key part. He even married his wife based on the compatibility of their charts.

With small wobbles from time to time, astrologers and their industry ruled from the second century B.C. until the year A.D. 357, when no-nonsense Christian Emperor Constantine made star-gazing a capital offense. Although modern astrology harkens back to ancient ways, it differs substantially in its concepts, having added extra planets, minor aspects, and the notion of transits or progressions.

❖ ❖ ❖ ❖ **PANCRATES** ❖ ❖ ❖ ❖
Of mice, men, & magic

Even sane, stolid emperors had high superstition indices—including Hadrian, one of the more sensible guys to wear the purple. The man spent so much money on fortune-tellers, he could have put their descendants through college. Hadrian was an omen addict, an entrail second-guesser, an astrology freak.

Despite his years of peaceful rule and his goodwill travels to meet his subjects around the empire, Hadrian was haunted by a sense of disaster. By degrees, he began to tinker with the darker side of the spirit world, an obsession that came to a head in A.D. 130. In that year, Hadrian sought out the services of famed magician Pancrates in the suitably spooky city of Heliopolis, Egypt.

Now fifty-four, skeptical Hadrian had seen a long line of charlatans work their spells and predict their predictions. Still hoping, however, he offered Pancrates a huge sum to conduct an experiment in necromancy.

Pancrates exuded confidence about his surefire recipe for murder via black magic. As he worked, he gave the emperor the details, some of which were: "Take a field mouse and deify it [that is, drown it] in spring water. Take two moon beetles and deify them in river water, and take a river crab and the fat of a dappled goat that is virgin and the dung of a dog-faced baboon, two eggs of an ibis, two drams of storax, two drams of myrrh, two drams of crocus, four drams of Italian galingale, four drams of uncut frankincense, a single onion. Put it all into a mortar with the mouse and beetles...after pounding thoroughly, place in a lead box and keep for use."

An hour after the magician compounded this appetizing mixture and recited the spell, a man showed up at Pancrates' lair. In two hours, the man fell sick; on the seventh hour, he died.

Despite the glaring possibilities for fraud in this setup, Hadrian was blown away. Then Pancrates announced that he would send the emperor dreams to confirm the power of his spell! Completely bowled over, Hadrian paid Pancrates double the agreed-upon fees.

The mouse-beetle-dung spell survived the centuries, materializing in our time as a fragment of papyrus unearthed from the Egyptian sands. On the papyrus were found other spells of coercion, attraction, and protection, some of them darkly poetic.

Pancrates, who possessed literary gifts as well as masterly con artistry, had another golden opportunity to bamboozle. During the imperial stay in Egypt, the emperor's foxy young lover Antinoos disappeared. His body was never found. Pancrates sped to the emperor's side and laid a rosy lotus on him—accompanied by a tragic poem he'd dashed off. In it, he likened the lotus to Antinoos, since it also sprang from the earth and had received the blood of a lion.

Already on the emperor's supernatural A-list for pulling off the death-by-black-magic thing, Pancrates scored even higher with his maudlin flower symbolism. Before he left Egypt, the grieving emperor rewarded Pancrates again—this time with a permanent chair at the Museum and Great Library of Alexandria, the most carefree sinecure any scholar (or magician) could hope for.

❖ THREE ❖

AVOCATIONS UP & DOWN THE ALIMENTARY CANAL

❖ FARMER ❖

FARM PRICES DOWN, SERFS UP

Except for the growing of olives, grapes, and figs, Greek farmers were often out of luck; arable land was scarce, terrain flat enough to plow even scarcer. Italy offered richer soil, more than enough to feed its early population. The average farm, however, measured five acres or less. Even with help from his slaves, a small farmer held on by his dirt-encrusted toenails.

A famous case tells the story best. A freedman named Chresimus got higher yields from his small spread than his neighbors, who accused him of magic spells to "entice away" their crops. The indicted freedman brought his evidence into court: well-kept iron tools, ploughshares, several nicely dressed farm slaves, and two fat oxen. Pointing to his exhibits, Chresimus said, "These are my 'magic spells,' citizens—sorry I can't show you my midnight labors and my sweat as well." Although he was obliged to clean up the appalling mess his oxen had left, Chresimus was acquitted.

Archaeologists have found twelve-month "almanacs" carved in stone that show how Italian farmers worked in tune with the seasons and the

heavens. Here is an example:

> May, 31 days; nones on seventh
> Daylight 14½ hours, darkness 9½ hours
> Sun in Taurus. Protector: Apollo
> Weed wheat, shear sheep, wash wool
> Break in young bullocks
> Cut vetch
> Bless the cornfields, sacrifice to Mercury, Flora

Elite Romans loved to get nostalgic about the good old days when everyone, even scruffy plebs, owned small farms, and politicians retired to their country holdings. True enough, politicians owned farms on which most of their provisions were raised. They also had spreads near Rome where their slaves produced another income stream by raising luxury items, from fatted boars to peacocks and dormice. (The slaves' diet? Bread, figs, sub-standard olives, and cheap wine.)

The days of small indie farmers, however, were numbered. The trend became to let tenant farmers work off their debts by sharecropping.

By degrees, wealthy investors acquired vast tracts in Italy, North Africa, and Sicily, planted with single crops like wheat or lentils, stocked with huge herds of livestock, and worked entirely by slaves. A typical spread might have 2,000 cows, 1,000 mares, 10,000 sheep, 15,000 goats, and 500 slaves to care for them. Agribusiness had arrived with a vengeance.

On these megafarms or *latifundia*, slaves were branded, then savagely whipped to reach their quotas by an overseer, himself a slave. When not laboring daily, the men were chained in the prison found on most farms. Ethnic groups were deliberately mixed to keep revolts to a minimum; most were POWs, men with no future. Except for the mines, this was the worst job a slave could endure.

Something had to give. And in 135 and 104 B.C., it did. Sicily exploded with rebellions called the Servile Wars, which gave some runaways freedom for a few years, after which the revolts were put down with great cruelty.

Agribusiness slavery was never abolished. As the Empire's main sources for cheap slaves dried up, it became cheaper to use free tenants called *coloni* to work the land. Slaves and coloni worked side by side, married to the land, their status gradually melding into rural serfdom as the Roman Empire disintegrated into a mosaic of medieval holdings.

❖ BEEKEEPER ❖

SWEET WORK IF YOU CAN GET IT

Since honey was the ancient world's sole sweetener and a key ingredient in medicines, beemen who raised the insects in apiaries were looked upon with great favor.

Connoisseurs gave the greatest acclaim to the honey from Attica, the area around Athens. There, the bees swarmed around the abundant flowers of wild thyme, watered by the sea breezes. In later Roman times, some beekeepers nearly equaled that fabled honey's quality by establishing hives on the plains of southern France.

Ancient apiarists went the extra mile for their bees. If local blooms weren't sufficient, beekeepers took a hike with their hives. In parts of Italy, hives were placed on boats and taken miles upstream. At dawn, the bees would swarm out to feed. When the boats began to sit very low in the water, the beekeepers knew that their busy charges

Instrumento per le Api

 had filled the hives. In Roman Spain, the apiarists worked even harder, carrying their bees from place to place on mules.

To encourage the industriousness of their bees, apiarists sometimes fed them raisins, dried figs, or wool soaked in raisin wine. They also put out carcasses that had gone bad under the mistaken belief that bees spontaneously sprang from rotting meat. The other cherished myth? Beekeepers believed that a king bee ruled, not a queen.

The tall domed hives were fashioned from bark, fennel, cork, dried dung, or osier reeds, tightly woven and daubed with mud and leaves. (A few ritzy beemen had brick hives or expensive glass ones so insect activity could be observed.) Greeks thought that beehives should always face the east wind, not the rougher north and west winds.

Harvesting took place twice a year. When the Pleiades were seen in the sky, beemen knew it was time for the spring harvest. After extracting honey, beekeepers went after the wax, using a system of washing, drying, then melting it in earthenware pots. The best kind, called Punic wax, was heavily used in medicine preparation, giving beekeepers another source of income.

Disaster could also hit apiarists. When bees fed on the nectar of poisonous plants like rhododendrons and mountain laurel, the honey turned toxic. The Greeks called it "mad honey." It could cause sickness and death in cows, dogs, and whole armies of men.

The Greek army commander Xenophon, who for some masochistic reason wrote a detailed account of his own military failure in Persia, also included another honey of a disaster in his book. While near the Black Sea, he and his starving men raided beehives and became, as he put it, "like raving madmen." His troops collapsed by the thousand—some never to get up again.

In modern times, the toxin in mad honey has been identified as acetylandromedol; a breathing inhibitor, it acts on the nervous system and heart. Small comfort to Xenophon and his men, who had to make do with the traditional Greek "cure" of mixing rue with old honey wine and downing it with bites of salted fish.

❖ ❖ ❖ ❖ PHRYNE ❖ ❖ ❖ ❖

Budding beauty

Agricultural work in Greece was often low-status, done by slaves or the poor. Around 328 B.C., a toothsome young pauper named Phryne was slaving away in the hinterlands, picking the unripe fruit off caper bushes. As she plucked caper buds, an eagle-eyed Athenian sculptor named Praxiteles happened by.

One "Eureka!" later, Phryne found herself swept away, established as his mistress, and duly launched as a red-hot model in Athens, the Big Pomegranate itself.

Her new squeeze had a soft, blurry sculpting style (detractors called it "simpering"). For greater shimmer, he rubbed the marble flesh of his statues with wax. She posed for many of his sculptures, but the work that got them both talked about was a Venus commissioned by the islanders of Cnidos, said in awed whispers to be the finest marble statue ever.

In his studio, Phryne watched as Prax pioneered the use of daring, off-balance poses, using supports disguised as trees or drapery. For her Venus statue, he used an egg-shaped washtub and a towel.

She may have been a Boeotian from Thespiae, the Greek equivalent of a hillbilly, but Phryne was no fool. Although she had major doubts about the Venus-washtub symbolism, she hung out with Praxiteles, dropping hints about how she deserved a gift—say, for instance, one of his best works. When a reluctant Prax offered her a much-praised statue of a satyr, Phryne said, "I'll get back to you."

The following day, Phryne's servant rushed up, shouting that the sculptor's studio was ablaze and most of his artwork destroyed.

In despair, Praxiteles cried, "I'll have nothing to show for all my labors if the fire's gotten my satyr and my cupid!"

Phryne restrained him, smiling. "There's no fire. I'll take the cupid, too." Five hundred years later, both masterpieces were still on display at the shrine of Delphi, where Phryne in turn had given them to honor the gods.

Before long, Phryne didn't confine her favors to Praxiteles. Modeling and world fame were all very well, but a girl had to make a living. She more than made ends meet as a hetaera, a high-priced courtesan who could pick and choose her paying suitors.

One of her gentleman "friends" included an orator called Hypereides. When Phryne got accused of corrupting women by starting a club to worship a Thracian god—a capital crime—she called on Hypereides to defend her.

As he orated away, he could see the jury wasn't won over. Turning to Phryne, he muttered "Trust me," then ripped off her blouse, leaving her topless. At the sight of her amazing maracas, the male jurors were struck with religious awe—or helpless lust. In any event, they acquitted the goddess-like beauty, who went on to even more notoriety.

Praxiteles' statues of the satyr and cupid have vanished. His statue of Phryne no longer exists, either, but a not-very-awesome Roman copy can be ogled in the Vatican Museum. Phryne was right; the washtub was all wrong.

❖ COOK ❖
FLAUNT BEFORE EATING

Parasitic Roman poet Martial once told a wealthy patron, "You're not content to be a glutton—you want to be seen and known as one." Belching, the fellow agreed.

It wasn't easy being filthy rich. You never had a moment's rest, buying armies of slaves, flaunting the length of your client list, blowing obscene amounts on comestibles and potables. Gluttony was a wealth index, extravagance a yardstick that measured who had fuller coffers—and wider waistlines.

In more austere times, Greeks and Romans waited for the cooking slave to prepare a meal, and that was that. To throw a big dinner or a wedding party, a more elegant chef could be rented in the agora or the Forum.

As early as the fifth century B.C., demented cookbook authors began rearing their pretentious heads. At least fifteen books entitled *The Art of Cooking* circulated. One author gained glory for a go-with-everything sauce made of honey, vinegar, milk, cheese, chopped herbs, silphium (a flavor enhancer), and fried blood.

Once the humblest household slave, the cook gained status as cooking became an art form. Junior chefs who showed promise got sent to cooking schools. A cook who earned praise could win freedom and even go on to own her own set of kitchen slaves and washers-up.

Gastronomic one-upmanship ruled. In Athens, cooks in ritzy households favored peacocks' eggs over hens', and routinely served canapé trays of sea urchins, wine-soaked bread, cockles, and sturgeon, followed by roast pig. Dice—square loaves made of cheese, oil, and anise—were a hit. So were songbirds roasted on a spit.

Romans pushed the banqueting envelope even further. Their cooks had to ensure that the ham was from Gaul, the oysters from Britain, the pickles from Spain. Many cooks were imported, just like the kitchen's peppercorns and cinnamon sticks.

Moneyed folk stalked the hottest chefs of the hour. Egged on by foodie celeb and cookbook author Apicius, the quest for culinary gems (Cajun-style sow's udder, dormice flambé) and bizarre ingredients (flamingo tongues, braised camels' heels) grew fiercer.

By imperial times, cooks as working professionals were well organized, having formed guilds as far back as 200 B.C. As a result, they got paid generously, especially those magic-fingered cooks who'd won reputations at the range.

That would have included the chef who created a theme dinner once thrown by Emperor Domitian. At this feast, guests walked into a darkened room where tombstones were erected as place-cards. The cook charred the Hades out of the meat, and the plates it sat on were black. Naked boys, inky black as Roman ghosts, served the food. During the meal, the emperor talked only of murder and sudden death. After an interminable evening of ersatz smiles, bogus compliments, and listless plate-picking, the guests gloomily went home, each expecting a hit man to arrive at any moment. Instead, a messenger brought each guest gifts, from cleaned-up gold goblets to the serving boys, now dressed in spiffy tunics.

Chills and thrills: that was foodie-mania circa A.D. 90, a time when cooks and consumers had to contend with the likes of Domitian, who also enjoyed tormenting flies with his sharp stylus—a habit only an emperor could get away with at the dinner table.

❖ PHYSICIAN ❖
MIRACLE DRUGS & QUASI-CURES

Respect for physicians wasn't that common a couple of millennia ago. Oh sure, everyone loved that warm and fuzzy Hippocratic Oath; but when it came to treatment, the sickly often scuttled in the other direction, saying: *"Aegrescit medendo*—The remedy's worse than the disease."

The best career move an ambitious medico could make was to develop a new cure for some ailment, then find a glamorous patient—or failing that, a loquacious one—to survive it.

A Greek ex-slave named Antonius Musa did just that. As physician to Rome's first emperor, Ant hit the jackpot. Augustus used to double over with periodic pain; an abscessed liver, it was thought. Musa changed all that. He forbade warm-water spas, insisting on a diet of lettuce and ice-cold water, plus a cold-water bathing routine at a spring north of Rome.

The emperor perked right up after his icy, multi-day ordeal. Because he was to be pain-free and warm again, he gave Musa money and gold rings— then exempted Ant and all physicians, present and future, from taxes! Others naturally clamored for Ant's touch, including the poet Horace, whose inflamed eyes got the cold-water treatment, along with head-dunking.

As chief physician, Musa got enchanted anew with the betony plant, writing voluminously about its miraculous cures for forty-seven diseases. (The sedative action of betony could cure a nasty headache, and its astringent leaves made good wound compresses, but that was about it.)

Another Greek miracle worker showed up during Nero's administration. Andromachus, the emperor's personal physician, had long used an evil-smelling compound called theriac to combat the poisons of dogs, snakes, wild animals, and crazed neighbors. Its contents were about as worthless as ear wax (which was in fact the other popular "cure" for bites), but people ardently believed in theriac. Placebo power did the rest.

His breakthrough notion was to turn theriac into a cure-all, a super drug. He began experimenting, eventually developing a proprietary formula of sixty-four secret ingredients. Since theriac had originally been used to combat snake bites, he put a nice chunk of viper flesh into the mix.

The other wow factors in Andy's recipe? He added some cannabis sativa and amped up the opium content five times.

Soon the imperial physician had scores of enthusiastic patients—plus repeat business from all the addicts he unwittingly made. (Or maybe wittingly; who can know?)

Life as a celebrity doctor just got better and better. When famed physician and medical writer Galen came along, he also found Andy's theriac to be a real panacea.

Post-Nero, Galen made buckets of the stuff and administered it to the emperors he served. For Emperor Marcus Aurelius, sick much of his adult life with stomach problems, possibly cancer, Galen prescribed theriac in huge, addictive doses. Whenever the emperor was in the field with his army, he ate nothing in daylight hours except a chunk of it. It's doubtful that Galen's prescription would pass FDA muster these days. Nevertheless, by all accounts his snaky opium milkshake helped Marcus Aurelius control chronic pain enough to rule effectively for twenty years.

❖ AQUARIUS ❖

TOTE THAT AMPHORA

Brains born between the years 1940 and 1950 are hardwired to respond to certain things. Get in an elevator and start humming the "Age of Aquarius" song from the 1967 musical *Hair,* for instance, and every middle-aged person will helplessly join in.

But the true age of aquarius occurred thousands of years ago, and it wasn't pretty. The ubiquitous *aquarius* or water carrier was looked down on as the lowest form of life in Rome. Most of the poor devils were male slaves. Their job? To spend all day toting huge pottery jars of H_2O up the narrow, unlit stairways of the plumbing-free apartment houses in the city. Other water carriers lugged bath water into the homes of the rich, while still others worked for the public baths. These fellows toted jars in and out, filling waist-high basins and pouring water over the bathers.

Water is unconscionably heavy, 8.34 pounds to the gallon. A typical amphora held about six gallons, and the clay container itself added more pounds to the load.

Another group of public slaves, also called aquarii, had more interesting and autonomous jobs. They worked for the *curator aquarum*, the alpha drake in charge of the Roman aqueducts. This large workforce occupied between 460 and 700 aquarii full-time, depending on the administration.

Their apparent job was to assure consistent service—but their main mission was to make bloody well sure that no individual or business got more aqueduct water than they were entitled to by law. This being Rome, home of the bureaucratic worker bee, their jobs were divided into a number of watery specialties.

The *circuitores* worked the circuit, going from one area of an aqueduct to another, monitoring its flow and overseeing other laborers. When a section of aqueduct required servicing—clogged by a mislaid corpse, perhaps—a group of slaves called *silicarii* removed the paving covering the channel, after which the *villici* got to work on the pipes themselves. For actual repairs, the *tectores* were called in to fix masonry or build new sections. Aqueducts had multiple reservoirs, called *castella,* which were located inside Rome and outside the city. Workers called *castellarii* were responsible for the maintenance of these reservoirs.

Being a Roman aquarius of any sort wasn't for sissies. But ordinary women, free and enslaved, also hauled jars of water from wells and fountains, and had done so for centuries. What's more, they looked forward to the outing, if not the chore itself, the neighborhood fountain being a prized center for female gossip and socialization.

❖ FRUMENTARIUS ❖

WHEAT WHEELER-DEALER

Exasperated Romans were fond of grumbling that even Jupiter himself couldn't please everybody. That maxim certainly rang true about the unglamorous position of *frumentarius,* the government grain officer. As the man responsible for supplying, warehousing, and selling grain, no one loved him. In an average work week, the frumentarius was cursed and threatened as much as fawned over.

Why did the grain guy figure so prominently in the lives of people? His influence over their daily bread—or its lack. In Rome alone, one million bread-lovers chomped down an average of one and a half pounds of bread per day. (Roman loaves, made from emmer wheat, may have had twice the protein of modern breads.)

Since its beginnings, the city of Rome had considered the grain supply to be a government obligation. For centuries, a fixed quantity of wheat was supplied monthly to the public (not just the poor) at well below market price. No means test, either: just show up in person to claim it. The poorest folk got theirs free of charge, using a system of Scrabble-sized tiles—the B.C. equivalent of food stamps.

Anxious to keep the populace happy, rulers and administrators kept relaxing Roman laws. By the reign of Augustus, as many as two hundred thousand recipients may have received the equivalent of twelve million bushels of free or at-cost wheat, rye, and barley each year—all of it supplied by the provinces.

The crops came largely from huge plantations in Egypt, Gaul, and Spain. Arranging long-distance transport became a key part of the frumentarius's job. After harvesting and drying, broad-beamed ships brought the grain to Italy. The grain was then stored and sold from warehouses at the port of Ostia. It took a thousand shiploads of grain to feed Rome for a year—if all went well. If storms, shipwreck, or war disrupted the supply, results could be disastrous.

The frumentarius official was constantly being evaluated. Although he could make a very prosperous living from his job, penalties for shortfalls, interruptions, or grain scandals were dire: heavy fines, exile, even (gulp) execution.

As more towns like Rome, Antioch, and Ephesus grew into cities, the number of frumentarii rose like good bread. Their duties also expanded, getting even more people furious at them. Most working people had to hand over a grain tax that went to pay for the standing army of Rome. Other taxes were imposed on middlemen or customers like bakers wanting to buy grain in large quantities. To build granaries for storage, middlemen were at times compelled by the frumentarius to take out high-interest loans—invariably from local lenders like the city itself.

At some point in the Hadrian administration, the job of frumentarius took a curious turn. As if it weren't difficult enough to be a grain officer, what with the public abuse he had to endure, he was now called upon to spy in the provinces. Was this some weird moonlighting quirk? A money-saving gesture on the part of a penny-pinching administration? The grain-spy enigma is a mystery as tough as a week-old loaf of Roman rye.

❖ LABORER ❖
HARD-EARNED BREAD

Whenever there's talk about big-city welfare programs or government policies to pacify citizens, pundits invariably bleat about Rome's "bread and circuses." That pithy phrase from Juvenal's book of satires actually refers to an important right lost in A.D. 14 by non-aristocratic citizens (that is, any freeborn person not of senatorial or knightly rank). In that year, new emperor Tiberius abruptly took away the rights of plebeians to elect their own magistrates, giving that privilege to the Senate.

At the stroke of a pen, a huge majority of Roman citizens lost their political power. In his poem, Juvenal assumed that all of them immediately turned to gobbling down the bread dole and watching subsidized entertainment. An upper-class satirist who'd been exiled once for a too-vigorous lampoon, Juvenal now courted favor with another emperor by writing sassy but patrician-pleasing remarks about the idle mob he imagined to have existed 116 years previously.

It's quite true that up to twenty percent of all Romans received the *annona,* the free monthly wheat or bread; in addition, prices were kept artificially low for half a million more residents. But households at poverty levels could not live on bread alone—nor did they.

They worked. Many of the jobs they took were invisible, a humble yet critical part of the Herculean task of feeding a million Romans. Today this plebeian man would be called a temp, a casual laborer, but there was nothing casual about the labor he did. May to October, he put in long hours at Rome's port, Ostia, unloading grain from superfreighters, nicknamed "firs" or "pines" for the giant trees that formed their masts and keels.

Already in place at the port were well-organized, better paid guilds of stevedores, grain carriers, and amphora carriers. They expertly handled some of the arrivals, from construction materials to exotic animals for the arena. But they couldn't cover all of it.

A 1999 study done by classics and archaeology professors analyzed data and crunched the numbers to calculate how much food was unloaded and the amount of labor needed to move it from big ships to riverboats and then into warehouses.

The numbers are staggering: over eighteen hundred shiploads just to carry the wheat, olive oil, and wine to feed Rome for a year. That represented 20 million liters of oil, 100 million liters of wine, and 4.7 million sacks of grain.

Most ships arrived during the one-hundred-day window of peak sailing, creating a stack-up worthy of O'Hare International Airport. Some three thousand laborers were required to unload the ships the first time—and more thousands to load the riverboats to haul foodstuffs upriver to Rome.

Who filled these off-again, on-again jobs of back-breaking labor and few benefits? Not guild members or slaves, but the city's freeborn plebeians, the same men whose modest resources entitled them to the dole—Rome's edible answer to food stamps. Thanks to their part in the complex system that fed the city, Rome survived hundreds of years without widespread shortages or famine.

❖ BAKER ❖

HOME OF THE HAPPY DOUGH

For a carb-loving culture like the ancient Romans, the man who made fresh bread was bound to make dough of another sort. Romans were fussy about quality, too—only the best loaves got stamped "*primus*" for prime.

The profession of baker went back a long way. In Greek times, bakers used beehive ovens, and their products were sold in the marketplace by yeasty saleswomen noted for their abusive language. As a lark, one Greek baker invented the breadstick dildo, a biodegradable item that proved a hit with lonely housewives.

Roman bakers also had a reputation for earthy fun. Over many a bakery entrance appeared the words "here dwells happiness," along with a giant phallus, protective symbol of the god Priapus.

Like a few other trades, bakers were equal-opportunity employers, hiring a mix of freeborn, freedmen, and slaves. The bakers' *collegium*, or guild, was one of the original worker associations in ancient Rome, which boasted 254 bakeries at one point.

At times, bakers might also be millers, pounding their wheat in huge mortars or grinding it with stone querns, still seen at the ancient bakeries of Ostia and Pompeii. Stone-ground breads, while healthy, were full of fine grit that gave your teeth a terrible hammering.

Bread occupied a central place in stomachs and hearts; being a traditional item used in religious rituals, it filled a sacred need as well. Maybe that's why Roman-era bakers as a group were astonishingly prosperous—based on the evidence of their houses, bakeries, and tombs.

One eccentric example was Vergilius Eurysaces, an ex-slave with careers as contractor and baker in republican-era Rome. For himself and his wife, he built a sepulcher in the shape of a huge bread oven, complete with dough-mixing vessels, mosaics, and a jolly inscription, similar to a "We're all out of doughnuts" notice, saying, "The esteemed baker within will not appear today."

Pictorial evidence about bakers' success in life includes two of the best-known yet most puzzling images ever found in Pompeii and Herculaneum.

The first is a crudely painted image of two men and a child receiving bread over a counter from the hands of a well-dressed man, surrounded by stacks of round loaves baked in pizza-like slices. Some theorize this depicts the *annona,* the free or at-cost bread distributed to a large percentage of the populace. Others argue that it represents an honor held by the baker during his lifetime. Maybe it's the ancient version of a photo opportunity for an ambitious, apron-wearing candidate for office.

The second, a wonderful portrait of man and wife, is nearly as enigmatic. Found in the entry hall of a Pompeiian home, this encaustic painting on wood has been identified as the baker Terentius Neo and his spouse. Dressed in their finery, awkwardly holding upper-class symbols of literacy, the couple glow with embarrassed pride. Here dwelt happiness indeed—at least until the morning of August 24, A.D. 79, when their world disappeared in a rain of volcanic ash, deadly fumes, and white-hot stones.

❖ GARUM MANUFACTURER ❖
THE SULTANS OF SAUCE

Every culture has its well-loved national dish, often a substance that puzzles or nauseates people of other cultures. (Favorites like haggis and poi come to mind.)

Romans were no exception. Their catsup, their Marmite, their blue cheese dressing was called garum. This exquisite topping was composed (more accurately, decomposed) of fish entrails and blood squished into a paste, layered with salt and spices, then allowed to ferment and reduce for twenty to thirty days. The result? A fish sauce, sometimes dark as night, that Romans dribbled over eggs, meat, and vegetables, or spread on bread. They loved its tang on everything—even honey cakes.

What did garum taste like? That depended on quality and price. *Liquamen,* the primo stuff, was made from mackerel or fat sardines; *allex* and *muria,* the bargain-basement juice, from anchovy dregs. High-grade garum may have resembled a paler, fishier Worcestershire sauce.

Who were the gurus of garum, the strong-stomached entrepreneurs who produced this queen of condiments? Originally, the Greeks had dreamed the stuff up. Over the centuries, a number of locales gained renown for its odiferous manufacture, including Clazomenae in Asia Minor, Leptis in North Africa, Gades in Spain, and the cities of Pompeii and Cosa near Naples.

The father-son enterprise of the Sestii family of Cosa made famously good garum, but perhaps the biggest commercial fish in the sea of the first century was a freedman named Aulus Umbricius Scaurus. Pompeii's leading garum exporter and manufacturer, he also had retail shops. The Umbricii family's palatial split-level home overlooking the water had not one but three reception halls.

These families and others made fortunes, partly because they were astute enough to control other parts of the process. They owned kilns and manufactured clay amphorae, the shapely terracotta packaging of choice in ancient times. Garum, wine, and olive oil were shipped by sea and stored in amphorae. The amphora holding fish sauce had a distinctive hollow-toed shape and held up to twenty gallons. An average ship could carry five thousand amphorae of garum.

Always eager to have items made to order, wealthy Romans used slaves to produce their own designer garum at their country villas. Most people, however, bought the ready-made stuff, the best if they could afford it, such as the Umbricius amphora whose label said: "the flower of garum, made from the mackerel, a product of Scaurus."

As Rome grew as an empire, the use of garum spread throughout its subject nations and provinces with amazing speed—perhaps via smell. Archaeologists have followed the words of ancient writers (and maybe their own noses) to find garum sites and salting installations all around the Mediterranean, confirming the historical record.

Moreover, countless amphorae, some retaining an unmistakable fishy whiff, have been found in marine shipwrecks from Marseilles to Spain to Tunisia, many of them bearing a painted label or clay stamp of approval from the folks we might term the First Families of Fish Sauce.

❖ FISHMONGER ❖

FISH GOTTA SWIM, MONGERS GOTTA MONG

Even though his subjects snickered at Emperor Trajan's hokey provincial Spanish accent, he knew what people liked even before they did. Between A.D. 107 and 110, he put his favorite architect to work on a pedestrian-friendly, semicircular, multi-level complex of 170 offices, shops, drinkeries, and eateries. Before anyone could say gross excess ad infinitum!, the world's first shopping mall came into being.

Looking at the white stucco and shiny red bricks of Trajan's Market, the emperor must have hugged himself with glee. So beautiful! So...empty. By Jove, business clients to rent the spaces, that's what was missing—an old duffer with high-end togas for sale, a jeweler or two to give it that true mall feel. But what about a commercial anchor, something to bring in the foot traffic? Yes! A sassy-mouthed fishwife and her surefire draw of savory seafood.

Your average Roman fishwife was, like her counterpart in Athens, a streetwise gal of utmost independence, and a purveyor of much coarse merriment. Often joked about in comedies, Greek fishwives were notorious for their stout builds and beefy arms, which they used to good effect, slicing up huge tunas into steaks and flinging their finest fish at their customers. Their raucous voices were part of their stock-in-trade. Fishwives were loud enough to give stiff competition to the speakers at a Metallica concert—and glib enough to keep argumentative bargain-seekers in line.

Given the quick-ripening flavor of the merchandise and the need to wash down the stands at day's end, seafood shops were probably under the covered shopping arcade leading to the Via Biberatica, the main walkway that made a half-circle through the mall. Although the imperial circle might enjoy snow-chilled wine and other delicacies on a regular basis, the average fishmonger might never see ice in her lifetime except on the tip of her nose in December.

Like her competitors from Greece to Cádiz, the Roman fishwife arose before dawn to fetch the catch from boats at the port. She had to get there and back before the sun came up; no vehicular traffic was allowed within the city by daylight. Only a major disaster would force her to buy sardines or mackerel from the middlemen who drove cartfuls of more dubious-quality seafood into Rome.

Like others in the mall and throughout the city, the fishwife's shop opened for business at dawn and closed around midday. She sold wild-caught fishes and seafood but probably made more profit off the farmed oysters and eels that were grown in special ponds.

Male and female fishmongers, who sometimes fished for their own catch as well, had their own collegia or associations to ensure a nice crowd to party with (plus a savings plan for your funeral). Each June 6, they got together on the banks of the Tiber River to celebrate the Ludi Piscatorii, their own fisherfolks' festival, complete with lavish spread and assuredly the best seafood in town.

❖ DENTAL SPECIALIST ❖

OPEN WIDE

Fans of Brian Blessed and the BBC series *I, Claudius* might be downcast to learn that the toothy smiles of Emperor Augustus were historically impossible. The emperor's actual choppers were described by historian Suetonius as "small, few, and decayed."

Scribonius Largus, a dental specialist and author, cooked up a special toothpowder for Augustus, combining chamomile, fresh brine, salt, and spikenard. It was supposed to make teeth firm and white, but apparently didn't perform.

Undeterred, Largus invented another dentrifice for the emperor's sister Octavia, composed of barley flour, honey, vinegar, salt, and more spikenard, the whole mess burnt over charcoal. No word on its efficacy, but Largus remained an imperial favorite into the time of Claudius, and in A.D. 43 was sent to Britain with the military invasion.

In Roman times, the profession of dentist didn't stand on its own. Barbers, not dental specialists, took care of simple extractions and minor problems like bad breath, employing cypress-berry mouthwashes and purslane, chewed like gum. Physicians, usually Greek professionals, handled tougher dental emergencies.

Dental health was helped enormously by the foods eaten (or not) by almost everyone. Sugar was unavailable, honey used sparingly, and most people ate more vegetables than carbs. Decay did occur, however, among the great and the humble alike. Simple folks attacked the pain with wine and catmint infusions. The experts, however, believed that tiny worms caused tooth decay. To combat said worms, dental specialists fumigated patient's mouths with a charred mixture of narcotic henbane and soft tar, then said, "Rinse, please."

Other things went wrong in Roman mouths. All that stone-ground bread and porridge—with its many residual bits of grit—wore down the teeth of poorer people and soldiers. Teeth got knocked out. Archaeological research on skeletal remains show that pregnancy and childbearing were very hard on women's teeth; a large study of the Poundsbury population of Roman Britain showed twice as much tooth loss among females as males.

Once serious gum disease or an abscess occurred, most of the recommended options were gruesome. Celsus, who wrote extensively on medical matters and dental surgery, was a great one for taking a red-hot iron to the gums, preferably without anesthetic, although he grudgingly admitted that poppy juice would ease the pain. Of the "kill 'em or cure 'em" school, he also liked to stick peppercorns or a fish-resin mixture into the holes left by freshly extracted teeth. For mouth ulcers or jaw gangrene, he swore by a mixture of honey and burnt papyrus, washed out before and after with lentil gruel.

Even cocksure dental "experts" like Celsus made no attempt to copy or improve on the wizardry of the Etruscans. Seven centuries earlier, Etruscan orthodontists had manufactured cunning sets of false teeth, including bridges made of flat gold bands to hold them in place. Archaeological findings seem to suggest that only women wore the shiny prosthetics—and that tooth removal was deliberate. A fashion statement for the Etruscan matron, perhaps? You decide.

❖ FORETASTER ❖
SALIVATING TO GET TO WORK

Say what you will about imperial decadence, four centuries of gluttonous emperors created a smorgasbord of interesting job opportunities—including the key post of *praegustator* or foretaster.

Most of the new jobs were generated by the imperial households, beginning with Augustus, the first emperor. Once he had a foretaster, every imperial home had to have one. Paranoia ran rampant. Or maybe it was simple prudence, given the size and no-holds-barred ambition of imperial families, and the equally spectacular number of unexplained expirations and near-miss cases of poisoning among them.

What did it take to become a praegustator? Once a candidate passed the background check and the visual inspection for good grooming, the intake interview was a breeze. Have a discerning palate or wish you had one? Live on water but have a thing for fine wines? Willing to risk an agonizing death while on duty?

Job benefits were sweet. No heavy lifting or washing-up; able to take countless mulled-wine breaks in a warm kitchen; get to lord it over the cooks and waiters. Best of all, several times a day the foretaster got to be first to dive into meals fit for a king, the best bits smoothly washed down with wines from the imperial cellar.

Many foretasters were freedmen, while others were chosen from the ranks of trustworthy household slaves—a boon for upward mobility, since these slaves, provided they avoided death and weren't indicted on conspiracy charges, often became freedmen.

By the hyper-suspicious, toxin-hysterical reign of Emperor Domitian, the praegustators had their very own association, where they gathered periodically to snipe at their patrons' poor taste in wines. Off-duty, they probably gobbled fast food and knocked back gallons of swill until they passed out.

Most job-holders faithfully carried out their gourmandizing tightrope walk, saving the lives of the worthy and worthless alike. Those whose names were remembered tended to be corrupt souls who figured in conspiracies of one sort or another.

The most infamous? Halotus, foretaster for Emperor Claudius. A eunuch of high standing in the household, he was also the emperor's conveyor of secret messages. After Claudius's suspicious death, suspected of being caused by a toxic mushroom dish engineered by those tired of waiting in the wings, one would think that Halotus would lose his job or be banished to Bulgaria.

Instead, this probable co-conspirator continued in a position of gastronomic confidence throughout the fourteen-year reign of Nero.

He and other foretasters were genuinely needed by those around Nero. The pimply young emperor had ambitious plans to poison nearly everyone, including the entire Roman Senate. Among Nero's victims was his stepbrother Britannicus, who was bumped off at dinner in a feat of legerdemain talked about for centuries. In this case, the boy was given a drink, duly tasted by the foretaster, but too hot for Britannicus's liking. A servant in on the plan then cooled the drink with toxin-laced water.

Halotus, unflappable superstar of victual nibbling, went on to greater career moves in A.D. 69, the year of the revolving-door emperors. Appointed to a prestigious post by Emperor Galba, he probably outlived him, since Galba had just six months in office before being stabbed in the neck.

❖ STERCORARIUS ❖
MANURE ENTREPRENEUR

Roman engineers built aqueducts able to bring clean water to more than a million people each day, and a complex system of canals, pipes, and sewer mains to carry waste away. Refined for centuries, the city water disbursement and sewage disposal was, as that scatological joker Caligula might have said, a magnum opus that made one flush with pride at being a Roman.

A thousand fountains, all the great public baths, the public latrines, and Rome's important buildings were connected to the sewerage system. Now here's a shock: most Romans weren't hooked up. The poor and working class, who lived mainly in apartment buildings sans plumbing, sure weren't. Neither were folks who lived in low-lying areas; when the Tiber River rose, so did the sewage, with distressing results indoors. Even owners of mansions and villas on Rome's hills often opted out. The S-bend pipe hadn't been invented yet, so bad smells easily traveled from the sewer into the house. Vermin and other sorts of wildlife were a common problem. A local octopus even gained lasting notoriety by using the Roman sewer to get access to a house, where it regularly ate up the pickled fish.

So where did the end result of the digestive systems of a million Romans go each day? Enter the *stercorarius*—the smelly, unsung hero of the city's economy. A man of strong back and rare daring, for a fee he emptied the cesspools and slop buckets of the citizenry, then hauled the contents in a cart to the outskirts of the city.

The stercorarius was a recycler. He hauled away neighborhood dungheaps and collected at houses. At the other end, farmers bought his noisome product, since they routinely used all sorts of dung

Even the man who hauled manure and urine had symbols for his gross national products.

89

on their crops. Thanks to two-thousand-year-old graffiti, we even know what the stercorarius got for manipulating a cartful of manure. He received eleven copper coins, the smallest denomination but probably enough to buy his daily bread, figs, and wine.

❖ WINEMAKER ❖

MAKE MINE UNLEADED

In the ancient world, grape growers became winemakers and vice-versa. Greeks and their grapes had thousands of years of history together, making wines high in natural sugar that ranged in color from straw to blackish-red. Italian winemaking came along in the third century B.C. As the Roman Empire came into being, winemakers and growers moved into new provinces, such as Gaul, Spain, and the North African coast.

It was an unstressful time to be a winemaker. No striving for ribbons or reviews, no appellations to fuss over, no shelf competition, no fretting over clever label copy. Wine tastings happened at festivals or in homes. Most vintages were extremely ordinary, yet even sour rotgut found ready customers at dockside dives, snack shops, and any business near military troops. Advertising? Not a problem. Every tavern had ivy on its signage or walls, shorthand for "We've got the wine god's product inside."

The grapes, harvested from vines five years old and up, were collected in wicker baskets in September or October, and stomped (usually to live music) by two or more slaves on the pressing floors. After separating the juice from stems and seeds, it was then fermented for six months in huge earthenware jars called *pithoi*. After fining with strainers, most vinos were considered drinkable and were transferred to slim six-gallon terracotta amphorae for shipping and storage.

Greek and Roman winemakers leaned on luck. And magic. In vineyards, they hung masks of the wine god. As the breeze blew, wherever he "looked," the vines would be fruitful.

Although glass bottles might seem more practical, vintners of old swore by amphorae. Their voluptuous shape allowed the two-handled amphorae to be tightly packed into ship holds padded with pine needles or heather—up to four hundred metric tons of vino at a time. To unload the cargo, longshoremen simply rolled an amphora on its pointed "toe" or toted them on their shoulders.

Cork stoppers were seldom used; winemakers preferred clay seals with detailed labels. Those labels on wine amphorae, found by the gazillions through shipwreck archaeology, have revealed the unquenchable thirst of ancient populations—and the stunning quantity of wine that whizzed around the Mediterranean and Black seas.

Winemakers of the time made some darned good tipple, although you'd need to be a Roman senator to afford certain ones. The most princely vintage was Falerian, grown on the hillsides around Naples. Made from late-harvest grapes, it was one of a handful that aged well. Falerian, Caecuban, Massicum, and other famous names were laid down in smaller containers—even, at times, in costly glass-blown amphorae.

Since their products oxidized easily and had to travel by sea, winemakers sealed their containers inside with pitch and other substances. Customers didn't mind the resiny tang. Seawater itself became a common additive—as did smoke! Lesser and finer wines alike got an array of weird additives: mastic, myrrh, cinnamon, parsley, black pepper, and even more powerful ingredients from opium to absinthe. (We have to remind ourselves that ancient wine was utilized as a medicine as well as a beverage.)

Although downright phobic about the insanity potential of intoxication, Greeks and Romans were adventurous oenophiles in other ways. Environmentally speaking, the worst idea to catch hold was the Roman notion of sweetening old wine with sugar of lead (lead acetate). Called *mulsum,* this sugary wine was allowed to simmer for hours in a lead pot, then served in a fancy lead goblet. Beside the buzz, mulsum may have let sippers ingest as much as a gram of lead a day, according to modern researchers who have field-tested such mixtures—by methods, let's hope, other than tasting them.

❖ WINE CRITIC ❖

A MUCH SOT-AFTER POST

There may be veritas in vino, but wine one-upmanship began even earlier. It was no stroll in the Forum being an ancient wine critic. For one thing, you couldn't natter on about a vintage's color or its "legs" since you drank from pottery cups or metal vessels. You couldn't compare wines from different winemakers, either—only from districts.

Greek wines dominated the tasting and swilling scenes from the fifth to the second centuries B.C., island wines from Cos, Lesbos, and Crete being the hotly contested favorites. The majority were white wines, short-lived and potent.

Early wine connoisseurship was a clubby males-only bastion, its supreme expression an elaborate ritual at drinking parties called *symposia*. Someone would be elected that night's winemaster, in charge of the *krater* or vessel that would hold the beverage. Before anyone quaffed, the winemaster decided how much the wine was to be cut (the norm was to add two or three times more water). As the evening's head critic, he led the guests in sniffing, tasting, and judging.

Anyone who chose to drink unmixed wine, called "Scythian style," was shunned as a barbarian. Modern debate still rages about this issue; it's as difficult to believe that ancient wines were substantially more potent as it is to imagine that ancient drinkers were less able to handle their drink.

Italian wines had promise. The stuff made around Pompeii, while plentiful, was infamous for its hangover potential. Others, like Holconii, were terrific.

Once Italy began to produce high-quality wines, it left Greece the dregs of the market. At Roman parties, it became almost obligatory for seasoned bibbers in the crowd to bemoan the present, and sigh nostalgically for 121 B.C., the incredible year that had produced Italy's Opimian wine. Although most wine experts were upper-class and didn't lower themselves to accept payment (except in beverage), both Greeks and Romans wrote voluminously about their favorites.

In the fifth century B.C., an oenophile named Hermippus waxed poetic over Greek wines: "Sweet generous Magnesian, and Thasian over which the scent of apples plays, this I judge much the best of the other wines, after fine and harmless Chian. There is a certain wine they call *saprias,* from the mouths of whose jars when opened there is a smell of violets, of roses, of larkspur, a sacred smell through all the high-roofed hall."

Hermippus might have been describing a wine made from grapes infected with Botrytis, the "noble rot" still sought by some winemakers today.

Five hundred years after Hermippus, veteran boozer Pliny critiqued some nearly two-hundred-year-old Opimian, a remnant left from 121 B.C: "...the wines of that year still survive, though they have now been reduced to the consistency of honey with a rough flavor, for such in fact is the nature of wines in their old age. It would not be possible to drink them neat or to counteract them with water, as their over-ripeness predominates even to the point of bitterness, but with a very small admixture they serve as a seasoning for improving all other wines."

His comments confirm the ancient tilt toward sweet wines and mixing vinos. Less poetic than Hermippus, pithy Pliny would chuckle if he knew his critiques were still being read.

❖ FOUR ❖

THE LAW & DISORDER PROFESSIONS

❖ ARCHER-COP ❖
A BULL'S-EYE FOR COMMUNITY POLICING

The city-state of Athens was famous for its volunteer-based democracy. Local citizens had a reputation for doing things "their way," which included giving unpleasant and dangerous jobs to public slaves owned by the state. One employment curiosity had its start around 490 B.C., when Athenians got a great deal on Scythian prisoners of war. For a song they purchased three hundred low-mileage archers, big beefy specimens wearing barbarian-style long-johns and goofy headgear that passed for high style back in Scythia.

The ways and means committee, including commissioners called "the Eleven" who oversaw the prison and law enforcement, soon came up with a keen idea: why not use the new archers as community crime-stoppers?

Small-townish Athens wasn't a hotbed of crime, but the numbers of rapes, murders, burglaries, and arsons were already high enough to merit a full-time executioner slave. Besides, the bow-and-arrow bunch could also handle public gatherings, theater crowd control, and night-watchman duties.

Then there was that pesky quorum business. The peoples' assembly met every nine days and needed six thousand male citizens to reach a quorum. Without one, Athenians couldn't even ostracize anyone. The most tedious part of democratic rule was rounding up the late sleepers and slackers trying to play truant from assemblies.

Once the new archer-cops were installed, they moved through the Athenian marketplace, carrying lengths of fat rope between them. The rope, wet with red dye, besmirched the starchy white garments of any male citizens who hadn't made it up the hill to the assembly. Marked men had to pay fines.

The "rope of shame" was such a success that the archer-cops were given new firepower: whips. Even though they weren't what we'd call arresting officers, the Scythians nevertheless had the authority to wallop, handcuff, and hogtie rowdy citizens—and do the same to noncitizens, from uppity women and misbehaving slaves to nonresident ruffians.

Everyone loved the big lunks—uncouth, dim-witted fellows who couldn't even learn to speak Greek properly. In no time, Aristophanes and other writers used them as running jokes. Scythian archer slaves and their Keystone-Kop ways became mainstays of Greek comedy.

What were working conditions like for Scythian archer-cops? Far better than what most slaves encountered. The corps, eventually numbering one thousand, received food and clothing stipends. Initially, they were put up in tents, later in better housing atop Ares Hill. Although slaves, archer-cops were free to take part in the numerous religious ceremonies and festivals of Athens and could accept tips of food and wine from grateful citizens.

An especially sharp Scythian (if that isn't a contradiction in terms) might even become captain over his fellow archers. If so, he could then marry, have a house of his own, father children, and smirk at his countrymen while basking in the poetic title of *toxarch* or "Lord of the Bow."

❖ VIGIL ❖

SMOKE-EATERS BY DAY, CRIMEFIGHTERS BY NIGHT

Sure, Nero fiddled (lyred, actually) around while Rome burned in A.D. 64, but that blaze was merely one of countless monster fires the city suffered. This propensity to kindle was understandable when most temples and houses were built of wood. But later, when marble covered everything in sight and even cheapie structures were mostly concrete? Archaeologists blame the lack of chimneys and the use of open fires to heat and cook.

Historians, however, also point to arson for financial gain. Before imperial times, street gangs ran Rome, in turn controlled by crooks who got rich on flammable ventures. Residents only had ill-equipped bands of state slaves to turn to for help in dousing fires—or their own slaves.

The arson business came to a critical crossroads in A.D. 6, when fire demolished nearly a third of the city. That tragedy galvanized Emperor Augustus into creating a firefighting force called the *vigiles* by freeing six thousand slaves. The carrot he offered was the chance of Roman citizenship if they lived to complete a six-year contract. To run the corps, he recruited citizens with military experience as officers. The ranks of vigiles were replenished by freedmen at first; but by A.D. 160 or so, men of free birth could also join.

Training firefighters, building station houses and barracks in Rome's fourteen districts plus the port city of Ostia, and supplying equipment all cost a bundle. To fund the service, pragmatic Augustus levied a five percent surcharge on the sale of slaves.

The vigiles made an immediate impact on the overcrowded city. Organized in military fashion, tended to by four doctors, the corps eventually stabilized at about 7,200 men.

Three specialties emerged in the vigiles: the *aquarius, siphonarius,* and *uncinarius.* The first organized bucket brigades and supplied water to the heavy pumping engine; the second operated the siphons or pumps; and the third used large hooks to pull off burning roofs. Besides ladders, axes, and buckets, firefighters used heavy blankets soaked in vinegar and esparto-grass mats to smother fires. It wasn't long before they were dubbed "mat men." The vigiles' most useful tool? Acetum, a fire-extinguishing chemical put in a clay vessel, then lobbed into the flames like a hand grenade.

These early firefighters had the authority to levy fines on households that failed to keep supplies of water, vinegar, and buckets on hand—and even got to flog the grossly negligent.

Vigiles did their jobs so vigorously that before long they were given another—albeit with no increase in a salary already lower than that of your average legionary. Armed with truncheons and short swords, vigiles became street cops by night, busting burglars, tracking down runaway slaves, and arresting lawbreakers. Each station house had its own lockup for wrongdoers.

New recruits got duller tasks, such as looking after the valuables of bathers at the public baths, the equivalent of parking-ticket duty.

Rome continued to be flammable, averaging, it's now thought, about one hundred fires per day, two of them serious. Between A.D. 15 and 54, the city suffered six major fires. Despite the odds against them, the vigiles vigorously carried out their dual missions to protect a million-plus residents for five centuries. The spirit of the vigiles was such that many crime-cum-fire-fighters stayed active for a full twenty-six-year term before honorably retiring.

❖ PRAETORIAN PREFECT ❖

PUPPET MASTER

If the real Lucius Aelius Sejanus, played with silky villainy by Patrick Stewart in the BBC series *I, Claudius,* possessed half the evil intelligence with which Stewart infused the role, Romans must have endured sixteen years of terror during the regime of Emperor Tiberius.

Nailed in print by historian Tacitus, Sejanus easily takes the immoral-immortal sweepstakes as history's most notorious Praetorian prefect. Interestingly, he was simply one in a long line of hidden string-pullers.

Before imperial rule, prefects or commanders were appointed for a fixed period. Prefect posts ranged from the official who handled the pension fund for legionaries to the fellow who governed Judaea (which would include Pontius Pilate, history's favorite ditherer).

Beginning with Augustus, their powers were extended to include military and civil duties, and their selection became the sole prerogative of the emperor. The Praetorian prefect was suddenly the Big Cheese, the commander in charge of the personal guards of the imperial family.

As the importance and numbers of the Praetorian Guard climbed, so did that of its commander, now number two man in the empire, with the ear of the emperor himself. That firepower brought wealth, prestige, and the abilities to reward underlings who toed the line and to punish almost anyone else.

A dedicated social climber, prior to his appointment Sejanus had married his way into the wealthy family of Apicius, the nonfrugal gourmet of the day. Once he got the call from the palace, he jettisoned wife number one, insinuated his way into the good graces of the Senate and Emperor Tiberius—and into the beds of imperial females.

Sejanus loved his work, persecuting people accused of high treason. Proximity to the throne made him even more ambitious. Only when Sejanus's overthrow plot was discovered did Emperor "I'm-busy-with-unspeakable-vices" Tiberius lose confidence in him. By that time, he'd engineered the deaths of a great many people and had consolidated the Praetorian Guards into one camp, a menacing practice that made imperial coups easier.

Sextus Burrus, one of the "good" Praetorian prefects, spent eight years trying to keep the government on an even keel—meanwhile compensating for and (when desperate) covering up the vicious habits of young Emperor Nero. At length, despite his position, Burrus knuckled under to Nero's lethal demands. Like almost everyone in that circle, Burrus ended up on the mortuary slab, possibly poisoned at the emperor's wish.

The many-tentacled reach of the Praetorian prefect office continued its ambitious expansion for 170 years. By the third century A.D., some of its office holders were overthrowing emperors with laughable ease. Rulers cycled in and out of the top spot faster than the coinage could keep up.

Instead of carrying out his civil and military duties, the Praetorian prefect had become the rogue alpha. Only when Emperor Diocletian took the purple in A.D. 284 did he wrest away their control in a sweeping governmental reform. In later centuries, the post became more democratic, making it possible for a soldier to work his way up through the ranks to this exalted office, which commanded most of the military troops in Italy.

❖ **LICTOR** ❖

BODYGUARD ON BOARD

In Rome's republican times, if you were a husky pleb with nicely firm abs and a mean, don't-mess-with-me expression, you too could have a crack at becoming a *lictor*, the prestigious post established to escort the power-mad few. (A few centuries later, the job was made available to freedmen as well.)

As ceremonial bodyguards, lictors got more awe than action. Most of the time, their duties were the proverbial piece of cake. In essence, they walked around Rome carrying the *fasces*, a symbolic bundle of birch sticks, on their left shoulders, rifle-style. They also opened gates, stood next to officials while they were giving speeches, dipped their fasces to higher ranking officials before passing, and knocked on doors. Lictor paydays were respectable: about two-thirds the salary of a legionary at one-tenth the sweat and risk.

From time to time, the actual guarding of important bodies did occur; if a lictor had to escort an unpopular magistrate, for example. Mostly, though, the job involved a lot of standing around: outside the baths, outside the temples, outside the brothels. (As lictors aged, varicose veins were an occupational hazard.)

Lictors were status symbols of the political pecking order. Only certain officials got to have lictors fore and aft. Consul, the highest ranking officer, got a dozen lictors; the praetors merited six. If a crisis arose and a dictator were appointed for six months, he got maximum lictoration— twenty-four men.

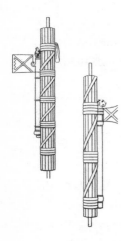

Lictors on board were also the privilege of governors of provinces (of which Rome had many), commanders of legions, members of the imperial family, and Vestal Virgins. The lightest duty took place in Greco-Roman Egypt. There, one lonely lictor was required to keep Apis the sacred bull company at its temple. Rome's lesser officials or magistrates—the quaestor, aedile, and censor—had to go lictorless.

The uniforms were great. While on duty in Rome, lictors wore laurel wreaths and freshly pressed togas. Outside Rome, or traveling with the brass, lictors wore snazzy military capes, sometimes over red and white tunics. Dark glasses and cordless headphones were not required on the job, only because they had not yet been invented.

Lictors went weaponless except for the long menacing fasces they carried. When lictoring outside Rome, an iron ax was lashed to this phallic bundle of birch or elm. At a general's triumph, the fasces were topped with laurel sprigs; at a funeral, the lictors carried their fasces upside-down.

Back in the days when Rome had kings, lictors actually arrested troublemakers and did crowd control. In that misty past, the wooden rods they carried may have served to lash malefactors, and the ax to execute—or seriously maim. To the average person, the clunky fasces didn't look like much use in an emergency. Nevertheless, it, and the sometimes thuggish men who carried it, symbolized the brute-force aspect of Roman power. Perhaps that was why that Italian dictator Benito Mussolini later found the fasces such an appealing symbol for his new movement—which he dubbed "fascism."

❖ ❖ ❖ ❖ **LUCKY BULLA** ❖ ❖ ❖ ❖
Bandit godfather

Bulla the bandit, popularly called "Lucky" by everyone in Italy, was an enterprising crook with an altruistic streak—a Roman Robin Hood. Over the course of several years in the third century A.D., he pulled together a band of some six hundred ruffians. Some bandit leaders demanded experienced highwaymen; Bulla, however, chose men he could relate to.

With his staff in place, Lucky proceeded to plague all of Italy. He was a real pain for Emperor Severus, who expended manpower and military troops to hunt the man down. Whenever there was a Lucky sighting, somehow it turned out to be as insubstantial as a UFO abduction. Whenever the emperor got word that Lucky had been captured, invariably it transpired that no, he hadn't been.

To rub more salt into Emperor Severus's wounds, a great many of the slaves at the imperial palace, angry at the absence even of slave wages, had run away from his employ and into the ranks of Bandit Number One.

If you get the feeling that Lucky Bulla had as much community support as luck, you're right. Bulla was generous with his loot, lavish with his presents, and in constant communication with his network of eyes and spies. His modus operandi was enlightened: in a holdup, he only took a share of what each person was carrying and released them at once. When it came to common folk, such as craftsmen, Lucky actually kept them around for a while fixing banditry gear—then set them free after paying the men a fair wage.

This pay-and-release philosophy made the emperor even madder. So did Lucky's gutsy way of rescuing his own men on the rare occasions when they were caught. Once he pretended to be a magistrate from his own hometown and went to the jail where two of his guys were being held. Their sentence was *ad bestias*, to be thrown to the beasts in the arena. A natural at disguises and accents, Lucky talked a load of convincing baloney to the jailer and got him to release the men into his "custody."

Bulla's luck eventually ran dry. The classic failing: forbidden fruit, the wife of a fellow brigand. While Bulla was busy getting a bit of adulterous sex in a cave, the cuckolded husband cooperated with the authorities upon the promise of immunity. Bulla, wakened from a post-coital nap, was brought before the provincial governor, who thundered, "Why did you engage in robbery?" Bulla had to smile; to his mind, there were no greater thieves than government officials. "For the same reason, guv, that you're governor," he replied.

That answer got poor old Lucky thrown into the arena and eaten alive by wild beasts. His public death put a real damper on his men, who allowed themselves to be captured, one by one.

Although Bulla was a historical figure, written about by Greek historian Dio Cassius, his story, which anticipates the tale of Robin Hood by nine centuries, is thought to represent an even more ancient oral tradition of the noble robber.

❖ ❖ ❖ ❖ **LUCINIUS LUCULLUS** ❖ ❖ ❖ ❖
Lots of WMD in warfare B.C.

Greeks and Romans weren't sure about love, but they did believe that all was fair in war. They were old hands at dealing with nasty tricks and unusual weaponry—and weren't shy about using biological or chemical warfare themselves.

For instance, when cities in Asia Minor revolted against Roman rule in 131 B.C., one general put a quick stop to the fighting by poisoning the water supply of the city of Pergamum. Earlier on, Greeks had done the same thing near Delphi, using hellebore in the water to bring the city to its knees.

Alexander the Great also met with disaster in the form of biological warfare. When he and his army attacked the Harmatalians (in today's Pakistan), soldiers who received even minor wounds died ghastly deaths, convulsing and turning gangrenous from arrows and swords that had been dipped in the toxin of the Russell's viper.

Roman general Lucinius Lucullus, however, knew his history. A veteran of numerous campaigns, he was savvy to every underhanded tactic. He'd catapulted red-hot sand onto foes. He'd tossed metal shrapnel and pots full of venomous reptiles onto enemy ships. He'd even utilized that old favorite, "mining" the battlefield area with booby traps to immobilize the enemy's chariots.

When he got wind that the Roman Senate and other leading politicos fancied the idea of subduing the lands where Iran and Iraq sit today, Lucullus said, "I'm your man."

Around 74 B.C., the general and an army huge enough to lift even his ego made for the fortified Mesopotamian cities between the Tigris and Euphrates rivers. He began by besieging the first city, an ordinary-looking place called Samosata. To his utter shock, those blasted Mesopotamians began to pour burning mud on his men and his wooden siege engines. The stuff was awful—sticky, flammable, and impossible to quench once afire.

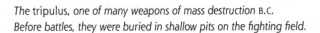

The tripulus, one of many weapons of mass destruction B.C.
Before battles, they were buried in shallow pits on the fighting field.

Lucullus beat a hasty retreat, his army enveloped in flames. He had just met that area's most potent arms—one that 2,300 years later would still be a deadly weapon, and an economic bludgeon as well. The Samosata WMD was a mixture of naphtha and pure petroleum.

It just wasn't Lucullus's day. Or decade. In his later campaign in Armenia, he and his army had to battle nomads who used a variety of chemical and biological weapons, including arrows especially designed to fragment inside the body. Then there was the painful episode at the Black Sea, where enemy forces released hornets and wild bears into his siege tunnels. The final ignominy? In 67 B.C., General Licinius Lucullus was recalled to Rome like a defective chariot wheel.

Future Roman armies would try for centuries to conquer Mesopotamia, only to meet with more petroleum warfare, along with such unpleasant add-ons as "bombs" filled with live scorpions.

❖ LEGIONARY ❖
PACKING IT IN, BRINGING IT ON

In earlier centuries, neither Greeks nor Romans had trouble filling their military quotas. They used a means test: own some land and a horse, badda-bing, you're a knight—eligible for active duty until you're dead or sixty, whichever comes first.

This changed during the manpower crisis around 100 B.C., when the Roman army went through major reform, allowing landless men and the unemployed to join. Ranks were reorganized into cohorts and centuries to make a legion of 4,800 soldiers, who, for the first time, got paid in coin. (Much earlier, men were paid in salt, origin of the word "salary." Or, at times, nothing.)

During the fray, Roman fighting units listened for the signals given by their horn players and their whistle-carrying officers.

103

As Rome conquered its way into an empire, somebody had the cunning idea of enlisting males from recently whipped provinces. Candidates were offered a decent incentive: serve twenty-five years as an auxiliary and win Roman citizenship.

Retirement options were equally attractive for regular soldiers: after a twenty- to twenty-five-year hitch, leave with cash and land. Roman legionaries earned their retirements. Even in peacetime, they worked like hell, building roads, digging canals, drilling constantly. At night the men shared leather tents and cooking chores, grinding grain to make porridge from scratch. Hard to believe after all those movie banquet scenes, but this was a heavily vegetarian army.

Legionaries were kept on the move, typically marching twenty miles a day. Counting weapons, long red cape, and body armor, each soldier carried ninety pounds of gear, hoicked onto a pole holding tools, water, rations, and tent. Soldiers were nicknamed "mules of Marius," after the general who'd invented this fiendishly clever way to pack gear.

Discipline was serious stuff. For major offenses, like sleeping on watch or abandoning weapons in battle, the guilty soldier would be clubbed to death with heavy sticks. That wasn't the worst part—the clubbing had to be done by his fellow legionaries.

To keep morale high, exemplary behavior in battle won public praise and rewards from the brass. Then there was booty call. After a victory, legionaries usually received a share of the spoils. Some booty (slaves, for example) was sold, the proceeds divided among the men. Spoils taken in battle were the best; a legionary who stripped an enemy twice got promoted.

Legionaries learned tactics that let them inflict heavy casualties, even when greatly outnumbered. They stood shoulder to shoulder, their shields nearly touching as they thrust forward with swords and spears. To refresh formations, officers using whistles signaled every half-minute to their men, whereby the front line would fall to the back to rest and get fresh weapons if needed. If a soldier fell, the badge he wore showing his position in the ranks was passed to his replacement.

High-stress soldiering: the man who carried the sacred standards of the legion. Embedded in battle without armor or shield, he had to rely on fellow legionaries for protection.

Always visible in battle were the Roman standards. Each century had a *signifer*, a legionary with an animal pelt over his helmet who carried the tall, disc-laden emblem. The *vexillarius* carried a brightly colored flag. A third man, the *aquilifer*, proudly hoisted the gold or silver eagle, symbol of Jupiter and the army's most treasured icon. These legionaries, who slept in a special tent with the standards, had an onerous burden. The images they carried into battle were sacred; their loss, the biggest disgrace an army could endure.

❖ ❖ ❖ ❖ AMANIRENAS ❖ ❖ ❖ ❖

Keep an eye out for a warrior queen

Octavian, newly Roman emperor by an eyelash, had just gotten over the scare of almost losing Egypt to Mark Antony and the ambitious Cleopatra when he got a second blow. Another bellicose female showed up in "his" Egypt!

This aggressor was Amanirenas, ruler of the mysterious Meroe empire of Kush. While Roman troops were stretched thin, fighting a conflict in Arabia, she led her army north and made an audacious attack on the strategic Egyptian cities of Elephantine, Philae, and Aswan. In a trice or maybe two, she defeated three cohorts of legionaries, wrecking the defenses they had built. Her success was humiliating. Even more creepily Amazonian were the reports that the woman warrior had either lost an eye in the fighting, or was one-eyed to begin with.

Amanirenas was a statuesque woman of Afro-Egyptian appearance, armed with ample buttocks and a wicked way with a sword. From a long line of hereditary queens called kandaces, Amanirenas ruled lands along the Nile between the first and the sixth cataracts. Her desert homeland, with its strip of fertile green along the river, was called Kush or Nubia in Roman times (and the Sudan today).

The Egyptians coveted her lands—and her sophisticated trade networks for ivory, gold, copper, jewelry, animal skins, and exotic woods. So did the Romans. Amanirenas had no intention of letting Egyptians, Romans, or anyone else steal them or her country's most important trade secret: the smelting of iron ore at carefully guarded sites to make armaments and swords.

At the emperor's urging, General Petronius hurried to regain control of the situation by pushing south to the Kushite religious capital of Napata. He destroyed it, deeply irritating the robust ruler, who trudged back north, deep into Egypt, with her army. After several battles, she and the general tried for a negotiated peace.

With her envoys, Amanirenas traveled to the Greek island of Samos, where the Roman emperor Octavian (soon better known as Augustus) planned to spend the winter. In 21 B.C., the two sides hammered out an agreement called the Treaty of Samos.

For their part, the Romans agreed to withdraw their military forces from Kushite lands and refrain from taxing Amanirenas and her people. This admirable peace between the Meroe empire and Rome remained in force for centuries, the legacy of a sterling leader of her people.

Like other kandace queens, Amanirenas was laid to rest beneath the "tombstone" of a slender, sharply pointed pyramid, the signature architecture of Kush. These chocolate-brown isosceles triangles, still clustered in semi-ruined glory around the Sudan, were built by an ingenious method quite unlike that used in the pyramids of Egypt. Counterbalanced by manpower on one side, Kushite workers used a simple crane called a shadoof to lift heavy stone blocks into place. Farmers in the region still use shadoofs; instead of erecting pyramids to queens, their devices hoist water from canals into irrigation ditches.

❖ WAR-ELEPHANT COMMANDER ❖

PACHYDERM PHOBIA FACTOR

Starting as commander of one elephant, an ambitious army officer with a zest for heights and a way with large animals might climb the ranks to become phalanx commander of sixty-four Asian or African elephants.

As it happened, the officer rarely rode the beasts he commanded; instead, the elephant carried a driver and three archers, sometimes protected by strap-on towers. The animal wore armored breastplates, metal spikes on its tusks, and colorful headpieces designed to dazzle and horrify.

Psychologically, elephants were scary. Very scary, at least to first-timer opponents and their horses, who tended to flee at the sight and smell of huge gray trumpeting objects.

Hannibal may have gotten most of the press for his use of a thirty-seven-elephant force, but Greeks, Romans, and their enemies all fielded elephants at one time or another. Alexander the Great made hay with them—in the process discovering that the beasts also devoured hay in industrial quantities. Fortunately, elephants could carry masses of fodder as well as equipment.

A wise elephant commander made use of his huge quadrupeds in four ways: as defensive screens, as attack wings on infantry and cavalry, as camp disrupters, and in siege warfare.*

Battle stories of elephant-enabled victories are, shall we say, legion. Roman warrior Antiochas ordered sixteen elephants to crunch a cavalry attack from either side, panicking his Gaulish attackers. Macedonian general Seleucus formed a screen of 480 elephants (the Macedonians always were show-offs) that kept enemy cavalry from the battlefield. The Carthaginians often stormed Roman camps with elephants, letting the animals trample men and equipment.

War elephants were handy after the battle, too. By positioning them as portable barriers upstream, armies could safely ford swift rivers.

Elephantine warfare went on for centuries. To immobilize the animals, many techniques were tried, from cutting their hamstrings to laying down layers of iron spikes on the battlefield. Finally, however, the Megarian Greeks found the secret to effective anti-elephant warfare. After a long and desperate siege, and down to their last decent meal, the Megarians oiled up

---

* There's nothing new under the sun. Some of the strategies developed long ago for elephants are still used in modern tank warfare, including the four discussed above.

their remaining pigs, set them alight, then headed the squealing herd toward their elephant-equipped besiegers. Chaos ensued. The elephants, more crazed by the high-pitched squealing than the smell of barbecuing pork, destroyed their own lines and trampled their own troops.

After such fiascos, the career of elephant commander took a nosedive. Finally the job disappeared, along with the elephants, after the Romans had rounded up thousands upon thousands of the poor beasts to be slaughtered for entertainment in the arenas of the empire.

In A.D. 363, Roman armies once again faced elephant-equipped enemies, this time the Persians. Since Roman troops hadn't seen battle pachyderms for centuries, they nearly collapsed with fright. Not a soul remembered the pig stratagem, either.

❖ ❖ ❖ ❖ **MARIUS** ❖ ❖ ❖ ❖

Spoiling for a fight

Imperator! That's what every Roman general B.C. wanted to be called. That grand title specified a commander who'd whipped his enemy, although later the word came to mean "emperor." To qualify, a commander had to lead his troops into battle, not just watch from horseback or make a post-match tour of the carnage.

A leader who led—that was General Gaius Marius. Although elected consul of Rome seven times, plain-spoken Marius was a rough soldier at heart, at ease with his troops, whether breaking bread or breaking barbarian heads. As commander, Marius skillfully whipped the armies of Numidia and defeated antlike numbers of Cimbri and Teutoni tribesmen, saving Italy from invasion by three hundred thousand raving Celts.

Was he declared Imperator and given a triumph? Was he ever. The word "triumph" really meant something in his day. Not just any old skirmish qualified; civil wars didn't count. At least five thousand legitimate foes had to be killed in a single battle. Bellicosities with little bloodshed won a mere ovation, meriting a short on-foot parade through Rome and the sacrifice of one crummy sheep.

Like other triumphs, Marius's celebration was a lavish day-long display of virility, excess, and kick-'em-in-the-face military might. After the general spoke to his legions and handed out goodie bags filled with booty, he headed for the Triumphal Gate.

The procession began with senators, magistrates, and trumpeters, followed by horse-drawn carriages piled high with the juiciest swag taken from the losers. They were followed by flute players, priests leading white oxen for sacrifice, and some exotic animals for color. By now the route was laden with dung, through which slogged high-profile prisoners, wearing golden chains and fetters. Wooden placards informed parade-watchers which particular set of losers these were.

Finally the horse-drawn chariot of the triumphant Imperator came into view, flanked by elite bodyguards. Marius, dressed in a flamboyant gold-embroidered robe, held a scepter in one hand, a laurel bough in the other. Later generals, notably Marius's younger relative Julius Caesar, would also paint their faces with red cinnabar for the triumph.

For the moment, the world was his *Ostrea edulis*. The hoopla of triumphs, however, was short-term glory. Although Marius would suffer defeats, his lasting triumph was his reformation of the Roman army. Not only did he open recruitment to the poor and landless, he made it possible for thousands to pursue careers as military men—and work their way through the ranks to centurion and even higher office.

Gaius Marius had sensible ideas and the will to implement them. He introduced an army-wide system of uniforms and provided the same weapons and gear to each soldier—with part of the initial resources coming out of his own pocket! Hard to imagine modern generals outfitting a battalion or two.

In addition, General Marius enabled his men to be paid in cash. He also pushed for retirement benefits in the form of land; vets, however, didn't get any substantial land awards until Julius Caesar. Later, Emperor Augustus founded vets' colonies from Corsica to Spain, Asia Minor to Gaul, southern Italy to a recycled Carthage.

These benefits and ideas, now accepted as commonplace, were bombshells at the beginning of the first century B.C.; future commanders and troops would have ample reason to thank Gaius Marius.

❖ MERCENARY ❖
THE FINE ART OF FREELANCING—WITH
REAL LANCES

The word "mercenary" has a sordid, metallic ring to our ears. At the mention of Spartan military might or the deeds of the armies of Alexander, we never think of hired help. The fact is, armies from early Greek times up through the late Roman empire used mercenaries. The famed Ten Thousand? Hoplite mercenaries all—including the officers, one of whom was fighter-author Xenophon, who later described that awful march from Babylon back to Greek lands in a classic eyewitness book called *The Anabasis.*

Even ancient Greek sailors turned mercenary in peacetime, hiring themselves and their ships out to fight. There were plenty of countries, Egypt for instance, that needed men for unwarranted attacks and land-grabbing forays on neighbors and foes.

Warriors who chose to become mercenaries had a lot going for them. First of all, they were courageous, seasoned survivors on the battlefield, on the sea, and in foreign terrain. An independent bunch, they were willing to travel to where the carnage was. These men worked for pay (sometimes in the form of booty), received ration allowances, and viewed killing as a necessary albeit unpleasant task. (Obviously the field also attracted men for whom bloodshed was the big draw.) Mercenaries often specialized, a fact many generals used to advantage.

Archers, on foot or on horseback, often worked as mercenaries. The most deadly attack force in the ancient world, they were the elite, the bow-and-arrow Marines of their day. The best archers came from the islands of Crete and Rhodes and from the land of Scythia. Another mercenary specialty was the slinger, the specialist who fired mini-missiles of lead or stone.

Some of these bellicose freelancers had big dreams. For instance, when the Sicilian city-state of Syracuse hired Italian soldiers to fight Carthage for them, they contracted for a good fight, crushing the enemy if possible—then closure. Once that was accomplished, however, the now-unemployed mercenaries swarmed across Sicily, grabbed the prosperous Greek city-state of Messina, renaming it and calling themselves "children of Mars." Their actions triggered a hullabaloo called the First Punic War between Rome and Carthage, with Sicily as both prize and battlefield.

Other mercenaries clearly possessed management skills. In Emperor Tiberius's day, for instance, a Numidian soldier named Acfarinas deserted the Roman auxiliary force in which he was serving, then formed his own large mercenary army. For six years, Acfarinas ravaged North Africa, became leader of the Musulamii people, beat the Romans in several battles, was captured, escaped, and in A.D. 22 pertly threatened the emperor with "perpetual war." It took the Roman generals an embarrassingly long time to catch and kill this troublesome man, viewed as a foe by some—and a hero among mercenaries by others.

❖ SLINGER ❖

FIRING RED-HOT LEAD FOR A LIVING

Mud-slinging is still popular among politicians and tabloid hacks, but these days no one slings much of anything else. The Greeks and Romans, however, knew the value of a literal sling made of leather or flax cords and loaded with stones or projectiles of cast lead.

Certain towns and cities were famed for their strong-armed pebble-firers, Patrae and the island of Rhodes among them. The real marksmen among slingers came from the Balearic Islands off Spain. In order to eat, young boys of the Balearics had to brain their dinners with slung stones before mom would dish up a plate of food.

Expert slingers, dubbed *funditores* in Latin, were praised by war historians and readily found work in the armies of Greeks, Romans, Persians, and other ancient cultures. Although the sling might sound frivolous and low-tech, it was anything but a toy. As a weapon, it had many tactical virtues. A skillful slinger was more accurate than an archer—and could hit targets twice as distant. Longer slings could kill a man as far away as two hundred meters. When flung in unison, the fast-moving projectiles often caused more serious injuries than arrows.

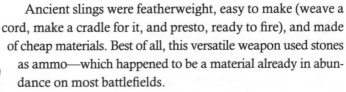

Ancient slings were featherweight, easy to make (weave a cord, make a cradle for it, and presto, ready to fire), and made of cheap materials. Best of all, this versatile weapon used stones as ammo—which happened to be a material already in abundance on most battlefields.

Some super-slingers sought out stones up to one pound. Elite troops, however, didn't rely solely on river rocks or pebbles at hand. They made ammunition from clay, iron, or lead. The most aerodynamic shapes resembled acorns or almonds, and were made from simple two-part molds. At a pinch, a slinger could simply poke his finger into the sand, then pour molten lead into the hole. (Armies in those days were much more DIY; troops had to cook up their own lead missiles, along with their own daily meals.)

Sling bullets of lead had additional advantages: dense and small, they had minimum air resistance and proved difficult for the enemy to spot, especially with bright skies. "Incoming sling bullets!" "Where?" "Uff!"

Although few ancient slings have survived, plenty of slingstone lead bullets have. Some carry symbols, from lightning bolts to scorpions. Others bear the names of commanders or military units scratched onto them.

Still others give glimpses of the rough-and-ready humor of military life. More than one declared "Take this!" or "Ouch!" Another was labeled "For Pompey's backside." But the award for Best Message Discovered on an Ancient Slinger's Bullet goes to the piece of lead that simply read: "Catch!"

❖ SAILOR ❖

HOISTING SAILS ON LAND & SEA

Greek tyrants came into vogue during certain tumultuous centuries B.C. The secret to a good tyranny, as despots were fond of saying, was a fleet—which meant that the Corinthians and the islanders from Corfu boasted the first Greek navies. Athenians, on the other hand, were still doodling around, working out the kinks in the democratic process. Once they got cracking, however, Athenians built two hundred trireme ships and developed a superb corps of sailors to man them. For decades, Athens had a slick protection racket going with the smaller Greek islands and city-states. Later they lost the title to the islanders of Rhodes, who became the new, less thuggish maritime power.

Greek triremes, speedily powered by three banks of rowers and a small crew for rigging the sails, had ferocious beaks on the bow for ramming the enemy. Some vessels carried more than one beak. The officers, helmsmen, and other crew sat in the stern on elevated decks.

Ships carried one to three masts, each carrying a square sail. Sailor specialists called *velarii* worked the rigging and tackle, put up removable bulwarks in high seas or when engaging the enemy, and kept the poop deck tidy.

Romans got involved in marine warfare with reluctance. Although the average man in uniform was ferocious on land, Romans were wimps at sea. Despite recruitment posters promising "See the world while earning a pittance!" almost no one signed up. With a sigh of relief, Roman officials made sailing into an auxiliary force, its navy soon filled with young draftees from the provinces.

Once on water, Roman strategy called for engaging the enemy as though on land. Their ships carried iron grappling devices called "ravens," enabling sailors to easily board enemy vessels and fight.

During prior centuries, the main objective had been to clear the Mediterranean of pirates. Later, sailors sailed to protect the grain ships carrying Rome's lifeblood from Egypt. The duty station everyone tried to get was Misenum, the huge ten-thousand-man base on the Bay of Naples, where the nightlife rocked.

Soon, however, the job sailors fought over most wasn't even on the water. Gladiatorial games had become very popular, especially when the Flavian Amphitheater (later called the Colosseum) opened in A.D. 80. As the sun beat down on the body heat of fifty thousand spectators, assorted wild beasts, and nervous gladiators, the atmosphere in that oval structure became far from fragrant.

To solve the problem, some bright spark invented removable awnings to partially shade amphitheaters and

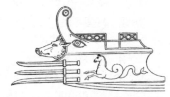

To help new sailors tell the back end of a warship from the front, the Greeks designed prows with pointy things called rostra. *Rostra also turned out to be uncannily useful at ramming and sinking enemy vessels.*

theaters. Architects visualized them as ships with sails to be furled and unfurled, using a system of masts, ropes, and pulleys. And who better to work sails than velarii sailors? For the Colosseum alone, it took a cadre of seasoned riggers (stationed outside Rome in a detachment from Misenum) to extend the awning or velarium over two-thirds of it. Besides rigging cotton or linen panels, sailors read the skies for signs of high winds or rainstorms, since those conditions canceled the programs.

Theaters were smaller facilities, but more numerous. Their smaller awnings could be made of pricey silks in brilliant colors. In Rome alone, it may have taken a thousand sailors to keep theater crowds and gladiator fans in the shade.

For a TV documentary, scientists attempted to build workable proto-types of this ancient Roman invention. Their efforts to rig them over a small bullring in Spain gave them new respect for the work of those long-ago sailors, who had to deal with wind gusts, tangled lines, and other problems—but not, thankfully, with seasickness.

❖ ROWER ❖

SLAVE ONLY TO AN OAR

Who could forget the galley slave—that noble, Charlton Heston-esque figure, sweatily chained to his long oar? Heart-rending, yes. Factual, no. The Greek or Roman galley slave was a fond myth, fabricated by the overheated imaginations of historical novelists and fleshed out by Hollywood.

The real scoop on ancient rowers? In Homer's day, military troops from Troy, Sparta, Athens, and elsewhere did double duty, picking up sword and shield to fight on dry land, then acting as rowers once at sea.

In classical times, merchant ships were tubby affairs with small crews, using sails to move. Warships were long and sleek, built for speed and powered by hundreds of rowers. As fleets grew in size, the task of moving them through the water required more trained men. Free men from poorer families filled these jobs.

By the fifth century B.C., the trireme, with its triple banks of oars, was the B-52 of its day. A 120-foot trireme held 170 rowers who pulled oars in sync; "beaten together," as the Greeks called it. Deep in the hull of the ship sat the *thalamitai*, 27 men to a side. On a tier higher up sat the *zygitai*. At the top sat the *thranitai*.

The rowers sat on leather cushions greased with tallow for good slide action. To dip their oars, the men got to their feet, then threw themselves back onto the bench to muscle the stroke. The rowing done by the fellows with the longest oars was the most arduous; as a consequence, they often got higher pay than the other rowers.

Besides the skill it required, the job was hellish hard work, up to seventeen hours a day, made somewhat easier by men who kept musical time with drums or flutes. Over the din of music and oar noise, the ship's mate bellowed out or whistled commands regarding the movement of the trireme to the rowers.

If the ship were going into battle, the oarsmen didn't row the entire trip; instead, sails were used to save their strength. During battles and other high-alert times, rowers ate combat rations, a mix of barley bread, wine, and olive oil, at their seats. Otherwise, trireme crews went ashore to prepare meals, since ships had no cooking facilities.

For decades, Athens maintained a large navy, paying well for rowers and employing thousands of Athenians full-time. What with near-constant wars between city-states, the demand for skilled rowers stayed high. In sea battles, however, losses aboard a trireme could be ghastly. During the Athenians' two-year siege of Syracuse in Sicily, they supposedly lost two hundred triremes, representing thirty-four thousand men.

Over time, city-states were forced to crew their ships with mercenaries, many of them non-Greeks. There were proud exceptions; the islanders of Rhodes continued to use their own citizen rowers.

In contrast, Romans exhibited little interest in sea duty; instead, they staffed their ships with rowers from subject nations. Although under Roman command, these naval auxiliaries were not enslaved. If a rowing recruit signed up for the full decades-long hitch, he won his "diploma" or honorary discharge and full citizenship—that is, provided he and his aching back both survived.

The people of Corcyra (called Corfu today) took such pride in their rowers and warships that they put them on the local currency.

❖ FIVE ❖

SLICK TALKERS & MUSE SEEKERS

❖ ❖ ❖ ❖ **APELLES** ❖ ❖ ❖ ❖

Image maker

Alexander wasn't called "the Great" for nothing. A champion warrior, he stirred people with his larger-than-life persona and exploits. Some of his charisma came from the gene pool—but an eye-opening amount of his image-building came from the gifted hands of a painter named Apelles, a Greek from the island of Cos.

As a young man, Apelles learned painterly precision from master teachers at Ephesus and Sicyon, then headed north to the court of Philip the Second in Macedonia, where he quickly elbowed his way into the job of court painter.

Straightaway, Philip's son Alex saw that this artist had a huge talent for heightened realism and the portrayal of masculine beauty. When he wasn't fighting his mother or other enemies, the young Great-to-be sat for Apelles, having already forbidden anyone else to paint his portrait.

Although incredibly paintogenic, Alex was not an ideal model. As he sat, he would pontificate nonstop about rules of perspective and other artistic matters.

Finally, Apelles had had a gutful of his Greatness. "You might want to drop the subject," he said. "The boys who grind the colors for me are laughing at you, Alex." That blistering remark silenced the Great one, since no heroic demigod in the making wants to be a figure of fun.

Apelles' reputation as hotshot painter to the reigning star of the Mediterranean gratified him, but he was more interested in feedback from everyday people. When his paintings went on display, he used to hide nearby to hear candid comments—and sometimes act on them.

He also maintained friendly rivalries with other painters. He'd heard raves about Protogenes and sailed over to Rhodes to meet him. The painter was out; in his studio sat a panel freshly prepared for work. Picking up a brush, Apelles drew a fine line across it and told the cleaning lady: "Tell him this came from Apelles."

Examining the line later, Protogenes recognized his rival's touch. He drew a finer line above the first and ordered the cleaning lady to show it to the artist if he turned up again. Inevitably Apelles returned. In the final paint-off, he drew a most delicate line between the first two—and the painters finally had a face-to-face meeting. That famous panel with its three enigmatic lines supposedly ended up at Julius Caesar's place, which later went up in flames.

Lionized and favored by fortune in his lifetime, Apelles was unlucky in terms of posterity. None of his works—not even his crowd-pleasing portrait of Alex throwing a thunderbolt—survived the lottery of time. One of his masterpieces, *Aphrodite Rising from the Waves*, was much copied by lesser lights. A version found on the walls of a Pompeiian mansion, however, only gives a feeble inkling of the Apelles magic.

Like the Greek sculptor Lysippus, the other "official" artist tapped by Alex, Apelles' key legacy will remain his visual role in making Alexander great. That is, unless the ancient gods—or maybe global warming—allow an undiscovered Apelles to surface one day.

❖ MASKMAKER, COSTUME DESIGNER ❖
JACK-OF-ALL-TRADES

Aeschylus, Sophocles, and Euripedes, the trio who wrote the finest tragedies in the world, became household words. For decades, they were successively adored by rapt audiences and garlanded with prizes from the Dionysia festivals of fifth-century-B.C. Athens. In reality, an ancient playwright had to be a jack-of-all-trades. Writing deathless lines of poetry? Just for starters.

The first tragedies had a chorus and one actor—played by the playwright himself. Aeschylus thought that was pretty lonely; he brought in a second actor, but still took the protagonist's role.

Want to guess who auditioned the chorus of fifteen to fifty men, wrote the songs, choreographed the dance, and rehearsed everyone for the tragedy's performance? Yep. The hyphenated playwright.

As if overburdened playwrights (at least until late Hellenistic times) didn't have enough to do, they also became maskmakers and costume designers.

The real forehead-crinkler was creating an otherworldly ambience. First, they tried painting actors' faces—then turned to making serene, open-mouthed tragic masks of white linen and plaster. Each mask was unique, taken from a clay mold of the thespian's own face, the whole affair sewn to a cap fitted to the actor's head. Underneath this wigged rig, the simmering actor wore a sweatband. Three holes, bowling-ball fashion, made each masked head portable.

Aeschylus added color to masks, then upped the fear factor by creating hideous ones for his Furies. Black of skin, hair crawling with snakes, these masks oozed blood from the eyes, causing audiences to faint and women (allegedly) to miscarry.

By 400 B.C., there were twenty-five tragic mask types, from pale-faced brunettes distinguishing female leads, to curly-haired images with high foreheads and raised eyebrows, depicting haughty youths. Since male actors played male and female, old and young, mortal and god, a variety of masks allowed three men to put on complex tragedies. Comedy followed a similar path, its forty-four masks usually exaggerating features for comic effect.

Costumes let audiences identify stock characters through colors and styles. Actors wore padded pot-bellies and donned red wigs to portray slaves; for harlot roles, they flounced in flowery outfits. Broad-brimmed hats and capes denoted young cavalrymen. The leads wore elaborate, long-sleeved gowns, banded with colorful embroidery. Tragic getups had a sculptural quality, especially those of the chorus. As the actors moved and sang, their fine robes fell into folds and swirled like smoke.

In crude contrast, the outfits worn in satyr plays, the brief but outrageous playlets between tragedies, turned actors into priapic half-beasts. All it took was a fake tail, an erect leather phallus, and a very hairy loincloth.

Thespians had to be quick-change artists. Sometimes the actors got a break after the first act, as the chorus sang and danced. Otherwise, offstage pauses were few or none. Actors had six lines or less to shed one role and jump into the next.

In later centuries, the artistry of masks and costume, once the province of Athenian playwrights, became full-time jobs, proudly carried on by professionals in theatrical guilds called "the artisans of Dionysus."

After winning a prize, a thankful actor might dedicate his mask on the altar of Dionysus, his patron god—the spiritual equivalent of the Oscar acceptance speech.

❖ ACTOR ❖
CALLING ALL HYPOCRITES

Twenty-five hundred years ago, being called a hypocrite wasn't an insult—it was a job description. The first actor given speaking lines in a Greek play was a hypocrite, meaning "answerer." When playwright Aeschylus added a second hypocrite to his tragedies, the thespian profession (at least for males) was off and running.

The notion of organized theater began at the Dionysia in Athens, a spring whoop-te-do to honor the god of wine and emotion that eventually included a playwriting competition. Audiences of seventeen thousand thrilled to day-long performances by actors who emoted in a trilogy of mythology-based tragedies, then changed gears to play naughty satyrs and, on the last day, racy comedies written by the likes of Aristophanes.

Actors played multiple roles, switching costumes and masks to go from elderly slave to goddess. Much rode on the individual's ability to emote, move well, and hold a gesture. Set speeches by the actors alternated with songs and dance by the chorus, who were costumed to fit the tragic situation and involved in it. Ancient hypocrites needed stamina; typically, three

actors had to cover thirty or more roles in one day's acting.

While theater structures were paid for by the city-state, wages, props, costumes, and other expenses were financed by well-heeled Greek citizens, who competed to be that year's producer. This voluntary burden, called a liturgy, gave the theatrical community a reliable source of underwriting.

Poet-playwrights, on the other hand, competed with two other finalists during the twice-yearly festivals—and only the winner walked away with a fat fee. For decades, Aeschylus, Euripides, and Sophocles submitted tragic trilogies plus a satyr play in each competition. After their deaths, comic playwright Aristophanes wrote *The Frogs* in tribute to them because, as he said, tragedy had no worthy successors. Despite his brilliance and popularity, Aristophanes himself was often an also-ran in the prize department.

For the city-state of Athens, drama (not democracy) became its most successful export. By 300 B.C., countless Greek cities scattered from Asia Minor to Sicily sponsored play competitions, put on festivals, and paid cash in advance to performers, now organized into guilds called "the artisans of Dionysus." These professional acting families included actors, musicians, and

support crews. As the guilds grew, that translated into better pay for all, plus exemptions from military service, tax breaks, and "safe conduct" protection while on the road.

When the Romans got into theater, they borrowed Greek plots and dialogue wholesale, then pumped up the gore, vulgarity, and melodrama to reality-TV levels. Romantic comedy in five acts, notably from Plautus, ruled the roost; among his hits was *The*

How to keep a fifty-man Greek chorus in line? Give the chorus leader wooden shoes with snappy percussive soles. This key player provided the musical heartbeat for ancient tragedy and comedy.

CXXVII   *Scabillo degl'Antichi*

120

Brothers Menaechmus, which Shakespeare later lifted for his *Comedy of Errors.* After each show, audiences laughed or groaned to "instant replays" of certain scenes, performed by understudies of the lead actors.

Roman actors mainly came from the ranks of slaves or freedmen and got little respect, comforting themselves with fat wages instead. Average fees in the first century A.D. were five hundred sesterces per performance, about six months' pay for a soldier. Top actors made upwards of two hundred thousand sesterces a year.

Whether sniffed at or fawned over, actors were paparazzi fodder, glamorous plebs that everyone wanted to rub elbows with, even patrician senators who pretended otherwise.

❖ DIE ENGRAVER ❖

CASHABLE ART

When they got fed up with bartering, the Greeks of long ago tossed around currency ideas and came up with version 1.0, iron nails. Easy to make but clunky and worthless for tipping, they quickly fell from favor. When a bright lad in nearby Lydia designed something called a coin for his king, the Greeks jumped on the concept.

In a flash, die engravers called *celators* began carving hardened bronze to create circular masterpieces in miniature. How'd they do it without magnification? Practice. Greeks had cut intricate designs into gems for centuries, using iron chisels and bow-drills tipped with abrasives.

Between 600 and 300 B.C., artistic rivalry arose between Greek engravers, a ferment that led to genius-caliber imagery on coins still sought after today, at prices no sane celator could imagine.

The most famous die a celator ever put a chisel to was the silver drachma of Athens, with patron goddess Athena on one side and an owl representing her wisdom on the other. When nudged, other city-states even accepted "owls" as legal tender.

Only the Muses knew why the prosperous Greek cities of Catana, Syracuse, and Camarina on Sicily spawned so many superb coin artists; Heracleidas from Catana, for instance, who designed the most splendid Apollo portraits ever seen.

But the artists to watch were the celators from Syracuse, so celebrated that they signed their bronze dies: Cimon, Eucleidas, and Euainetos. Formidable engraver Cimon designed a ten-drachma coin honoring the protectress of his city. On it, beautiful Arethusa faced front rather than in profile—an innovation that knocked the sandals off other celators and inspired imitators everywhere.

Like his rivals, Eucleidas had an exquisite grasp of perspective. Syracuse being famous for racehorses, his coins typically bore images of four-horse chariots in motion, the animals quivering with life.

In those silvery, golden centuries, lesser known celators also produced unforgettable portraits, from Hercules wrestling a lion on the coins of Cyme, to General Lysimachos on the currency of Pergamum.

An artistic masterpiece in miniature: the Greek coin.

After a celator finished his precision work, the hammerman took over. Using a hammer and punch, he smacked a blank of the appropriate metal into the die on his anvil, then stamped the reverse side of the coin. Even the finest die would only make about ten thousand acceptable images.

As the world came under Roman rule and coins were produced by the millions, artistic quality and metallic purity sometimes faltered. Nevertheless, superb coins, made at the correct size and purity, were the rule rather than the exception for hundreds of years.

Why was metallic currency so important? In a world without mass media or instant communication, it represented a durable medium of exchange, a way to store wealth, and a potent advertising tool. Coins were portable, readable, accessible to all. Some depicted icons of cultural importance, from Olympic victors to city logos like the winged horse of Corinth. Other issues served as propaganda pieces, emphasizing the ties between earthly rulers and deities.

Coins gave those in power an invaluable item that also worked as publicity, reminding everyone of wars won, foes beaten, prosperity gained. Small wonders: that's what coins were back then. And small wonder indeed that die engravers like Cimon enjoyed job security and lasting fame.

❖ MUSICIAN ❖
PAYING THE PIPER

The Greeks not only dug music; they believed it healed wounds and calmed mental patients—pretty sophisticated notions for a culture that hadn't yet gotten the hang of singing in harmony.

Greek and Roman streets and marketplaces rang with blessedly unamplified melody. Workers sang work songs, accompanied by panpipes, tambourines, or raunch riffs on the cithara as they painted, potted, stomped grapes, or did dirty laundry. Soldiers marched into battle accompanied by fierce horns, while rowers rowed to the sound of the aulos and drum, keeping time.

Athletes, especially wrestlers and boxers, practiced to live music; discus throwers and long jumpers almost "danced" to tunes as they competed at Olympia.

Funeral processions had properly mournful music, low oboe-like notes blown from long curved horns. Harvest festivals, entrail readings, weddings, and mystery religion conga-lines had their trademark tunes. Even gladiator matches and other beastly entertainments got horn backups and melodies played by a water-organist.

The poetic lines of tragedy and comedy had background music. Spoken passages alternated with songs sung by the chorus and actors. At festivals and play cycles, huge choruses competed for prizes.

Besides their raucous fun, the comedies written by Aristophanes must have had marvelous musical scores. His work *The Birds* contained arias imitating the songs of the hoopoe and the nightingale. His *Lysistrata* featured a dance number to the sound of a Spartan bagpipe!

In Roman times, the comedies of Plautus and other playwrights often featured music so fast and raucous that actors complained of the breakneck pace.

Mighty lungs and strong shoulders: that's what the cornu player needed. He carried eleven feet of brass tubing, supported by a wooden crossbar.

123

To "learn their strings," youngsters attended professional music academies in Greece and Italy to study the lyre, or its bigger brothers the barbiton and cithara. These seven-stringed forerunners to the harp and guitar were held upright to pluck and play. Sappho the composer-poet was a famous lyricist in several senses, having also prototyped a smaller lyre for her tiny hands.

Brass musicians played G-shaped horns and long trumpets. For woodwind, Romans preferred the flutelike sound of the tibia, Greeks the rich sound of the aulos, the paired pipes with three to sixteen finger-holes and a double-reed mouthpiece. Often mistranslated as "flute" or "pipes," the aulos looked and sounded more like a modern clarinet.

There were plenty of paying gigs, not all of them classy, for pipers. Randy male dinner parties called for female musicians, where women were sometimes pressed to play sexually as well as musically. Aulos music was also needed for sacrifices, athletic events, and dozens of other occasions.

The more highfalutin tooters, like virtuoso Greek rivals Dionysodoros and Ismenias, sniffed at such goings-on; they stuck to classic tragedy or poetry, wearing highly decorated crocus-yellow gowns and cool headdresses to distance themselves from the woodwind riffraff.

By the fourth century B.C., most musicians belonged to associations and their fees improved. In 290 B.C., for example, an aulos soloist received the gratifying sum of 2,400 drachmas for two performances at the Dionysia and Demetria festivals. By imperial times, the floodgates had opened, allowing some gifted musicians to pull down mega-fees—some from adoring fans.

❖ AUTHOR, PLAYWRIGHT, POET ❖
PLAGIARIZE AWAY, PLEASE!

Here's a giant surprise: neither publishers nor booksellers nor readers paid royalties to authors of long ago. Poets and playwrights and authors, being the powerless twits many still are, readily acquiesced to this state of affairs, often shelling out to put themselves into print.

Some were well-to-do to begin with; otherwise, they would not have authored anything. That too is why much Greco-Roman writing has an upper-crust attitude, with the wonderful exceptions of students of humanity like Greek comic playwright Aristophanes and storytellers Herodotus and Pliny.

Then, as now, writers had their idiosyncrasies. To write his complex plays, Euripedes couldn't be creative in noisy Athens; instead he fled to a cave on Salamis island. (Archaeologists excavating it found a cup with his name on it.) Pliny the Elder, who today would be under medication for chronic hyperactivity, dictated thirty-seven volumes of his *Natural History* to scribes, working through meals, at the bath, and while jolting along in a litter. (Your heart goes out to the poor devils who took his dictation.)

Poets, playwrights, and book authors were first "published" by being read aloud. Favorite venues were festivals, from the Great Games at Olympia, Nemea, Isthmus, and Delphi, to Rome's numerous events.

Readings became big. Very big. In fact, the auditorium (the place where one goes to hear something) came into vogue to fill that need. By the second century A.D., however, listener overload hit Rome. Reading burnout became common—especially since by now almost everyone who could dictate had put his priceless words onto papyrus. The only cats worth listening to were satirical poets like Horace and Juvenal, whose sarcasm—literally, "flesh cutting"—remained as sharp and full-bodied as unmixed wine.

To get published in print form, the author (or a slave stand-in) read the works aloud to a group of slaves, who copied them onto rolls of blank papyrus twelve inches wide. Finished scroll rolls were about the size and shape of a cardboard tube. To catch reader mumblings and typos, diligent authors had to proof every single copy.

Since copyright didn't exist, plagiarism abounded—often without attribution. So did censorship and *quid pro quo*. Many poets and authors were literary dependants with patrons hanging over their shoulders, suggesting themes and twittering over the wording of their dedication. Other writers held day jobs as court officials or secretaries. If their subject matter was indiscreet, it could mean losing a cushy post; that happened to Suetonius, author of a page-turner called *Lives of the Twelve Caesars*. Or being exiled to (gulp!) Romania for life by a touchy emperor, the fate of Ovid, the author of *The Art of Love*.

Plagiarized, preyed on, unpaid, exiled: what more could possibly befall a writer? Read on. While honeymooning with his first wife on Lesbos, Aristotle spent hours wallowing around rock pools and scribbling notes, intending to write a book. Then he got terribly busy, tutoring Alex the Great, founding a philosophical school, and other minor matters before expiring at age sixty-two.

That is, Aristotle expired; but his ramshackle lecture notes did not. Treasured at first, then buried in a damp cellar for 150 years, the moldy remnants were unearthed by another enthusiast and "reorganized" into a book. Sort of. The Aristotle that college students wade through today would horrify the author, whose shade may still be moaning "If only I'd had a chance to revise and polish…"

❖ POTTER, VASE PAINTER ❖

A POT FOR EVERY PURPOSE, EVEN X-RATED

"Mass production" is not a term that comes to mind with pre-Industrial societies like the Greeks. Yet they mass-produced a number of brilliant items, from coins to pottery.

Somehow the term "Greek vase" got stuck onto a mishmash of terracotta objects—hardly any of which were vases. Most held a trio of liquids: water, wine, and olive oil. The range of useful clay artifacts was prodigious. Potters made *lekythos* for olive oil and wider mouthed chamber pots for another liquid; they created wee perfume vials and storage-locker-sized *pithoi*, the kind in which cranky philosopher Diogenes lived. On potters' wheels, they threw shallow drinking cups called *skyphos* and bowl-shaped kraters to mix wine and water. Of amphorae alone, they created forty-plus styles.

Each shape related to its use. A mushroom-shaped cooler held snow to chill wine. Slender white *loutrophoros* jars held special water for wedding-day baths, and equally special water to wash a corpse (but not the same person or day, one hopes). Even more specific was the phallic-looking *alabastron* flask. It held olive oil—used by dutiful wives to oil their husbands' organs before and after sex! (As Galen the physician noted, the rub-up was for hubby's health and pleasure, not hers. Naturally.)

By the sixth century B.C., over a hundred pottery workshops did a thriving business in various city-states and Greek colonies. A medium-sized workshop might have an owner-overseer working with four throwers, a painter, and a furnace man for the kiln.

In later Roman times, potters copied and simplified Greek styles. They often signed and/or stamped their wares, revealing that most were Greek freedmen or slaves. Instead of the black-figured work traditional in Greece, the Roman market preferred red, achieved with an iron oxide gloss. Roman redware traveled well, so plentiful and cheap that any household could afford it.

Arezzo was the most prestigious area for redware production, and the bigger workshops had branches

Potters as well as painters of pottery sometimes signed their work. Potters often put their monikers on earthenware handles or rims.

127

in Gaul and other provinces. For decades, when *terra sigillata*, a bright red pottery with a shiny smooth surface, was fashionable, the potters of Arezzo had a near-monopoly on it. Fortunes were made; workshops grew huge by ancient standards; some employed sixty or more enslaved workers or indie craftsmen. They used shaping equipment to mass-produce simpler plates, bowls, and pots. To keep items consistent, workers made one hundred clay balls at a time.

Roman earthenware was seldom hand-painted. The Greeks, however, routinely decorated the rounded shapes of their pottery with magical scenes of myth, divine madness, and everyday life. Before firing, semi-dry pots were handed over to the Greek pottery artist. He sketched figures freehand with charcoal, its lines disappearing upon firing. His palette was select: white paint for women's flesh, red for blood and inscriptions, brown for shadings. For the finishing touches, the painter used a syringe with a pointed tip to make relief lines, put an ochre wash on certain areas, then polished the surface with bone or agate pebbles.

Certain Greek masters combined pottery and vase painting, including Sophilos, Nearchos, Amasis, Exekias, and others who signed their works. The amphorae painted by Amasis and Exekias have catch-in-the-throat qualities, never yet surpassed. Only men of this stature were asked to create the breathtaking, art-covered amphorae given as the prizes at the Panathenaica festival.

Lesser known potters took pride in their work as well. One red-figure amphora bore the saucy inscription: "Euphronius never did anything like this!" And among religious dedications found in the Asia Minor city of Ephesus is one from a triumphant potter named Bacchius, proving that this city and others sponsored pottery contests and gave crowns to its winners.

❖ SCULPTOR, ET AL ❖
ARTFUL TEAMWORK

The Etruscans preceding the Romans possessed genius when it came to bronze-working. One of them, a sixth-century-B.C. sculptor named Vulca of Veii, created visceral masterpieces of gods and men. His greatest work?

128

A bronze called the Capitoline she-wolf, which became Rome's totem animal and an iconic symbol still popular today.

Once word spread about the artistic possibilities of bronze, Greek and Roman sculptors lined up to use it. So did the highly skilled artisans who worked with them. For centuries, the creation of so many world-class bronze pieces was, in reality, the product of painstaking teamwork.

Small bronze pieces could be produced by a sole artist. In contrast, the life-sized and larger statues the Greeks and Romans craved for their temples had to be cast in pieces, the molten metal in each section no greater than two men could lift and pour. Arms, legs, heads, and torsos were cast separately, using the lost-wax method. The resulting body parts had a dull, often flawed surface, which workers put together with rivets or hidden joins, then polished with rasps and burnishers. At the sculptor's direction, they used chisels for the final details, including those lush folds and drapes that still delight the eye.

Meanwhile, other artisans were busy carrying out the subcontracted jobs. A specialist called the *oculariarius* delivered eyeballs of ivory, glass, or stone—giving the figures startling life.

Another specialist fashioned finely wrought hairdos, usually in wig form. This technique was carried to ingenious heights by Roman sculptors, whose commissions often included lineups of emperors and empresses, living and dead. To keep statues from getting that dated bell-bottoms look, the specialist periodically replaced the coiffures with bronze wigs in fresh new styles.

Other artists created mini-masterpieces in metals. Silver was preferred for teeth, fingernails, and eyelashes of statues. Nipples and lips? Copper, please. Many statues also were bedecked with gold or silver jewelry. Some statues were given locks of hair, cast separately from bronze or lead.

As demand for the highest quality work grew, bronze artisans specialized even more. A marvelous head-maker would stick to portraiture. A genius at feet might concentrate on those body parts. Some pros devoted themselves entirely to bronze genitalia, which helps explain the occasional "family jewels" resemblance between male bronzes.

Although we tend to think "marble" when it comes to sculpture of the classical world, the best sculptors, whether Greek or Roman, preferred bronze to marble. Lysippos, Polycleitos, Praxiteles, and Myron (of Discus-thrower fame) all created their most important works in bronze.

So too the pieces themselves; the most prestigious projects, the largest sculptures, the group commissions were in bronze. The thirty-foot-high Athena created by Phidias for the Acropolis was worshipfully admired by Greeks for centuries; later it became an object of awe among the Ottoman Turks of Constantinople until 1203.

The sculpting community's unbending notions of *arete* or excellence lasted much longer than the empires they worked for. The Romans had a cliché they used about something eternal, like friendship. They said it was *"aere perennius"*—more durable than bronze. That could equally well be said of these creators, known and unknown.

❖ MURALIST ❖
MORE THAN MERE COPIERS

Although the top ten abductions from Greek mythology or a bit of bestiality never failed to please as subject matter, a handful of bold Roman artists chose to depict the everyday. One streetwise up-and-comer did such skillful paintings of donkeys, street people, and other grimy topics that they sold for glorious sums.

These Roman painters weren't the only pioneers. During the reign of Augustus, Spurius Tadius introduced the radical notion of murals as home decor. Covering walls with gentle landscapes of villas and rivers, he also peopled them with peasants gathering grapes and elegant couples gliding in gilded boats.

Tadius's work became fashionable. Every other Roman, it seemed, was having a villa built—and they all wanted murals. This yen for large-format paintings coincided neatly with technological know-how from the building trades. Frescoes, the art of painting on fresh plaster, made murals at once splendid and durable.

Commissions started pouring in. Muralists began to produce works that honored great contributions from Greek art while taking them to a whole new level. On the walls of a first-century-A.D. villa, an unknown artist paid homage to a Greek vase painting created six hundred years earlier. In his mural, however, the artist improved on the stiff figure of a woman working wool. His woman is drawn in a freehand style of great poetry, at once stronger and more graceful. Moreover, she is placed as a painting within a painting upon the wall, revealing worlds within worlds.

Despite their material success, nay-sayers like Pliny the Elder dumped on muralists, saying that public art (i.e., on temple walls) was far more important than private art (i.e., walls in homes). Ironic, therefore, that the murals which survived the vicissitudes of time were mostly in private homes.

How did these artists do their work? The muralist did preparatory drawings, called *sinopia* after the brownish-red substance used to make them. Afterward, the walls were covered with fresh plaster and the muralist attacked them with mineral-based paints. As the plaster dried, the colors got trapped, becoming an integral part of the wall.

Fancier villas had distinct color schemes and pictorial themes for each room: birds, sea creatures, masks, landscapes, portraits, and those old standbys, Venus and Mars.

The Villa of the Mysteries, famed for its huge salon of larger-than-life figures painted by an unknown master, got an extra fillip of extravagance. Brilliant Pompeiian red was applied to the walls of the room. Once it dried, the artist had the walls polished, which also made the glowing surface stronger. Only then did he paint the lifesized figures carrying out enigmatic tasks, their actions possibly part of a Bacchanal religious rite.

The Greeks also produced mural art, but none has survived. If it had, Roman muralists might again be dismissed as mere imitators. In all media, their artists have gotten a bad rap, their work often labeled as "Roman copy of a Greek original."

Roman artists owed a debt to the Greeks, just as the work of modern artists owes a debt to both. In the twenty-first century, villa owners are once again commissioning murals, giving today's artists opportunities to pay homage to the fresco masters of two thousand years ago.

❖ MOSAIC ARTIST ❖

MASTERLY PIECES

The most enduring Greco-Roman art was largely underfoot: the mosaic. Some have withstood twenty centuries of foot traffic and still gleam gloriously from the floors of villas, palaces, and baths.

Although many unnamed artisans labored away, ruining their backs and knees, exceptional mosaic artists were recognized by others and often signed their work.

In the Macedonian capital of Pella, their skill reached superlative heights during the lifetimes of King Philip and his son Alexander. A ten-by-ten-foot masterpiece called *The Stag Hunt* has "Gnosis made this" on it—the earliest signed mosaic ever found. His work was made from simple pebbles, sorted by size and color and tightly set.

Gnosis and other mosaic-makers drew inspiration from artists in other mediums, such as the large-scale paintings on the walls of luxury homes around Macedonia. Their new knowledge gave their mosaics perspective and foreshortening. Some artists used sophisticated materials, such as terra-cotta spacers, outlines made of lead, even jewels for eyes, to create their effects. Not Gnosis; he created fine detail using tinier pebbles. This level of artistry, and the labor it required, would not be equaled again. Pebble mosaics from Rhodes to Spain continued to be made for several centuries, but in much simpler form.

Although mosaic artists played around with mixed mosaics of pebbles and marble chips, the next breakthrough was the tessera—a neat little square of cut stone or glass. Suddenly a huge palette of color and shading possibilities was available to the mosaicist. Around 150 B.C. an Alexandrian mosaic master named Sophilos created a portrait in minute glass tessarae, an artistic first, and the trend was off and running.

Alexandria's competition, the Asia Minor city of Pergamum, also had a rising star. Sosos was much copied by talented others—lucky for us, since none of his originals survived. Around 140 B.C., he created a piece called *The Drinking Doves*. Using tiny tesserae, some made of glass, Sosos "painted" highlights on silver, ripples on water, and even the shadows cast by four lifelike birds. He followed that triumph with an outrageous work called *The Unswept Room*. On a dining-room floor, he created trompe l'oeil images of chicken bones, fish skeletons, nutshells—even a mouse nibbling the leavings.

As time went on, mosaic artists turned to emblemata, smaller format mosaics from twenty to forty inches square, set in stone trays to be displayed on walls or inset into floor mosaics.

The giant exception was the emotionally compelling Alexander mosaic, sixteen square meters of genius. The damaged original is believed to owe much to a painting by Philoxenus, made soon after one of the two great battles between Alexander and Darius, King of Persia.

Speaking of debts: we owe a great one to mosaic artists of long ago, whose extant work provides the richest "picture book" as to how the Greeks and Romans lived, dressed, worked, and played. And more kudos to an international team of present-day artists who devoted two years (and assembled more than two million tiny tesserae) to recreate the Alexander masterpiece and install it in the House of the Faun, its original Pompeiian home.

❖ SIGNWRITER ❖
GRAFFITI-GRAMS & SIGNS OF THE TIMES

Humans have long been inveterate scribblers, doodlers, and graffiti artists. In Roman times, some even made a decent living at it.

Towns in southern Italy, especially Pompeii, Neapolis (Naples today), and Herculaneum, were hotbeds of vertical advertising. Exterior walls, gates, and houses carried political slogans, rental ads, warnings, maxims, obscene boasts, graffiti, schoolboys' pranks, humorous slanders, and announcements of gladiatorial games. Interior walls and cemeteries also got their share. Loan-shark receipts and running tallies for gambling adorned tavern walls; erotic personal ads were scrawled on bathhouse walls and jotted on tombstones.

Every March in Pompeii and the vicinity during the first century A.D., citizens who wanted to run for office made a public declaration in front of other residents. That kicked off the political campaign, letting signwriters called *scriptores,* hired by the candidates or their supporters, start work.

Unlike graffiti guerrillas and the ordinary folks who scribbled "beware of dog" and "bedroom to let" signs, the scriptores used black and red inks and fancy brushes to form their gracefully elongated messages. These visual displays were often quite striking. A community of talented young men did this work, often writing by torchlight or even moonlight, working late when streets were less crowded.

Some of the scriptores became name-brand artisans, signing their work and even making personal comments, like the artist who thanked a bar-owner for loaning him a chair to stand on. The fine calligraphed hands of Papilio and Astylus created messages that can still be read, two thousand years later, on the walls of a Pompeiian workshop on Abundance Street and near the Temple of Isis.

One busy chap named Aemilius Celer even labeled his own house so clients could find him with ease. He lived next door to a candidate and wrote a political plug for him with an afterthought that hinted at signwriter rivalries: "His neighbors urge you to elect Lucius Statius Receptus duovir with judicial power. He deserves the position. A. Celer, his neighbor, wrote this. If you spitefully deface this sign, may you become very ill."

Political candidates didn't worry overmuch about the relevance of their supporter groups. Quantity and diversity, that's what mattered. Over sixteen hundred election notices have been found in Pompeii alone. Groups of garlic-sellers, farmhands, goldsmiths, fullers, and more gave endorsements, usually formulaic, as in: "Vote for so-and-so, a good man." The signwriter often used key abbreviations: VB meant "a good man," OVF meant "I beg you to elect him."

Women, slaves, and ne'er-do-wells also paid signwriters to get into the action. Political plugs from a fun-loving group of waitress-hookers covered the walls of Asellina's tavern. Another ad read: "The petty thieves recommend so-and-so." (This and other joky "voting blocs" may have been the tags or nicknames of regular clubs or associations.)

When elections were over, scriptores turned to other work, from bereavement notices to entertainment. Over time, scriptores had fine-tuned their vocabulary of acronyms and abbreviations. One advert illustrates how the scriptores pruned Latin yet still were understood:

VEN.ET.GLAD.PAR.XX.M.TULLI.
PUGN.POM.PR.NON.NOVEMBRES.VII.IDUS.NOV

These laconic letters state that a certain Marcus Tullius plans to present a wild-beast hunt and twenty pairs of gladiators belonging to him in Pompeii from the fourth to the seventh of November.

If scriptores were alive today, they'd be welcomed by the subway-defacing communities—and could no doubt find immediate employment at the Pentagon.

❖ ❖ ❖ ❖ **SENTIA SECUNDA** ❖ ❖ ❖ ❖
People who work in glass houses

Even the most talented glass artisans of long ago seldom got recognized. Critical raves? Unlikely. Gallery openings with little canapés and wine? Not a chance. The artist who got to sign his or her work was a rare exception.

Meet Sentia Secunda, one of the rarities. A *vitrarius* or glassmaker of note, she lived in Aquileia, a Roman city on the Adriatic Sea. A member of the well-established Judaic community of artisans, Sentia may have been a slave herself—which made her achievements even more astonishing. She's one of a handful of glassmakers known by name.

Glassmaking traditions had been refined for centuries in the Middle East. In the first century A.D., however, it was a new and mysterious art to the Romans. Most glass objects were made by experienced artisans who'd fled Palestine and settled in Jewish communities throughout Italy, southern France, and Germany.

In her workplace, Sentia used time-honored ingredients (sand, soda, and lime) and a wood-fired furnace. The tools of her glasshouse haven't changed much in two thousand years. She handled a metal blowing pipe, worked with pincers and tongs to squeeze the molten glass, and shaped the mass on blocks of stone. Much of what she and other glassmakers did involved mold blowing or casting. Molds fashioned of stone, clay, or bronze were incised with designs. More elaborate effects could be produced by fusing slices of colored glass into a disc, then placing the disc into or over a mold.

To make the bottles that bore her stamp, Sentia blew molten glass around a four-sided mold. The finished product was usually bluish green, due to the iron naturally present in sand. For other hues, she added copper to produce ruby-red, cobalt for rich blue, or manganese for shades of yellow or purple.

When Sentia finished one of her sensuously beautiful, square-bottomed bottles, she attached a handle and spout made by freestyle glassblowing. She no doubt made other glass objects; to date, only her beautiful bottles have turned up. Found in Linz, an Austrian city along the Danube River, they carry the message: "*Sentia Secunda facit Aquileiae vitra*—Sentia Secunda made this glassware from Aquileia."

People in the Greco-Roman world used countless small slender glass vessels to hold perfume, ointments, and funerary libations. At first, glassmakers filled the demand by molding clay or dung over a metal rod, then forming a core in the shape of the desired vessel. Once it was dry, the glassmaker dipped the core into molten glass, sometimes finishing the vessel by adding decorative stripes or zigzag patterns in contrasting colors.

As the demand for glassware rose, glassmakers took up the technique of freestyle glassblowing with a pipe in a big way. With it, Sentia and her fellow workers could produce larger quantities of high-quality glass with less labor.

Unlike many of her fellow artisans, Secunda appeared to live and work in Aquileia. Glassworkers often became itinerant craftsmen, traveling where they were needed. Given the special needs of the equipment, it was far easier to send workers to glassmaking centers than vice-versa.

❖ ❖ ❖ ❖ **APOLLODORUS** ❖ ❖ ❖ ❖

Born litigious

Apollodorus had it all, scion of a self-made man, a wealthy banker and manufacturer named Pasion. Dad might have been a banking bean-counter to the core, but his real passion was his older son. Apollodorus (meaning "Apollo's gift") got the classiest of educations, from training in oratory to writing perfect Attic Greek.

Inevitably, god's little gift wanted more. He dabbled at banking in his dad's operation. He became a fine orator like his rival Demosthenes. And, thanks to his argumentative nature, he turned into a hotshot lawyer.

His dad's passing—that was a shock. But the real blow was his will: the family bank was left to Phormio, faithful ex-slave and right-hand bank manager. Furthermore, his mom Archippe was ordered to marry Phormio to keep the fiduciary beans in the family.

Apollodorus didn't care what mom thought, he set out to sue the sandals off old Phormio. He and his brother Pasicles had inherited loads of assets, including dad's war-shield factory—but into court he charged for a protracted nineteen-year battle with Phormio. This conflict spread into other legal cases. Apollodorus bumped heads with everyone, from local politicians to Demosthenes himself.

At least his training turned out to be money well spent, since Apollodorus ended up arguing both his own cases and a number of his father's outstanding legal matters in court. (Seven surviving cases, long attributed to über-orator Demosthenes, were written and argued by Apollodorus.)

Finally, however, Apollodorus found his thrill in 368 B.C. when he became one of his city's official benefactors. He accepted a liturgy, the most important obligation a rich person could carry out.

As liturgist or underwriter of a civic project, Apollodorus financed a warship and—more thrills—he'd have personal command of the vessel! Determined to rub everyone's nose in the most outlandish expenditures ever seen, Apollodorus poured cash into fancy fittings for the 150-foot vessel. When finished, his wooden beauty was the hottest three-banked trireme in Greece. A little pricier than anticipated, but never mind, dad wasn't around and there was plenty to spare.

Gleefully, Apollodorus set out to surpass himself in the matter of hiring the crew. Normally the going rate was a drachma per day per sailor, with half held back until the end of the tour of duty. Chickenfeed, Apollodorus thought. To make a memorable splash, he rounded up a seasoned crew, promising them a signing bonus, paid in advance. In the end his crew amounted to six deckhands, four archers, three officers, ten armed hoplites, and 170 rowers, into all of whose callused hands he counted out silver coins.

His wife squawked at his extravagance, but Apollodorus ignored her. Soon he'd be under way as commander of his own ship and wouldn't have to hear that noise. His mission came off without a hitch. For twelve months, he used

his trireme to escort the grain ships from the Black Sea to the port of Athens at Piraeus.

Everyone was terribly impressed—even the fellows at the barber shop. The only snag? Apollodorus found himself back on dry land but up a creek, a bankrupt blockhead at age forty-five. A real case of the tables turning on a banker's son.

❖ TEACHER ❖

GOLDEN OPPORTUNITY FOR CLOSET SADISTS

Conditions for modern-day educators haven't improved greatly, but at least teachers today can breathe a sigh of relief they weren't born B.C.

On the Ides, the thirteenth or fifteenth of each month, Roman teachers were paid a pittance from parents—for which they sometimes had to sue to collect! A teacher needed fifteen students to earn what a mule-driver did.

Educators had little motivation to go the extra mile. A fortunate few got rewarded for doing so. Freedman Marcus Flaccus held classroom competitions to stimulate the minds of his pupils and was chosen to teach the grandsons of Emperor Augustus at a fat per-annum of one hundred thousand sesterces. His case was rare; most teachers moonlighted to make their salaries go further.

Education was a stripped-down affair. Teachers had no building, no rooms, no desks, and no equipment to speak of—not even a measly blackboard.

School began each day before dawn. Kids brought wax tablets to write on and oil lamps to see by, which got abundant soot on the few book-scrolls on hand. Some teachers had to rent classroom space; others taught outdoors, using sidewalks and plazas in fair weather, covered porticos in the rain.

On the bright side, the teachers of yesteryear had no administrators, school boards, SAT tests, grant-writing, or over-involved parents to placate. No credentials were needed to teach—an ideal career for those who enjoyed discipline. Most teachers carried whips, and parents expected them to be used liberally.

Greece and Rome had no preschools with teaching toys and enrichment activities. Parents, however, did outsource lots of their early education chores to a tutor slave called the *paedagogus*. This employment pool contained many experienced people of good birth who'd been captured in war or by pirates. The tutor slave was often more educated than the parents.

Some tutors taught the three Rs, but their primary job was to instill good behavior while looking out for the child. Parents were as spooked as modern ones about sexual predators or precious little Claudius falling in with bad company, so the paedagogus stuck like a shadow to his charge.

In Greece, most children received basic reading and writing from a *grammaticus,* singing and lyre-playing from a music teacher, and physical education from a coach. Roman parents who couldn't afford private tutors sent their kids to the *magister,* an elementary teacher big on memorization and practical math. Roman ten-year-olds also went to the grammaticus, who pounded Greek into them, along with poetry, writing, philosophy, music, and public speaking. Girls rarely attended; affluent families hired tutors to educate their daughters at home.

By fourteen, a child's education was over. Most boys were already in the workforce. Most girls were married, the legal age being twelve.

A privileged few went on to study with a professor versed in rhetoric or oratory. This was the fast track, the only track to a future as an orator or officeholder. Besides classes, these elite students observed the *rhetor* at work. In the process, they absorbed the lessons for success: studying audiences; studying judges; learning the art of skillful argument; and thinking on one's feet.

No one knows for certain, but it's safe to say that few of these students ever decided to become real educators.

❖ TOUR GUIDE ❖

DELIVERING WHOPPERS IN ANCIENT TIMES

If dropped into tour mode two thousand years ago, we'd feel right at home, gawking at the pyramids or trudging around Troy. Then as now, the grandest attractions were easy to spot because they had the biggest gauntlet of tour guides, helpful child beggars, quasi-polyglot translators, and pointer-outers to run.

Tour guides of old rose to the noble challenge of giving visitors a wonderful experience by meticulous preparation and intimate knowledge of the site. To ensure accuracy, they steeped themselves like fine teabags in the subject matter at hand. Unfortunately, such paragons were always someone *else's* guide.

Seasoned travelers like Herodotus, Pausanias, and Plutarch, who later wrote detailed guidebooks about the regions they visited, often groused about the *mystagogi* ("mystery teachers" in Greek, although "mystery makers" might be more accurate) they encountered. On a sightseeing trip to the famed shrine at Delphi, a member of Plutarch's group snarled, "Our guide refused to cut his talk short, grinding through his standard speech instead."

Surviving graffiti from ancient times, besides the standard "Cleopatra was here" and "I was amazed" (the most frequently carved remark on ancient stones), included travelers' prayers, such as this passionate graffito from a Roman historian: "Protect me, Zeus, from your tour guides at Olympia—and you, goddess Athena, from yours at Athens."

Ancient travelers had several disadvantages compared to today's globe-trotters. Maps were rarer than griffin sightings. The few guidebooks available were for pre-trip study, being too valuable to carry and too difficult to open or close in a gale.

On the other hand, long-ago tourists had porters galore to carry food, gear, and extra clothing; everyone, even the most impoverished visitor, brought along one or more slaves. Thus these elite tourists had their own Berlitz guidebooks in human form—slaves who probably spoke Greek better than they did and might know other tongues as well.

Despite the drawbacks, almost every traveler hired a tour guide for rich sites like Delphi, where the monuments and artistic treasures were piled up in confused abundance. Ditto for temples, which were the art galleries and museums of the day. Since cameras wouldn't exist for another two millennia, visitors might hire a quick-draw artist or miniaturist to create painted mementos of their stay.

Ancient tour guides also had the twenty-first-century habit of segueing from the sightseeing mission at hand to nearby gift shops owned by moth-eaten cousins, where the traveler would be dazzled by gimcrackery from good-luck statues to cheesy pyramid carvings, and assured of "special prices."

When Christianity began to attract followers around the Mediterranean, globetrotters of that faith eventually developed a network of stops, called hospices. Each hospice, often located at sanctuaries or near monasteries, provided food and lodging. Even better, they furnished guides to show the visitor around—all of this on a donation basis.

❖ SIX ❖

SMALL-TIME OPERATORS, CORPORATE RACKETS

❖ OLIVE-OIL WHOLESALER ❖
THE OILMEN OF OLD

The tree, the fruit, and the oil of the olive had holy significance to the Greeks. Bestowed on Athenians by their patron goddess, they gave it special honor. In the sixth century B.C., Solon made the felling of olive trees a capital crime. At the Panathenaica, the annual Festival of Athens, winners of chariot races and other events received sleek painted amphorae filled with Attic olive oil. In another part of Greece, the organizers of the Olympic Games so treasured the tree that they made an olive-branch crown the only prize given to the victors.

Useful as food, cooking oil, medicine, sunscreen, lighting source, laxative, cleansing lotion, and a halfway decent contraceptive, this versatile liquid became the city's hottest export. Greek colonists soon brought olive cuttings to Italy. It wasn't long until groves of silvery leaves found fertile ground in faraway places, including North Africa and Spain.

Thousands of growers, pickers, processors, shippers, traders, and wholesalers made their living from the olive.

Farmers found that the hardy trees needed little moisture and grew well in clay soil on rolling hills, being happiest no more than fifty miles from the sea. Hand picking or lightly beating tree limbs with long reeds, workers harvested olives each December.

Once picked, olives were processed in a roller mill, then had the pits removed. For the first pressing of Athena's liquid gold, half-ripe olives were put in a beam press; a screw-press was sometimes used for smaller amounts. A team of four men could do over twenty pressings a day, yielding about six hundred pounds of olive oil.

Initially, Attic olive oil was the standard by which the rest were measured; for hot commodities like wine and oil, regular tastings were held for buyers in the Athens market. Traders who braved the seas to ship the distinctive baggy-bellied amphorae of oil to markets in Egypt and the Black Sea made fortunes. Later, Athens lost its grip on the slippery olive, and places like Rhodes, Crete, Sicily, and Asia Minor muscled in on their near-monopoly.

By Roman times, traders were shipping seas of oil from the ports of Cosa and Brindisi. From northern Italy, traders sold to the island of Delos and even to Athens, whose population had grown larger and oil production smaller over the centuries.

At the top of the heap, oleaginously speaking, were the wholesalers, like those from southern Spain's Baetica province, who by A.D. 75 had their own powerful guild. As the *corpus oleariorium*, they controlled oil output from Cádiz to Córdoba, their wealth of trees bearing the finest fruit. They also had the vertical integration so beloved by corporations, owning pottery factories to make their containers and fleets in which to ship them.

Oilmen like Aelius Optatus could have bought and sold Roman senators; at Monte Testaccio, Rome's man-made mountain of broken-up amphorae pottery, archaeologists have found vast numbers of shards with his name on them. Another well-represented wholesaler in the olive-oil amphorae mountain: Fadius Musa, patron to his regional guild, who donated monies to pay for yearly festivities and distribution bonuses for members.

Optatus, Musa, and their colleagues were the oil tycoons of their day—but the oil that made them rich was gold, not black. Thanks to their fat market share, oil wholesalers got the same tax privileges as the wheat suppliers. Sensible emperors never forgot that without its daily oil and bread, Rome as a city was dead.

❖ ❖ ❖ ❖ **PASION** ❖ ❖ ❖ ❖
Banking on himself

During the golden centuries of Athens, when great men ruled and wrote, moved and shook, a humble foreigner from Phoenicia achieved the improbable. Pasion came to Athens the same way countless others did, captured in battle and afterward sold as a slave. His new masters, bankers at the port of Piraeus, soon noticed the sharp wits of their Phoenician slave. Once Pasion learned to handle the table that was set up each day for currency exchange in the marketplace, they had him collect loan payments that were due each new moon, make loans at the standard ten percent interest, and attend auctions to offer credit and other bank services to buyers.

Despite his low status and broken Greek, Pasion became the man in whom locals reposed the utmost confidence. So impressed were his two owners with Pasion's honesty and reliability, they finally gave him his freedom.

Always a drachma-pincher, the new freedman moved decisively. He bought out his retiring bosses, then purchased a war-shield factory that would eventually net him the rough equivalent of $32,000 a year. Good choice, as it happened, since rival city-states Athens and Sparta were engaged in another interminable war and needed shields in mega quantities.

After decades of fighting Spartans, the city-state of Athens hit rock bottom, emotionally and fiscally. When his adoptive hometown reached financial crisis, Pasion stepped in, endowing Athens with generous gifts from his profits in banking and manufacture, including in-kind donations of one thousand shields and a trireme warship.

In return, the assembly decreed the unthinkable: about 400 B.C., they made Pasion a full citizen of Athens. (The New Yorkers of ancient times, Athenians rarely let outsiders become insiders, much less voting citizens of their city-state.)

Now a well-heeled hero, Pasion got married, dabbled in real estate, made high-interest loans on fifty talents he had lying around, and took up fatherhood. A super-indulgent dad, Pasion's relationship with his litigious and "I'm entitled!" elder son sounds strangely contemporary.

When Pasion died in 370 B.C., his wife, Archippe, and sons were staggered to learn that pop had willed his bank *and* his ever-loving spouse to Phormio, his own ex-slave who'd managed the bank for years. Among the pragmatic Greeks, that was par for the course in inheritance matters—but a decided bump in the road for certain beneficiaries with Great Expectations. (You can read more about this eccentric dynasty and the checkered career of Pasion's son Apollodorus in chapter five.)

❖ PERFUMER ❖
WRAP-AROUND SCENT

Scent dominated much of daily life in Greece and Rome. People not only wore perfume, they bathed in it, burned it, even drank it.

The Greeks believed that good aromas would please the heavenly nostrils of the gods. On their outdoor altars, they burned incense and myrrh; our word perfume (literally meaning "through smoke") is a reminder of this ancient practice. Frankincense was the top-of-the-line offering, popular for sacrifices and celebrity funerals—and the perfect gift to lay in a manger.

Mere mortals wanted to get in on good smells, too. *Myropolides,* or perfumers, found on every street corner, sold chewing gum in ginger and other flavors and whipped up perfumes to order. At their minibars, proprietors also prepared wine and soft drinks sweetened with violets, cinnamon, and other additives, making this a mix-and-mingle hangout.

A whole Martha Stewart etiquette of scent arose. Experts recommended dabbing feet with an orris-root and rose mixture, hair with sweet marjoram, arms with mint, neck with tufted thyme, and nipples with palm oil.

Even staunch believers in simplicity, like philosopher Socrates, adored perfume. He dipped the hem of his robe in scent, explaining that good smells travel upward.

Romans were sniffier, in both senses of the term, about the work performed by perfumers. Orator-writer Cicero, always scornful of the lower orders, clumped perfumers among the "shameful occupations, catering to our sensual pleasures." (His ideas were pretty weird, since he also included fishmongers in this group.)

Romans ignored Cicero and went quite potty over perfumery, the more exotic and rare the ingredients the better. Empresses and senators nearly ruptured themselves in the race to have exquisite combinations devised for their bodies and for the fur of their pet pooches. One heinously expensive favorite melded lotus, saffron, iris, Syrian cinnamon, cat-thyme, camel's thorn, wild grape, cardamom, all-heal, and gladiolus, plus other ingredients.

At banquets aimed to impress, guests lolled on scented cushions, were served by slaves reeking of musk and spikenard, and were beguiled (sometimes besplattered) by birds with perfumed wings.

During these sybaritic centuries, the government sometimes subsidized the provision of perfumes and unguents at the public baths. As a profit-making arm, the baths sold charming little scent pots in quantities that would floor even the marketing directors at Chanel.

Perfumers had no need to stress over business trends. Because perfumes weren't alcohol-based or long-lasting, public demand usually exceeded supply. Most scents were produced by expressing flowers and plants into fresh green olive oil or bitter almond oil, then adding stabilizing resins before bottling the mixture in alabaster containers that kept the perfume cool and hidden from the sun. Small-scale perfumery existed in Pompeii and other places, but Capua was the production hub, as was the fragrant rose-growing town of Seplasia and its generations of perfume families.

Some of the perfumers' recipes have survived. To make eight gallons of rose perfume, for instance, took masses of petals plus ginger-grass, sweet flag, and twenty-three gallons of salt!

Even the gladiatorial games developed an olfactory component; perfumers who won the scent contracts were the envy of their competitors. Besides the refreshing feel of scented showers, periodically sprayed by an attendant over the rows of spectators, and the sheer extravagance of the gesture, the gladiatorial perfumery served a more ominous purpose. The lovely aroma of crocuses, roses, and lilies was meant to overcome the stench of the arena: the rank odors of wild animals battling to their deaths, and the sweet nauseating smell of human blood, freshly spilled.

❖ AMBER SCOUT ❖

APPLICANT MUST HAVE BUILT-IN COMPASS

Amber had long been a seduction favorite of the Greeks. If a wealthy chap wanted to impress a woman, he bought her a nubbin of *electrum*, as amber was called. Women adored its piney scent, the way things stuck to it when rubbed. Greeks argued savagely over amber's origins. Some believed it was the solidified urine of the lynx. A more delicate school of thought declared the stones were the tears of mythical sisters. All agreed that laying hands on the stuff was a risky and difficult business.

As Roman armies conquered the far reaches of the empire, they discovered where the best amber came from. Rotten luck: those blasted barbarians along the Baltic Sea and other chilblain-producing places controlled the secret of its whereabouts.

No strangers to bartering, Roman soldiers on border duty traded with the barbarians and began to wear pieces of amber on their persons for good luck. As civilians clamored for the stuff, a middle-man job was created: the amber scout. All it took was fluency in barbarous tongues, diplomatic skills, and utter disregard for one's safety and comfort.

In A.D. 57, Emperor Nero put out an urgent call for an amber scout. Outdoing his own Julian and Claudian ancestry had become a dreadful problem. As their great-great-not-so-great descendant, he had people to impress, lots of them. It no longer sufficed to throw gladiatorial games and shower the mob with coins. Nero needed more pizazz: something rare, useless, and hard to obtain. Like amber. To Julianus, his carnage organizer, he gave the shattering news that a vast amount of amber must be procured. Deadline? Yesterday.

Cursing his lot in life, Julianus scurried around until he found the man for the job, a low-key fellow of the knightly class. In truth, the man appeared to have zero qualifications, but he owed Julianus a big one.

Julianus was careful to give his scout detailed instructions: "Go to the northern edge of the Roman Empire, cross the Danube River—you'll hit Upper Silesia, but don't stop there. It's six hundred, maybe eight hundred miles, tops."

Months went by. Just before the games were to begin, Julianus was about to fall on his sword when the stalwart scout dragged in, laden with masses of amber. One chunk weighed thirteen pounds! In his quest, the knight had trudged from Pannonia to Posen (from Italy through Hungary and Poland to the Baltic coast), waded through snow banks and rivers, and overcome ghastly local foodstuffs. He'd found the amber collecting places and faced the fearsome trade factories armed with hostile haggling warriors.

Needless to say, Nero's games glittered. Golden amber adorned the gladiators' armor, weapons, and the netting used to keep wild beasts from the crowd. Even the biers on which dead gladiators were removed bore amber decor.

Thanks to other scouts who followed the path blazed to the Baltic by the knight, amber soared in popularity—and price. Soon a small amber statue cost more than a large healthy slave.

And history's first amber scout? That dauntless fellow outlived Nero and other emperors to be admired (but unnamed) in the writings of Pliny the Elder.

❖ PUBLISHER-BOOKSELLER ❖
SO THAT'S WHERE BORDERS GOT
ITS MARKETING PLAN

Publishers who doubled as booksellers got into the game early. The making and merchandising of books started in sixth-century-B.C. Athens, given a huge boost by the popularity of Greek comedy and tragedy. The mega-hits of Sophocles, Euripedes, and Aeschylus were the first works to be published on papyrus.

Publishing in those days meant copying by hand. The system was more like "print on demand," with a roomful of scribes copying the same manuscript onto rolls of papyrus as it was read aloud.

Greek tyrants from Polycrates to Pisistratus were keen on recreational reading and took the lead in book-collecting, purchasing their favorites from booksellers around the marketplace of Athens.

For five hundred years, Rome was a blank slate, literarily speaking. One of its first bookshops belonged to filthy-rich Atticus, a publisher-bookseller and writers' groupie. His large staff copied Latin and Greek manuscripts, giving them wide circulation—the best fate an author could hope to achieve. Royalties? Dream on. The notion of copyright didn't exist, conveniently allowing publishers to snap up any manuscripts they fancied.

By the time Augustus became Rome's first emperor, the city had a community of publisher-booksellers, mostly freedmen who established businesses like Atrectus's place on Argiletum Street and Secundus's bookshop on Sigillaris near the Forum. Most of them published by category—poetry, history, salacious memoirs, and so forth. Or concentrated on a few brand-name authors they were pushing.

Outside their bookstores, advertisements touted best-sellers and remainder bins invited browsing. Scrolls took getting used to. This book-in-a-paper-towel-roll format had no paragraphs, no chapter divisions, and took both hands to scroll through the material. It was even more tedious than electronic scrolling today.

Inside the bookshops, a pleasant olfactory ambience reigned. To protect manuscripts from moths, scrolls were treated with oil of cedar, and deluxe editions often carried scent.

The papyrus for books came from Egypt, which the publisher bought from the warehouses of the *chartarii* or paper dealers. As literacy rose, books were duplicated in quantity by slave copyists. With their reed pens and cuttlefish ink, a hundred scribes could crank out one thousand copies in a ten-hour day. What Greeks and Romans called "books" were skinnier than novellas. Instead of chapters, they carried a tag with the number of lines, which established the size and cost of a title.

A standard offering might sell for the equivalent of twenty-five cents to a dollar—most of it fattening the bottom line of the publisher-bookseller. Coffee-table editions were also produced, centuries before anyone thought of actually making the coffee. These volumes, calligraphed with accents of gold, silver, and red ink, sometimes illustrated, captured the high-end market. One evergreen title? A fully illustrated erotic how-to by an impudent Greek named Philaenis, the *Joy of Sex* author of her decade.

Although publishers made limited editions by binding papyrus sheets or thin slices of wood between leather covers (a specialty of the city of Kellis), it was Pergamum that refined the format. They used animal-skin parchment, which allowed writing on both sides. This more book-like format was called the codex; it quickly became popular for Christian works.

Publisher-booksellers continued to sell papyrus scrolls, however, the format of choice for pagan fiction and nonfiction, right up until the last days of the Roman Empire.

❖ ❖ ❖ ❖ CEPHALUS ❖ ❖ ❖ ❖

Metic makes good

Like many a modern nation, the city-states of ancient Greece wrestled with immigration and resident-alien issues. In Athens and its port city, Piraeus, for example, lived twenty-five thousand resident aliens called *metics*. Most were attracted to the Athenian city-state because of its booming economy—not for its democratic political system, in which they could never play a part.

One venturesome metic was Cephalus, originally from Syracuse, Italy, who around 430 B.C. settled in Piraeus. As a metic, he had to abide by numerous finicking rules. He had to register with authorities, find himself a citizen sponsor, sign up for military service if called upon, and pay a special monthly tax for the privilege of living in or around Athens.

Most metics started businesses or small manufacturing workshops—activities the very thought of which gave freeborn Athenian males acid reflux. Having observed the number of wars that the testy Athenians got involved in, Cephalus put his startup funds into a shield-making factory.

In a few years, he'd built his business into a going concern. By the time his four sons had grown into teenagers, Cephalus had an operation employing 120 men—possibly the biggest business in Athens. "Employed" might not be quite accurate, since most or all of the workers were probably his slaves.

His hot, noisy factory rang with the sound of hammers on bronze. His men worked half-naked, using their caps for sweatbands. Crews showed up before dawn and spent fourteen-hour days working metal into a circular shield about thirty-five inches in diameter, then attaching it to an inch-thick wooden core. A typical shield weighed about twenty pounds; it had a lipped edge so a soldier could rest it on his shoulder when not in battle.

Evidence of the property tax Cephalus paid is still in existence, indicating that he must have owned a home and possibly his commercial property. By law, metics were forbidden to own real estate, so the exemption he got was unusual. Very likely it was due to his extraordinary efforts as a good citizen, even though he could not vote. He spent big sums to educate his sons as well as any Athenian. Over the years, he took on several liturgies, the honorary posts whereby people of means shouldered the financial burden for civic events and works, from festivals to buildings.

An honest man who paid his debts and kept his word, Cephalus must have been a fellow who could toss around philosophical ideas as well as twenty-pound shields. A long-time friend and social equal of Socrates and other thinkers, in his old age the metic was immortalized in Plato's book *The Republic*. The first chapter was even set in his house in Piraeus.

Cephalus never achieved Athenian citizenship, although one of his sons did. Remaining a resident alien wasn't necessarily a tragic fate—or an impediment. A number of metics achieved fame that still burns brightly: Herodotus, the father of historians; Hippocrates, the father of medicine; and Aristotle, whom we often think of as quintessentially Athenian.

❖ BARBER ❖

PUTTING YOUR NECK ON THE LINE

Greece being home base for shaggy, bearded philosophers, the Greeks had a more relaxed attitude about facial hair and hairdos. That is, the men did. In ancient times, women wrestled with female five o'clock shadow, a Greek tragedy that has continued to plague their mustache-prone great-great-to-the-*n*th-degree-grand-daughters.

Until the time of Alexander the Great, Greeks favored hairy faces and long locks. Shaving was for girly-men. Young Alex was quick to claim that he went clean-shaven only because the enemy kept grabbing his soldiers' chin hairs in battle.

Even post-Alex, Greeks often kept their beards and hair medium long, since only slaves wore cropped hair. In Athens, a few barbers did a modest business at the agora, their shops serving as news-exchange hangouts for males.

Meanwhile, further west a young razor-wielder with a flair for grooming and gossip emigrated from Sicily to Rome to become that city's first barber. After he talked high-profile general Scipio Africanus into a daily shave, the other Romans emulated him. Scruffy facial hair became taboo. The tonsor and his art were in business, his barber chair a morning stop for all males who could afford it. Only when in mourning, or if for some inexplicable reason they wanted to pass for Greeks or barbarians, did Romans let their stubble grow.

The rite of passage from youth to manhood involved a trip to the barber for the first whisker-whacking. Emperors threw big ceremonies for the occasion; Nero preserved his scraggly chin-hairs in a pearl-encrusted gold box and offered them to Jupiter.

Wielding a *novacula,* an iron razor with a crescent-shaped blade that would scare the pants off even the reddest-blooded male today, the tonsor oiled his man, then shaved him. In an era of soapless shaving, it was a slow, painful process. Razors didn't hold their edge well and needed frequent honing; shaving was almost never attempted at home.

By degrees, the *tonstrina* became a full-service shop that stayed open until the eighth hour, roughly 1 P.M. in summer. Besides shaves, the tonsor pared nails, plucked eyebrows, cleaned ears with a scoop, and pulled teeth on demand. (Roman Forum excavations at a barber's, or what might be a dental while-you-wait, have yielded nearly one hundred rotten teeth.) To stanch bleeding, all tonsors kept vinegar and spider's webs on hand.

Some customers opted for depilation and had the barber apply bat's blood, Cretan acid, or powdered viper, which apparently scared the whiskers off.

To finish up the well-groomed man, the tonsor cut his customer's hair with scissors and knives, afterward applying an early version of Brylcreem to treat dandruff, baldness, and other scourges.

Hair fashions followed the coiffures of the rich and famous; the facial hair of ruling males was sedulously copied. After 148 years of clean-shaven emperors, the entire Roman world grew beards when Hadrian began to rule. His shaggy look was chalked up to facial scars, acne, or his fondness for things Greek.

A number of deft and gossipy women also competed in the Roman marketplace as *tonstrices.* On their tombstones, these trailblazers took care to boast about their tress success in a mostly male world.

Prudent Roman barbers kept essential supplies on hand—like spider's webs to stanch the bleeding from all those razor cuts.

❖ GARLAND-MAKER ❖

HEAD TRIPS

Greek and Roman civilians rarely wore headgear—not even funny hats on birthdays or New Year's. Instead, folks in both cultures put on sweet-smelling garlands, wreaths, diadems, chaplets, and crowns to mark every occasion.

The earliest crowns dated back to the runners who took first place at the eighth-century-B.C. Olympics: simple wreaths, made from the branches of a sacred olive tree. As soon as they heard about it, sponsors of other athletic games and festivals wanted in on the crown thing.

Then somebody popped a wreath of leaves and flowers on their recently deceased, setting off a trend for rites-of-passage headgear. Before long, new births were announced on the door by a crown of olive leaves (it's a boy!) or wool (drat, another girl). For garland-makers, weddings looked like the next Big Thing. Finicky brides, however, decided it was bad luck to purchase nuptial wreaths and opted to weave verbena and other posies themselves.

Professional garland-makers didn't take that snub lying down, regrouping with more wreath-occasion ideas. Luminaries like Sappho the poet helped matters by writing that nine out of ten deities looked favorably on people wearing flowered crowns.

As it transpired, the serious cash for garland-makers came from the manufacture of tipsiness-prevention headgear. It was common knowledge that amethysts, ivy leaves, and roses were sure-fire prophylactics against drunkenness. Wearing protective chaplets became de rigeur for symposia, orgies, and other drinking occasions.

To make their creations, garland-makers sewed together roses, laurel leaves, violets, myrtle, ivy, parsley, and other flowers and herbs, selling them in the marketplace and door to door. The party sort were very inexpensive and could be recycled as offerings to the household deities on each family's hearth.

So far, the garland industry, now fully organized into associations with burial-club benefits, hadn't spread much beyond natural vegetation.

But change was in the air. Garland-makers would soon confront headgear hardware—and serious competition.

It might have begun when an Athenian official at a loss for honors bestowed a shiny gold crown on the man who got his ship in the best order that year. That opened the cupidity floodgates. Soon metallic crowns were being awarded left and right.

Roman emperors predictably went nuts. They began to award gold crowns decorated with turrets for the first man to scale the wall of a besieged city. Eventually they had three classes of triumph crowns for victorious generals—the biggest being too heavy to wear. The most ludicrous headgear had to be the *corona radiata,* a spiky number that can still be seen atop the Statue of Liberty. For ages only the gods and deified heroes like Hercules got to wear the spiky crown. But wouldn't you know it, Emperor Caligula, an early baldie and a constant garland-wearer, usurped it for his daily attire. Not for long, however; he died young, assassinated but gorgeously garlanded.

And what of the original garland-makers? The fad for metallic coronas never gained more than a small market share. Even among the most ostentatious gold-crown wearers, flowered wreaths and garlands remained perennial favorites—fragrant, lucky, and, best of all, lightweight.

❖ JEWELER ❖

WORKING WITH SCALPERS

Around the time of Alexander the Great, jewelers were the growth industry to envy. Highly trained, inspired by centuries of Greek and Etruscan tradition, the best had rock-steady hands and good eyesight. Not 20/20, though; short-sighted jewelers did better at close work.

Jewelers' exquisite pieces typically began with malleable gold, seventy-five to one hundred percent pure. Gems like emeralds, even when flawed and cloudy, were sought after. Rare rubies and diamonds were seldom used—too hard to work with. Diamond chips did serve as abrasives on the rotating tip of a lathe-like device, powered by a bow-drill.

Besides gold, the other must-have item was the pearl. Some ultra-fashionistas staggered under the weight of the pearl ropes they sported.

That is, they would have staggered if they hadn't been supported by a clutch of robust slaves.

For more modest budgets, jewelers fashioned earrings, bracelets, and rings of peridot, aquamarine, sapphire, and red garnet, the most popular choice. Amber was also big.

To begin a piece, the artisan hammered gold into a thin sheet for working, then cut strips and twisted them by hand into beaded spiral wire or wavy ribbon. The real experts in granulation techniques were Etruscan jewelers, who bonded minute beads of gold, using heat. Gold rings, rolled from sheets and thus hollow, were first filled with wax mixed with marble dust; in later Roman times, with liquid sulfur that became solid once set.

Using instruments of wood, bone, and metal, the jeweler created raised positives, such as cameos, or cut intaglio designs. His most useful tool? A small chisel with which he chased or displaced gold rather than carving it away. Preserving raw material was important. Usually supplied by the customer, it consisted of old coins and jewelry to be recycled. Jewelers got paid by the complexity of the piece and the time it took; something elaborate might consume a week.

Gem engravers used tools called scalpers to engrave designs and logos into carnelian and sard signature rings. Worn by almost every free person, these beautiful rings served as portable ID. With them, wearers could sign documents or stamp the clay stoppers of wine jugs and other valuables.

Although silver mines in Spain and Greece pumped out lots of ore, interest in silver jewelry was negligible. Gemstones, semiprecious stones, and pearls were a godsend to the jeweler, who enjoyed huge markups on them. As a guild member, he had ready access to wholesale materials.

Jewelers weren't always men, either. In the Roman period, women also became gem engravers, cameo cutters, pearl setters, and makers of gold-leaf jewelry.

The marathon ostentation of rich women ensured that jewelers of any gender would prosper. Take Lollia Paulina, one of the ex-wives of Caligula; this unbashful bimbo showed up at a casual engagement party draped in forty million sesterces worth of pearls and emeralds. Ye gods, said avid spectator Pliny, who was nearly blinded by the vision. Good taste might be lacking, but one could always depend on an excess of bling during Rome's glittering centuries.

❖ LITTER CARRIER ❖

LUXURY TRAVEL, BUT DON'T FORGET
THE WORMWOOD

Many Greek aristocrats considered it poor form to be seen walking from A to B. Instead they traveled elegantly from here to there, carried on a bed-like platform called a litter by four stout men.

The more stodgy Romans resisted such usage for the general public. To their minds, litters were reserved for long trips or to get around if wounded or sickly. Most importantly, they were meant for that last ride to the funeral pyre, letting the neighbors admire the corpse: "Uncle Rufus looks so peaceful—like he's sleeping."

Little by little, into this masculine decorum crept the female use of litters for nonmedical, nonfunereal reasons. Ladies ferociously engaged in decorative upgrades. It got to the point where leaders in 195 B.C. passed a law forbidding female litter usage. By Julius Caesar's time 150 years later, the law was still being honored in the breach, causing him to issue various decrees that were equally ignored.

By the reign of Emperor Claudius (whose gimpy leg and love of wine made him a litter-bug), these conveyances littered the landscape of Rome and other cities. Initially, most litters were the conspicuous property of the wealthy, who insisted on up to four pairs of matching, muscular, spiffily dressed slaves. (Bright red outfits were popular for years.) As the salesman said, these litters came fully loaded: custom paint jobs, leather roofs, feather beds, and the hottest craze, see-through windows of glass instead of curtains.

Pretty soon folks of more modest means clamored to get into littering. Enterprising souls in Rome started companies of litters for hire, stationed near the Tiber River (where out-of-towners arrived) and at strategic litter-load points around town, the equivalent of today's cab stands. When not engaged for use, the poles were removed and each litter sat on four wooden feet.

The load-bearers for these mass-transit litters were often freedmen or freeborn Romans, poor but energetic workers with no back problems—at least not initially.

Although the conveyance held no more than two persons, with the majority circulating as single-passenger vehicles, it still must have been tough on the *lecticarii,* as they were called. They probably wore thick pads on their shoulders where the poles rested. They knew the secrets of picking up evenly, setting down softly, and walking in the ideal rhythm for minimum sway and bump on the passenger. (Even today, during Holy Week celebrations in Spain and Latin America, we can admire the cunning footwork of the bearers who carry aloft the great religious floats in a similar manner.)

Despite the most expert littering, the passenger in ancient times had better come prepared. Famed physician Cornelius Celsus warned that the rocking motion was worse than a ship on the high seas. Another weary traveler was the writer Cato, who'd obviously spent many litter-bound hours. His blunt suggestion: "To prevent chafing, when you set out on a journey, keep a small branch of Pontic wormwood under the anus."

❖ SELLER OF PURPLE ❖
PURPLE REIGN

Internationally adventurous businessmen knew there were fortunes to be made importing the right sort of goods. Wine was one. "Flower of purple," the murex dye, was another.

The murex marine snail, a pretty little meat-eater that kills other invertebrates by injecting neurotoxins, lives around the shores of the eastern Mediterranean. When exposed to sunlight, the poison from three species of murex turns rich colors, from pink to deep violet; two thousand years ago, that venom was the source of a highly prized commodity.

Everyone loved the color purple, including a businesswoman named Queen Cleopatra VII. One of her best moves? In 34 B.C., she slick-talked Mark Antony into giving her the murex monopoly he held for the city of Tyre in present-day Lebanon.

How lucrative was Tyrian purple dye? Each small shell yielded only a drop, with the result that the dye cost up to twenty times its weight in gold. It took the essence of twenty thousand murex shells to color the trim on a couple of senatorial togas. Cleopatra, a conspicuous consumer herself, used it to color the sails of her warships.

Speculating in murex was risky. By sea, the *purpuraria* or merchants of purple sailed from Rome to Alexandria, Egypt, then on to the cities of Tyre or Sidon, where, two millennia earlier, Phoenicians had discovered the snail's brilliant secret. The sea trip took fifty to one hundred days. Travel overland took even longer; but in winter, it was the only option because of rough seas.

If the purple seeker made it back safely with a load, he could net huge profits. More than one murex mogul bragged on his tombstone about his membership of the Augustales, an Italian society that allowed freedmen to buy their way into status. Even freeborn men clamored to join this group, whose privileges and rank were nearly equivalent to those of mayors.

With such keen demand, a seller of purple could enjoy the highlife. Not so the people who extracted the venom, processed it, and used it to dye wool and silk. The stuff was nasty. Tyre was described as "unpleasant for residence;" its workers toiled in a miasma of rotting mollusks, a most singular stench among stenches.

To make the dye, huge quantities of snails were caught by lowering baskets baited with frogs or mussels into the sea. After crushing smaller murex shells whole and extracting the poison glands of the larger ones, workers steeped them in salted water for days. The liquid was then tested by dipping a woolen fleece into it. It took about eight thousand pounds of murex pulp to get five hundred pounds of prime flower of purple.

Afterward, the dyers heated the dye, now the optimum shade of lush, plush purplish-red—the color of kings and emperors. To keep its brilliance permanent, it was fixed with a mysterious mordant, possibly a seaweed alkali. Sometimes silk or cotton was dyed on-site; otherwise, the flower of purple was sold in dye form.

In later Byzantine times, Roman empresses always gave birth to their children in the Purple Chamber, a room swathed in murex-dyed cloth. These kids were porphyrogenitus or "born to the purple" and thus legitimate successors, as opposed to ambitious generals and other non-royal throne-jumpers.

❖ ARMPIT PLUCKER ❖
PLUCKY CUSTOMERS NEEDED

To describe a situation at its absolute worst, we're fond of saying, "It's the pits." However, one particular occupation in ancient times really *was* the pits.

Roman armpit pluckers (try saying that three times after a nip of ouzo) usually belonged to a bathhouse guild. By the second century A.D., almost all cities large and small around the Roman Empire had elaborate public baths. In these spa-like settings, men and women routinely had body hair removed.

During the prior century, it had become the fashion among aristocrats, masochists, and social climbers to indulge in whole-body depilation—face and neck included. After hair removal, special workers called polishers then buffed clients' bodies to a Parian white-marble glow.

Romans have always had high fashion sense. Back then, they must have had similarly high pain thresholds. At his disposal, the armpit plucker had tweezers and an unsavory looking sickle-shaped blade. Being iron, the darn thing wouldn't keep an edge well.

In lieu of the razor, he could apply pitch or beeswax to the customer who preferred it. Or he could call in his fellow torturer, the *dropacista* or depilator. That specialist would slather a variety of nasty nostrums into quivering pits, from ass's fat to powdered viper, from nanny-goat's gall to bat's blood, until something worked. Often, however, it took the sturdy tweezers of the armpit plucker to de-hair the client.

Armpit pluckers were a special breed. They had to have the stomach to inflict pain—and be strong enough to hold down the client while inflicting it. A brash and hard-sell bunch, they advertised their services verbally. And often.

Lucius Annaeus Seneca, tutor to young Nero and adviser thereafter, made a habit of writing in the rooms he'd taken near the public baths. He had this to say about the armpit gang: "...and the hair plucker with his shrill and high-pitched voice, continually shrieking in order to be noticed. He's never quiet, except when he's plucking armpits and forcing his customer to shriek instead of him."

Not all paid pluckers were members of the bathhouse guild, either. Some were slaves, male and female, called *alipilii,* kept on tap by the wealthy and the hair-phobic.

Freedmen and others of modest means went freelance, plying their trade on the green lawns and under the noble colonnades of the baths, where shops and street vendors abounded. It didn't take a fortune for an apprentice armpit man to set up shop. All it took was a strong arm and a pair of tweezers—a startup cost that wanna-be pluckers might have called "a pittance."

❖ SILPHIUM IMPORTER ❖
AND THEN THERE WAS NONE

From an unimpressive-looking weed growing on the limestone plateau around the city-state of Cyrene in North Africa, the Mediterranean world derived two amazing substances: a sought-after birth control agent, and a pungent condiment that heightened the natural flavors of other foods.

The wonder plant? Silphium. A distant relative of celery, silphium (now extinct) had heavy stems, strappy leaves, and yellow flowers. Discovered in the seventh century B.C., when Greeks first settled on the African coast, silphium quickly became the colony's most profitable export. As Cyrene's big moneymaker, the iconic plant was even stamped on local coinage.

Everyone craved silphium. In the bedroom, taken as tea or as a suppository, it kept away unwanted babies. Mixed with wine, it aborted them. As medicine, it was used to treat maladies from mange to tetanus, from gout to dog bites.

In the kitchen, silphium had dozens of uses—most importantly in sauces, where it married with other ingredients to give an exquisite flavor to chicken and fish. As time went on, affluent Romans—who'd been busy poisoning themselves with lead from their plumbing, their face paint, and their daily pint of boiled honey wine—craved a dab of silphium on everything. And no wonder; one of the unhappy symptoms of lead poisoning was the gradual loss of taste.

With any luck, a savvy silphium importer from Rome or Athens could make a fortune on a single shipload. The only downside of silphium was its pesky refusal to grow anywhere else.

Or even be cultivated. In fact, the city folk of Cyrene themselves didn't quite know where to locate the actual crop. They got it from nomadic tribesmen, who harvested the wild plants and brought them into the city.

Although export was tightly controlled, inevitably a few entrepreneurs managed to smuggle out cuttings and seeds. With them, the Greeks tried mightily to naturalize silphium, first on the Ionian islands and later on the Peloponnese mainland. All attempts at a crop were failures. Other relatives of the silphium plant, like asafoetida, were experimented with—but none came close.

The folks who ran things in Cyrene were delighted, of course. Their monopoly meant that importers paid through the nose for the plants and the white sap. Besides the cost of goods sold, importers had transport to worry about. Shipping silphium to Rome or Greece carried risks because of the high probability of shipwreck or piracy. (Buccaneers B.C. were no dummies; the careful wrapping given to silphium cargo made it easy to spot.) Still, limited supply and ever-growing demand meant that the risk was worth taking.

About the year A.D. 55, terrible weather struck the Cyrene region. That same year, the natives who collected the silphium got into a big beef with the city Cyrenites—and deliberately uprooted all the plants they could find. Sheep over-grazed the plateau, a final insult. Silphium importers arrived, only to find there was no crop. None.

One importer managed to obtain the very last specimen of the wild plant. This man took his lone silphium, unique in all the world, to the connoisseur he knew would appreciate it. Tragically, that buyer was a voracious, acne-ridden young emperor named Nero. After paying, Nero unceremoniously devoured the silphium—the first documented case of single-handed extinction of a species by a human.

❖ COBBLER ❖

SLIPSHOD? NOT LIKELY

Some things never change. Two thousand years ago, Romans were already mad about shoes; the cobblers' guild was even considered one of eight occupations "essential" for city life.

Roman shoe leather was dyed or painted, made into fanciful shapes, stamped or pierced in patterns. Certain Etruscan cobblers even embroidered their luxury footwear. Shoemakers worked with cowhide, which cost the most, followed by lambskin and goatskin. Shoes were made to order but might feel odd to twenty-first-century feet: they had no heels or insteps.

Shoemakers plied their trade along Sandalarius Street, its landmark feature a noble statue of the god Apollo, given to the guild by Emperor Augustus.

Most Roman shoes were gender- and situation-specific. For example, the toga-ed man about town wouldn't be caught dead in anything but *calcei,* sturdy numbers put together with layers of leather, nailed rather than stitched.

Indoor shoes for women and children, called *socci* or *soleae,* came in colors and were sewn from soft leather or fabric. Socci-wearing men provoked sneers, unless they were comic actors, stylishly hopeless Greeks, or nutters like Emperor Caligula, who made a habit of making public appearances wearing inappropriate dress.

Caligula, incidentally, got his name from footgear. *Caligae* were hobnailed affairs made of leather, slitted to ventilate the red-hot feet of a legionary on the move. As a child, Caligula or "little boots" was dressed up soldier-style, head to foot. The legionaries made a pet of the boy and gave him the nickname he came to loathe.

Bathers wore thick-soled wooden clogs at the public baths to protect their feet from heated floors. Wooden shoes had another traditional function: in lieu of handcuffs, a man found guilty of killing his mother was made to wear wooden shoes, then had a wolf-skin tied over his face before going to prison. And you thought foot fetishes odd!

When it came to shoes, Greeks weren't slipshod, either. Their shoemakers specialized, some as cobblers of men's footwear, others who did nothing but stitch uppers.

Although most slaves went barefoot, as did children and adults in warmer weather, Greek citizens had special shoes or sandals for outdoor wear and slippers for indoor wear.

In Athens, some businesses employed a shoemaking crew, each earning about a drachma a day like other skilled workers. By and large, though, cobblers cobbled solo.

One cobbler, Simon by name, even rubbed elbows with the great while he worked. At his workshop near the marketplace, city ruler Pericles hung out, as did philosophers like Socrates and Xenophon. A philosopher himself, between sandal repairs Simon wrote a now-vanished book of thirty-three philosophical essays, nicknamed "the leathery dialogues." At his workshop site, artifacts have been unearthed that let us time-travel back to fifth-century-B.C. Athens: hobnails for boots, eyelets for laces, and a simple drinking cup with Simon's name inscribed on the base.

❖ SURGEON ❖

AVOID THAT OPERATING ROOM!

Rome's first surgeon might well have been its last. Archagathus emigrated from Greece to Italy in 219 B.C., and at first, everything went swimmingly. Made a citizen, given his own shop at public expense, Archagathus found it thrilling to be called by the honorable title of *vulnerarius* or wound specialist.

Brandishing the ghastly tools of his profession, Archagathus set to work. His surgeon's knives saw action. So did his prods and irons for cauterizing wounds. One procedure, sometimes used on wrestlers whose arms kept dislocating, was to take a fold of skin in the patient's armpit, insert a white-hot wand (but not too deeply), cover the resulting burns with a lump of greasy wool, and let the whole festering mess heal. Doctors of the day believed the contracted scar left by such a burn would hold the arm in its socket better.

Archagathus used his bone-drills and skull-rasps to treat patients who'd been kicked in the head by a horse or taken a sling-stone on the noggin. To find a fracture, he would shave the head, enlarge the wound, lift the scalp, then plug the hole with barley flour and boiling vinegar. And that was just the procedure for day one! The rest of the treatment included a generous application of black goo, later scraped off, and sometimes a skull-drilling to allow blood and other fluids to escape.

Dismayingly, Rome's new surgeon had to operate without anesthetic. As a medical writer of the day put it, "A surgeon should have a strong and steady hand which never trembles, with vision sharp and clear, and spirit undaunted; filled with pity, yet not moved by his patient's cries..."

The savage operating-table manner of Archagathus and his patient mortality rate left something to be desired. Before long, he won the cruel but perhaps more accurate nickname of public executioner.

Although Roman army surgeons became very handy at setting bones and removing arrows, their skill and survival rates were the exception. For centuries, most surgeons continued to be Greek freedmen who routinely butchered their way through life and other peoples' deaths in the cities of the Empire. Given the state of the art, patients who went untreated often did as well as patients who got operated on.

There were some deft and clever surgeons—like Galen, who spent his formative years patching up disemboweled gladiators. The first man known to dissect animals in order to study anatomy, he even did clandestine autopsies on human cadavers, although mucking about with dead bodies was a huge taboo in Greco-Roman medicine.

Galen never dreamed of using a tourniquet; his favorite post-op wound dressings were wheat flour cooked in oil or dove's dung and ink. Nevertheless, he avoided killing an impressive number of patients and went on to minister to three emperors.

By the second century A.D., surgery on afflictions like goiter were routine albeit excruciating. The use of mandragora, atropine, and a few other pain-dulling drugs helped matters. Surgeons were gloomily accepted as practitioners of the Hippocratic art, although surgery remained a field no self-respecting Roman would enter.

❖ SEVEN ❖

AT LEAST I'M IN SHOW BIZ

❖ ❖ ❖ ❖ **HERODOROS** ❖ ❖ ❖ ❖

He blew 'em away

The Greeks thought it was perfectly okay to toot your own horn. At the 96th Olympiad, they even made it an event, called the *salpinktes* or trumpeters' contest. While they were at it, they inaugurated a competition for heralds, where many of the same iron-lunged men competed.

The pint-sized Louis Armstrong of trumpeteering had to be Herodoros of Megara, at 5ft 3in. His trumpet, a long keyless pipe with a bell at the end, was nearly as tall as he was. But he had the lungs of a rooster.

Jealous blowhards skulked around, pressing for the secret to his dazzling decibel levels. At length Herodoros confessed: a strict diet of food and drink in industrial quantities. Observers saw him devour seven kilos (over fifteen pounds) of bread and meat at a sitting, washed down with six liters of wine. The man had other idiosyncrasies. Copying his heroic idol Hercules, he slept on a lion's hide.

At his first Olympics in 328 B.C., he took first place in the competitions for heralds and trumpeters—then topped himself by winning firsts at the circuit of Great Games (Olympian, Delphian, Nemean, and Isthmian) nine more times. Forty years of blowing those high notes; as Satchmo might say, that is some fine embouchure.

Olympic events for heralds and trumpeters took place on day one of the games, according to some sources. Competitors competed in the echo colonnade, the winners then playing and announcing events during the rest of the festival.

Other authorities argue that the two competitions took place in real time during the five days of the Olympics. In this scenario, hopefuls took turns announcing the winners, doing trumpet starts for the chariot races, and blasting different commands for the listening pleasure of the judges and spectators.

Whichever the case, Herodoros was officially listed as winner of both the heralds and trumpeters at forty of the world's biggest competitions.

As a man who'd won crowns made from prestigious varieties of shrubbery, Herodoros could have rested on his laurels. Victors raked in myriad perks, from free meals to cash given by admirers and home cities. But once a salpinktes player, always a salpinktes player. Music accompanied many activities in Greece, including warfare, with high demand for trumpeters to blast away on the battlefield. Given his stamina and volume, Herodoros naturally got offers.

In 303 B.C., a Macedonian general named Demetrius approached him. General D. was busy besieging the city of Argos—a place that happened to be the sworn enemy of Herodoros's hometown. As the general complained, his soldiers couldn't seem to get up sufficient steam to move the heavy siege-engine into place against the city walls.

Herodoros said he'd help, and got the notion of playing two trumpets at once. That showy feat, and the amount of racket it generated, revved the troops into eager action. Before long, Argos and its city walls lay in itty bitty pieces. Picking up his paycheck, Herodoros strutted away, another Herculean job well done.

❖ COMEDIAN ❖

HEEEEEERE'S GAIUS!

Pro comedians, called *gelotopoios* or "laughter-producers" in Greece, got their start playing private parties, the symposia where aristocratic men drank and got rowdy. At them, "*asbestos gelos*," meaning unquenchable laughter, was the goal; of course that was back when "asbestos" was still an adjective instead of an environmental hazard.

In Plato's day, one of the hot comics was Philip, who specialized in impressions. He could imitate a political figure or ape a dancer with equal skill. Other laughter-producers mocked well-known boxers or musicians.

Professional comedy wasn't an everyday job. Even the uproarious comedies of Aristophanes and other comic playwrights were only performed during the special festivals in Athens.

It wasn't all that easy getting paid to knock 'em dead, either. In fourth-century-B.C. Athens, so many gifted amateurs got into laughter-producing that they formed a club. Calling themselves "the sixty," their membership of aristocrats and politicos met regularly at the sanctuary of Hercules. The fame of "the sixty" even spread to Macedonia, where King Philip (Alex the Great's father, a real prankster, but no relation to the comic Philip) was moved to request a written selection of their jokes—for which he prepaid in gold.

With that kind of cut-throat competition, the job market for comics was anything but funny. In a society that had no television, no Comedy Store, no nightclubs—how, and where, could stand-up comedy make it? In desperation, Greek laughter-producers started working weddings and writing jokebooks to make a drachma.

One of their jokebooks has survived, a collection of 265 hits and duds written about A.D. 250. More than sixty are jokes about places famous for their stupidity; thirty of them make fun of doctors; and one hundred of the jokes skewer nerds and eggheads. Here are two of the surefire numbers used by comedians of long ago.

In dire need of funds, a learned student sold his books—then wrote to his father, saying, "Congratulate me, Dad—I'm already making money from my studies!"

Groucho Marx must have had an early Greek ancestor, gauging by the following:

A patient went to a doctor from Cyme (a city whose residents had a reputation for idiocy) and said, "Doctor, when I wake up, I feel dizzy for about half an hour before I start to feel normal."

The doctor replied, "So, wake up half an hour later!"

Roman clowns and comedians flattered by imitation and wholesale plagiarism of the Greeks, as did comic playwrights like Plautus. The Roman public couldn't get enough of broad comedy, slapstick, and mime, provided by a host of clowns. Their comics were called *scurra*—the source of our term *scurrilous*.

Upper-class men with careers as orators often used wit to win judges over, and found it useful to study with comics and comedic actors. Author-orator Cicero was one. After getting tips from the most famous actor of his day, Cicero wrote pedantic essays about how witty speech should amuse—but in a dignified, high-class way. The orator's enemies got on him instantly. They knew how to hurt a guy, especially one like Cicero who'd scrambled up to his status instead of being born to the purple. They responded by calling him a scurra.

❖ ❖ ❖ ❖ THEOGENES ❖ ❖ ❖ ❖

He put Thasos on the map

A husky nine-year-old on the Greek island of Thasos, Theogenes was not your typical schoolboy. When he took a shine to the bronze statue of a god in the marketplace, he dragged it home—to indignation and horror all around.

Some citizens muttered, "Kill that impious kid;" cooler heads suggested returning the statue. Once Theo bench-pressed the bronze and returned it, his reputation as a Hercules in the making began.

At the 75th Olympiad, Theo's gameplan was to compete first in boxing and then the pancration, a bloody, almost-no-holds-barred event, more like street fighting than anything else. Pancratiasts slugged each other like boxers, used headlocks and strangleholds, tossed opponents and grappled on the ground, kicking guts and breaking limbs.

Theo, however, exhausted himself to win his boxing match and withdrew from the pancration—whereupon he was heavily fined by the judges. Greeks had an interesting way of levying punishments. They ordered Theogenes to pay half his fine to the athlete he would have competed against—and half to the god Zeus, the Big Cheese patron of the Olympics. Despite this setback, the young powerhouse went on to win an astounding fourteen hundred firsts in pancration, boxing, and running at five consecutive Olympiads and the three other Great Games on the circuit. Famous? And how. The poet Pindar, noted for his victory odes to Olympians, wrote eight of them to Theogenes. At Olympia itself, a statue of Theo stood in the place of honor for centuries.

In Theo's day, the fifth century B.C., most boxers and pancratiasts were still amateurs, awarded symbolic crowns for their big wins—although they often got showered with perks and gifts from fans and home cities. By 300 B.C., however, most athletes in these well-attended heavy events were paid pros, competing for fat purses at athletic festivals around the Mediterranean.

After Theogenes died, the people of Thasos also erected a statue to their hometown hero. One local athlete, disgruntled over having lost to Theo, began making nightly visits to the statue to thump on it. Good therapy for the attacker, no doubt, but the abuse made the statue come loose from its moorings. One evening, it fell on the sore loser and killed him.

No Greek would let a statue get away with murder—consequently, the bronze was immediately prosecuted under local homicide laws and tossed into the sea. (The Greeks firmly believed that all killers must be punished, whether they were higher primates or rocks from an avalanche.)

After the bronze received its watery sentence, locals moved on with their lives. They overlooked a key fact, however: the statue symbolized their real-life hero. Years later, when famine and plague struck Thasos, the islanders sent to the nearest oracle for advice. "Welcome back your exiles," the oracle said.

The islanders were still trying to unravel this message when a fisherman snagged the Theogenes statue in his net. The islanders set it up anew in the marketplace, and everyone made darned sure they honored their internationally famous homeboy. Bingo: good harvest, famine averted, happy ending to the story.

❖ FACTION MASTER ❖
OVERLORDS & UNDERLINGS OF THE
BIGGEST SHOW ON EARTH

The racetrack (*circus* in Latin) was every Roman's favorite venue. No mystery why: the circus had free seating, allowed gambling, and let men and women sit together, unlike the theater and the arena. Moreover, gladiatorial games were rare occasions, whereas chariot races were held regularly, on as many as sixty to eighty days a year in later imperial times. The circus became Big Business, its racing drivers the most visible participants in a hive of worker bees.

Four faction overlords managed the whole shebang, running the professional stables or factions, identified by their colors of red, white, blue, and green. This was no come-up-through-the-ranks position. To be a *dominus factionis,* your family had to have connections and wealth—at least until the late third century, when the Blues and Greens gobbled up the two weaker factions.

If any of these influential men disliked the terms offered for his faction, he could say no—even to an emperor. Needless to say, they were pandered to for centuries, since emperors couldn't afford a shortfall of racing events.

Huge support crews managed the show, the track, and the crowd control for two hundred and fifty thousand fans. The Circus Maximus described an elongated circle with sharp turns at either end. In the center was the spine. Besides altars to Roman deities, the spine held seven bronze eggs and dolphins to indicate the laps run, placed high so the crowd could see them. Starting gates were at one of the short ends. On the longer sides were three-story porticos of stone seats, separated from the racetrack by a ten-foot canal.

Each charioteer had a pit crew of five to ten men. At the starting gate was the *morator,* who held his team's horses for the start. A clean getaway was essential, since frontrunners often won. Also at the starting gate was the *tentor,* who operated the starting mechanism. Simultaneously, a "celebrity starter"—often the emperor—stood in full view and dropped a large white handkerchief.

Men called *sparsors* stood at the racetrack turns. Buckets at the ready, the sparsors threw water to cool their horses and drivers. A key task was to splash the wheels of their faction's chariots to prevent the wooden axles from burning up.

These pit-crew functions were lightweight compared to that of the *hortator* or "encourager." This daredevil rode horseback, moving around his driver without crashing into him (or the other chariots). His job? To hearten his man and give him frequent updates on what the competition was doing.

Races could have up to twelve rivals plus a dozen encouragers on the track—a crush that made crashes frequent and bloody. Racing drivers kept their horses' reins tightly wrapped around their bodies. In a pileup, if they couldn't reach their knives they stood a good chance of being trampled or dragged to death. Hortators ran similar risks of injury or fatality.

Roman racing fans worshiped the drivers and adored the circus ambience—so much that it became increasingly difficult to get the hyped-up, jovial mobs to go home. After trying various stratagems, the faction overlords finally found a workable solution: they gave away free food after the last race, usually as a mass distribution of *sportulae*, the ancient Roman goodie bags.

❖ CHARIOTEER ❖
AN AGITATED LIFE

In the high-speed racing frenzy of the first few centuries A.D., chariot competition became an early World Cup, a global addiction, not merely a local one. During earlier centuries, the Greeks had looked at chariot racing as a once-in-a-while contest, one that enabled the well-heeled to show off at the Olympic Games and a few other venues. Roman chariot racing, however, was plebian, from its drivers to its fans, a spectator sport for common folks that also hooked the affluent.

Rome itself boasted a number of rough, tough young *agitators,* the Latin name for racing drivers. Most agitators came from slave or freedmen backgrounds, with nowhere to go but up. An elite few became *milliarii,* members of "the thousand club," given to those who'd won that many races at the Circus Maximus and elsewhere.

A speedster named Pompeius Musclosus bagged 3,559 wins; another nicknamed "Golden Nose" won 2,048 times—only to die young and brutally. Some agitators gained their freedom and moved from faction to faction; hometown boy Polynices successively drove for the Reds, the Greens, and the Blues, ending his career (and his life at twenty-nine) with the Whites. Pretty-boy Scorpus took first in one spectacular race and won

fifteen bags of gold in an hour—plus adulation from poets and swooning admirers, before ending up dead at twenty-six, on a less lucky day.

Whenever racing days were announced, hundreds of thousands of fans jammed the enormous racetrack called the Circus Maximus for a full day of up to twenty-four races. At times, the grounds also hosted other activities, from religious processions and beast-hunts to gladiator matches.

Circus crowds made superstars of their favorite drivers, but also relished "shipwrecks," the frequent crashes that occurred when hell-for-leather competitors flew at breakneck speed for seven laps. Unlike those scythe-equipped, James Bondian models shown in the movie classic *Ben-Hur,* the working chariots used by race drivers were lightweight affairs, usually pulled by a four-horse rig.

Fouls, dirty tricks, and curses were part of the agony and the ecstasy. Drivers used whips on opponents' faces as well as on their steeds. Racers steered by shifting body weight, sometimes turning their chariots in front of others to force a collision. Men who raced, and the folks who bet on them, were superstitious to a fault. A lively market in curse-tablets tried to influence outcomes through spells, a typical one being: "Demon whoever you are, I demand of you this hour, from this moment, that you torture and kill the horses of the Greens and Whites and that you kill in a crash their drivers…and leave not a breath in their bodies."

The daring of these no-holds-barred athletes captured the imaginations of historians and writers in ancient times. More copious evidence of agitator glories has been found on bas-reliefs, mosaics, and statuary. By far the most poignant and interesting details about their lives come from official inscriptions left by their fans and the won/lost records on the tombstones of these human shooting stars.

❖ ❖ ❖ ❖ **DIOCLES** ❖ ❖ ❖ ❖

Superstar & free agent

Fully one quarter of Rome's million inhabitants gathered regularly at the Circus Maximus for maximum thrills. In a gala atmosphere, part Derby Day, part Billy Smart's Circus, they spent the day watching races between two- and four-horse chariots driven by wily and fearless drivers. Four wealthy factions or stables, known as the Whites, Reds, Blues, and Greens, fielded all the teams— and everyone from slave to senator rooted for one faction or another.

During the glory decades between A.D. 100 and 150, circus-goers got to cheer on a supernova named Gaius Appuleius Diocles, raved about as the world's best agitator or racing driver. Diocles' beginnings were inauspicious. Born in Portugal, as a teen he ended up in Rome and drove his first racing chariot for the Whites. He lost the race—and kept losing for two years. Still, management kept him on as a driver; there was something about the boy, his unflinching courage, or perhaps the intelligent way he analyzed each race and learned from the other agitators.

At age twenty, Diocles won his first race, justifying the Whites' belief in him. At twenty-four and already a star, he jumped to the Green faction. At twenty-seven, he left them for the Reds and stayed there for fifteen years. Diocles might be the first free agent we know about in sports history. Without a doubt he was one of the cleverest, on the track and off.

In his career, he took first place 1,462 times out of a mind-boggling 4,237 starts. Sixty of those wins were main events between the top-ranking drivers. At the Circus Maximus, the initial race of the day was the big-money event, held right after the competitors, accompanied by statues of the main gods, did a lap of the track.

A true professional, Diocles kept meticulous records, organizing his wins and losses into categories that reveal much about the workings of the circus. For instance, 1,064 of his victories occurred in races with one team from each faction, meaning four chariots in the field. As the number of chariots increased—up to twelve were permitted—his win record decreased. Crowded fields meant less room to maneuver and more bad crashes.

Unlike the flicks, where the hero comes from behind to win the race, Diocles' stats show that in more than half of his winning outings, he was the frontrunner. He knew it was vital to grab the lead where the chariots broke from their lanes. This white line was located at the end of the low walled area (called "the spine") in the center of the track, whereas the finish line was on the straightaway.

Diocles also competed in other sorts of races, and was the first man to win a seven-horse chariot race. Special races involving more horses or even other animals took place on training grounds, most likely for the private pleasure of an emperor and his pals.

173

This boy knew horseflesh; and he knew when to quit. Diocles amassed over thirty-five million sesterces, which made him richer than most Roman senators. Unlike the majority of his competitors, he got to enjoy it, retiring in one piece at age forty-two.

❖ HORSE BREEDER ❖
NO DARK HORSES IN THIS BUNCH

What was behind the centuries-long success of the Circus Maximus and its chariot-racing imitators across the Roman Empire?

The animals themselves were a powerful draw—horses like no one had seen since that fabled Greek military upset in southern Italy, when troops from Croton played dance tunes on the flute, throwing the cavalry of their Sybaris enemies into confusion because their stallions were trained to dance to music. As they pranced off the battlefield, the horses brought their reluctant riders right into enemy hands.

Roman horse breeders also took their work seriously. They owned stud farms in North Africa, Thrace, Thessaly, Sicily, Cappadocia, and Spain, where the best racing breeds, like Asturian and Lusitanian, were born and reared. Some breeders also raised horses for military use as pack animals or cavalry steeds. Since the army required mares and geldings, and the circus racetrack used stallions, the two markets were complementary. Cavalry horses required intensive training, as did racing stallions, meaning that equine whisperers were much in demand.

Stud farms were serviced by the *mulomedicus,* the vet-surgeon, who consulted the literature on equine maladies. Pedigrees and conformation were carefully documented. Although two-year-olds could be broken and trained for riding, horses had to be five-year-olds to be used in a chariot race. If a stallion stayed sound, its racing career on sand or dirt tracks could last until its twentieth year.

Some charioteers left records, citing horses by name, that show how much endurance these animals had. One stallion appropriately named Victor won 429 times for his driver; another, called Germinator, won 92 races for the same charioteer.

Some horse breeders were independent operators—but by no means minor players. Sent to check on several breeding farms, a Roman official said of one he bypassed, "The owner only had four hundred horses so I decided it wasn't worth bothering about."

Bigger breeders worked for one of the four official factions or stables, simply known by their colors as Red, White, Blue, and Green. The factions owned multiple stud farms, plus fleets of ships fitted with stalls to transport the animals safely to racetracks around the empire.

Winning horses often became more famous figures than celebrated humans. Status-hungry poet Martial moaned that popular horses were often recognized by sight, while he was not. Favorite teams had their images painted on children's toys and carved into knife handles. A charioteer called Polydus was immortalized in mosaic with his lead horse, Compressor. Other racing drivers posed with their named steeds for bronze and marble statues, and were also depicted on frescoes adorning the homes of horse-fanciers.

In a fit of race-mania or maybe just looniness, Emperor Caligula built a marble stall with an ivory manger at the Greens' stable for a stallion named Incitatus—then gave the prize-winning racehorse senatorial status. That honor provoked outrage—and more than a little fear among Roman senators that their jobs were being lost to quadrupeds.

In A.D. 47, steeds from the White stables won a special sort of immortality. After a popular driver named Raven got thrown off at the starting gate, his impeccably trained team continued to gallop. The horses took the lead, then jostled, maneuvered, and outfoxed their rivals, just as if there were skillful hands on their reins. To everyone's shock, the driverless pair won— and were smart enough to stop dead on the chalk finish-line before prancing a victory lap.

When the prize went to the White faction, the crowd went insane with joy. The horse breeder and the trainer were in heaven. Every charioteer at the track, however, shuddered at the thought: a breed of horses that no longer needed drivers? Uh-oh. There goes the gravy-train.

❖ TICKET TOUT ❖

HOT SEATS A SPECIALTY

Certain occupations—and not just prostitution—have always been with us; the *locarius* or ticket tout, for instance.

On the streets of Rome and other cities, the locarius worked music festivals and live theater events, making lucre by locating groups of seats and reselling them at maximum markup. Despite enthusiastic attendance at these events, most ticket touts couldn't make a full-time living from the job.

Once chariot races at Rome's Circus Maximus and other racetracks ushered in a new era of spectator sport, they attracted mobs bigger than all the theaters combined. The only fly in the olive oil? The racetracks' fluid seating and no-fee policies.

Hope appeared on the horizon in the form of the *munus* (*munera* is the plural), begun in the misty past as a somber funeral obligation to honor an important corpse by letting a couple of fighters spill blood. Having borrowed the munus from the ancient Etruscans, the Romans saw no harm in modifying it. By degrees, the event evolved into a splashy, pay-per-view gladiatorial performance.

Once the event went mass-market, it began to be held in wooden or stone facilities with gated entrances and paying audiences. During the bloodfest days of the December Saturnalia, a locarius could make a killing outside while gladiators were doing the same in the arena.

Julius Caesar increased his approval rating with a show featuring 320 pairs of fighters, but Emperor Augustus really pepped up the gladiatorial business by sponsoring eight flashy events in which ten thousand men fought. The tout community was in heaven.

Then, however, the Roman Senate intervened, passing dreary legislation to limit shows to two a year, with sixty-fighter maximums! Nearly deafened by boos from everyone, including the emperor's family, the Senate hastened to add that imperial displays would have no such limits. Another loophole, the aedile-sponsored show, was also allowed to stand.[*]

Red-hot tickets to Rome's latest play.

---

[*] Romans with political ambitions began their careers as quasi-interns called *aediles*, one of their obligations being to sponsor gladiatorial games. The splashier the sanguinary event, the more renown an aedile won in his quest for higher office.

As the Roman Empire grew, so did the mania for permanent amphitheaters. Ultimately there were nearly a hundred arenas from sea to shining sea—and ticket touts to service them all.

Seating in these edifices was a model of efficiency. Separate entrances and staircases channeled different classes of people to their numbered seats. Paid attendants worked inside the amphitheaters to keep order.

As at the Super Bowl, certain associations owned blocks of seats, and a few freebies were given to upper-class folks with pull. Nevertheless, the majority of fans paid entrance fees, as archaeological evidence shows. According to ancient writers, only twice did emperors allow free days at the gladiatorial games.

During especially grandiose events, like the memorable 117-day gorefest Emperor Trajan threw to gloat about his victory over the Dacians, ticket touts cleaned up. So too when gladiators with big followings appeared on the bill. Around A.D. 65, any time Hermes, a fighter also known as "the darling of the ticket touts," stepped into the arena, a locarius could wring double or triple from his seats on offer.

A locarius who was on the ball could make a ludicrous amount of money—which seemed only appropriate, since *ludi* was the playful name given to all spectacles, entertainments, and games.

❖ DOCTOR ❖

DOCTOR, MY EYE!

Ever wonder how gladiators learned to gladiate? After all, gladiators were made, not born. The men weren't special forces, although quite a few had been in the service of an army defeated by Rome.

Most gladiators entered the workforce unwillingly, as slaves or war captives. Being property, they were locked up in barracks at one of the training schools in Rome and other places in Italy. From time to time, freeborn weirdos voluntarily entered the gladiator workforce, but they were exceptional.

The man who trained gladiators was called a *doctor*. (The Latin word for the medical sort of sawbones was *medicus*; and gladiators had plenty of occasion to use them as well.)

Doctors had the personality of drill instructors, endlessly coaching the men. Most of the time, they practiced with wooden swords—which seems astonishing, given the difference in weight and feel to the razor-sharp gladius sword used in the arena. Some doctors came from the ranks of ex-gladiators who'd survived their careers and "received the *rudis*," the complimentary wooden sword with one's name on it, given to a man who'd survived long enough to retire.

Around 100 B.C., certain military leaders saw the benefits of using doctors to train army recruits. From that time on, doctors also found employment with the Roman legions, instructing the infantrymen in life-and-death fighting techniques.

❖ EDITOR ❖

NOT AS BLOODY-MINDED AS THEY USED TO BE

Lots can happen, etymologically speaking, in two thousand years. Take the word "editor," for example.

Way back when, an *editor* was a private citizen who set out to be a politician by holding the succession of offices leading up to Roman consul. To further that goal, the editor put on a beast-hunt or a gladiatorial event in honor of someone important and dead. At first, these events tended to be small, invitation-only bloodbaths. The event wasn't nearly as important as

the boastful inscription that got put up afterward. On the most durable and visible surface available, the editor placed an inscription, proudly touting his generosity as the "first to provide five wild cameleopards @ own expense" or some such superlative.

But along came Julius Caesar and other big noises, followed by a string of emperors, all of them vying to top the last showoff and give the biggest, goriest gladiator games yet.

What was an editor to do? Mortgage the family home, spend his wife's dowry, and splash out for an even more grandiose day of carnage, evidently. The Roman public had an unquenchable thirst for novelty, so an ingenious editor might schedule a bout between a battling dwarf and a female *gladiatrix,* or pit leopards against giraffes. Fads came and went. Straining to be original, some editors had fighters' armor decorated with peacock feathers. To augment the glitz factor, other editors ordered up shields made of silver and gilded helmets. One editor had the bright but short-lived idea of holding games at night, using torches and oil lamps.

The most gruesome variation on the theme was the *munus sine missione,* a fiendish version of domino slaughter where the editor decreed that no one would remain alive by the end of the day. (Naturally, gladiators and their managers demanded top dollar for that sort of dead-end job.)

By rights, the gilded chamberpot for most memorable editor should go to Gaius Terentius Lucanus. To honor his departed grandfather, he mounted a three-day gorefest with thirty pairs of gladiators. During the matches, he stationed artists in vantage points to capture key moments. Immediately after, Lucanus had huge paintings made of the whole affair and placed them in a high-traffic area, near the Temple of Diana. These scenes, and other gladiator portraits, became the new claims to editor extravagance.

Besides thrilling the public with "the best of the grisliest" vignettes from his very own gladiator games, the editor could add further niceties. He could commission a floor mosaic in his home to represent his spectacle more permanently. It even became the fashion among editors to put such vignettes on their own tombs.

❖ AUCTORATUS ❖

GLADIATORS WITHOUT BORDERS

The most unusual people to don gladiator gear were the *auctorati* or volunteer gladiators; some of them poor men who desperately needed money, others patricians who wanted to get down and dirty. Freedmen also became auctorati, including ex-slaves who'd won freedom in the arena but kept coming back for more gore.

It wasn't illegal to become a gladiator—you just gave up all your civil rights, sank to the social status of a pimp, and were denied burial in regular cemeteries.

To volunteer, you declared your intention to fight in front of a magistrate, then negotiated your contract with the sponsor, arm-wrestling over fees before swearing that creepy oath about third-degree burns, cold steel, and so forth. Volunteer gladiators got signing bonuses, the prime motive for poorer citizens and desperate debtors to enter this career field.

After acquiring the necessary gear, practicing your crowd-pleasing death thrusts and parries with your trainer, and putting your affairs in order, just in case—you'd get your first fight.

The day prior, you'd star at a public banquet, where carnage-lovers would ask you what it felt like to take one in the gut, and little old ladies would queue in line, wanting your hair for a love charm. You'd rub elbows with condemned prisoners scheduled as the noontime "entertainment" for the wild beasts, who'd be hitting the wine pretty heavily.

The next day, you'd swashbuckle into the arena in your parade helmet and gold-embroidered cloak, where you'd hang out until the afternoon gladiatorial events began. There could be twenty matches or more ahead of you. After your fight was announced and the swords tested for sharpness, you'd go to the center of the arena, where two referees awaited, together with two brass musicians who would accompany your grunts and moans. Your match might seem endless, but would last ten to fifteen minutes, by which time you'd be sweating like a boar and possibly leaking other fluids.

You'd rely on skill and endurance. Most fights ended with someone getting wounded or when one guy ran out of steam. If this were you, you'd raise an index finger or throw down your shield. Attacking an opponent when he'd given up was very poor form; so was running away from the fight. (Offenders got flogged or burned with red-hot pokers.)

Let's say you won your match. Amid the roars of the crowd, you'd get a palm branch and maybe a crown, after which you'd take a victory lap. With this victory or perhaps the next, you'd build a fan base, and the largesse would start to flow. In time, you could expect bags of coins and necklaces of twisted gold, gaudy enough to make a Mafia don writhe with envy. These goodies would be in addition to your fees as a voluntary gladiator.

As you improved at mayhem, you'd command bigger fees and prestige, especially with the ladies. In Rome, a surprising number of women thrilled to the vicarious brush with death that only a gladiator could provide.

❖ GLADIATRIX ❖

FLIRTING WITH DEATH BUT NOT GOING STEADY

It's always been impossible to keep female vixens in line, especially those with a yen for the high-risk, low-status job of female gladiator, or *gladiatrix*.

Roman senators kept passing laws to forbid women in the arena—and gals kept ignoring them. By A.D. 19, parents of such unruly young women were at their wits' end. Senators passed the Tabula Larinas law to make it even more unseemly and illegal; this "prohibited the gladiatorial recruitment of daughters, grand-daughters, and great-granddaughters of senators or knights…"

Matters predictably got worse under Emperor Nero; he sponsored games with gladiatrices in A.D. 55 and 63. At an exhibition in Puteoli, he even pioneered duels between ballsy Ethiopian gals.

Emperor Domitian was just as reckless, putting on events where women fought by torchlight. Like rock concerts, the late-night slots were reserved for the top acts.

A century later, Emperor Severus started whinging about females in the arena and banned single combat by them, citing "an upsurge among upper-class women." He might have saved his breath; a certain breed persisted, determined to adopt this career.

Not that gladiating was a prestige job. Most fighters were male slaves or war captives; the balance were volunteers who automatically lost their civil rights and were declared infamous. Women, however, had few civil rights to lose. That "infamous" label may have had its own allure; gladiators were scorned but ardently admired, with groupies galore.

Thus most gladiatrices were freeborn women who took the job for reasons of their own. Some wanted to flirt with the forbidden, play with terror. Others feared boredom more than death. Still others chose to test themselves as men did—test their ability to defend themselves, and to show courage in the face of the very real possibility of injury, disfigurement, or death.

Risk was a relative matter, however. A gladiatrix who was good at her job attracted fans and higher fees. As a volunteer, she was guaranteed a minimum sum per fight. Games officials had a vested interest in her long-term survival. Even though events were huge, days-long productions, they didn't occur all that often. Even seasoned gladiators might only see a week or two of work per year; gladiatrices, probably less.

Although the film *Gladiator* gave an inaccurate nod to the gladiatrix by having a chariot-driving female rip around the arena, the fighting done by women was on foot in one-on-one duels, just like male combatants.

A bas-relief found at Halicarnassus (in modern Turkey) has given historians and archaeologists many compelling details about female combatants. On it, gladiatrices called Amazon and Achillea—probably their stage names—fought wearing nearly thirty pounds of armor, including leg guards and rectangular felt-lined shields. Protection on one arm kept their sword arms from injury. The shields and huge visored helmets they would have worn were lined with felt. These gladiatrices used their short swords with finesse, slashing with quick, aggressive moves.

Women in the arena caused plenty of buzz in their day. Evidence of that is still around, including archaeological clues from Ostia to London that hint at the surprising frequency of fighting females.

❖ BEAST SUPPLIER ❖
RSPCA MEMBERS NEED NOT APPLY

Like many people today, Romans were spectator junkies and loved seeing exotic wild animals. One slight difference: they enjoyed seeing the creatures kill and be killed in novel ways. First the circus and later the amphitheater included large carnivores as part of the fun and games. In 186 B.C. at the Circus Maximus, lions and panthers were displayed between chariot races—more piquancy added by the fact that spectators had little between themselves and the ferocious big cats.

Once the gladiatorial spectacle got rolling, it expanded into much more than gladiators. As a novelty, exotic animals went on display between events. Oh wait, that's too dull, said organizers. Why not have them do something? And so ostriches ran races, and trained elephants "wrote" words in Latin in the sand.

But difficulties arose. Training took ages, and the supply of such animals was sketchy, so organizers brainstormed how better to exploit beasts, wild and domesticated. We'll have them fight each other! So they devised grotesque matches for the *venationes*, as the bloody animal-hunt spectacles were called: bull meets python; elephant versus leopards; rhino against bear; wolves chained to wild boars.

One twisted soul came up with a variant that also solved the pesky superfluity of condemned criminals. *Ad bestias,* it was called, or man (sometimes armed, at others not) versus beast. This new slot, scheduled for midday, was an instant smash hit. Another innovation recycled less talented gladiators into *bestiarii* or beast hunters, who used a variety of weapons and props in their quests.

In due course, more than a hundred permanent arenas circled the Mediterranean, plus countless private rings and circus racetracks where beastly events took place. Someone had to guarantee a steady supply of beasts to these facilities. So who oversaw this logistics nightmare? The job fell to a problem-solver who bore the sonorous title of *praepositus camelorum*: the official rounder-upper, cager-and-shipper, get-'em-to-the-arena-on-time honcho. Among other duties, he managed the activities of dozens of subcontractors and hundreds of workers, whose job it was to locate and capture thousands of animals. The PC had to keep an acceptable percentage of creatures, from crocodiles to camels, alive, from capture to shipping by sea.

Once the beasts arrived at their final destination, this CEO of carnage saw to it that they received adequate care and feeding, so that their live performances were lively. For lions and other predators, this meant holding back on raw meat for days to make the starving animals less choosy about their prey.

Human slaughter aside, this was an environmental holocaust. For seven hundred years, wild animals were dispatched in vicious ways at circuses and arenas throughout the Roman world.

Provinces from Syria to Germany were stripped of their wildlife to feed the insatiable appetite for murderous spectacle. Elephants came from Leptis (modern Libya); a nonstop stream of bears from Germany. Even milder emperors like Hadrian threw slaughter-house spectacles, such as one in Athens where a thousand beasts died. So many millions perished that entire species, such as the Mesopotamian lion, may have gone extinct.

Living in an age of greater empathy toward wild animals, it's difficult to understand Roman delight in their deaths. Animal sacrifice, however, symbolized two things: Roman might; and the power of man over beast.

Thus the prestige of the post of praepositus camelorum. More than one of its job-holders bragged of his career on his tombstone, often adorning it with images of elephants and other beasts that had perished in the course of his duties.

❖ WATER-ORGANIST ❖

ROCK ME ON THE WATER

In its heyday, Alexandria glittered as the Paris of the Roman Empire: cultured, cosmopolitan, and a center for learning. At its great library-museum, scientists and thinkers worked, talked, and invented.

But the most serendipitous invention occurred in a local barber shop. Endeavoring to counterbalance an adjustable mirror, the barber's son, a gadget-fixated fellow named Ctesibius, stumbled on the principle of compressed air. After his device made a few rude treble and bass noises, Ctesibius got the notion that it might produce music. (He never did get that mirror hung properly.)

A few trials and errors later, Ctesibius invented the *hydraulis,* and, with it, the field of hydraulics. Hydraulis meant "pipes powered by water" rather than water-organ, but the latter translation stuck.

His bronze-and-wood prototype sat on a heavy cylindrical base of marble filled with water reservoirs and pistons supplying compressed air to the pipes above. To the observer, the organ resembled a mechanized, upright version of the Greek pan-pipes. Its playable levers produced an octave or so of musical notes.

Ctesibius moved on to tinker around with other toys, including the first pump his world had ever seen. Meanwhile, his wife Thais started tickling the levers of the hydraulis. Her melodious playing proved a hit with those who heard it, helped by the fact that most musical instruments of her day sounded so darn mournful.

Over the next century or so, refinements were made by Heron, another local boy, and by Roman architect Vitruvius. By now, the hydraulis boasted dolphin-shaped valve covers and nineteen pipes, producing a powerful, resonant sound. Water-organ use spread around the Med, and a new career was born: hydraulic keyboardist.

Water-organists began to compete feverishly in musical contests. One talented enthusiast named Antipatros won glory at a competition in Delphi by playing for two solid days. Before long, no wedding, horse race, swearing-in, banquet, or theater production was complete without hydraulic accompaniment.

Since a woman had paved the way toward its acceptability, the water-organ was thought appropriate for female musicians too. When the water-organ was introduced onto the sands of the gladiatorial arena, women as well as men got jobs as keyboardists. Accompanied by a musician playing a spiral horn, the water-organist ground out tunes while the gore-covered combatants nearby ground through each other.

Boastful souls claimed to be maestros of the instrument, the most egregious being Nero himself. When not busy doing in his mother and other family members, he enjoyed tickling the keys. More of a murderous hobbyist than a musician, Nero played the hydraulis about as well as he drove a chariot. That is to say, not well at all.

As the Roman Empire withered, so did the number of gigs for hydraulis players. Proofs of the water-organ's long popularity, however, are numerous. Remnants and images of it been found from Libya to Hungary on mosaics dating as late as A.D. 500. On some of them, water-organists male and female alike grimly accompany the carnage of the gladiatorial arena, amid clashing swords and severed limbs. Would the health-and-safety people have approved? Unlikely, even with a hard hat.

EIGHT

HAVE T-SQUARE, WILL TRAVEL

❖ PLUMBER ❖
INTO HEAVY METAL

For the Greeks of old, bathing facilities were largely what nature offered, from hot springs to rivers. Upper-class gents, women, and other effete citizens might take a dip in a terracotta tub filled by hand, but most Greeks had more macho attitudes. Spartans, for example, were famous for not allowing any of *their* people to bathe in anything but a river, the icier the better.

Plumbers had more important tasks than bathtub hookups anyway. To protect their fresh-water supply, the Greeks used springs when available, or dug deep wells when not. They also insisted on underground aqueducts—some as deep as sixty feet. These water sources in turn fed cisterns and neighborhood fountains.

For waste disposal, plumbers dug cesspits and fashioned sewers flushed with recycled water, at least in the cities. Lead, the nicely malleable metal everyone loved, wasn't in wide use in Greece.

On the Italian peninsula, aqueduct and sewer building started as early as 800 B.C. And when Romans began to plumb, they soon plumbed with *plumbum*—the Latin word for lead. Even though lead was more expensive, lead pipes came to supersede the terracotta version 1.0.[*]

Roman plumbers fashioned their lead water-pipes in the shape of teardrops, welded together at the top. They came in lengths of ten feet or more, their width being measured in digits, one digit equal to ⅟₁₆ of a foot. A five-digit-wide, ten-foot-long lead pipe weighed sixty pounds; needless to say, plumbers (certainly their helpers) had chronic back problems.

Although some fountains and public toilets—the municipal latrines of Rome, for instance—had water flowing night and day, plumbers had the know-how to regulate flow. They installed devices from turnoff valves to bronze water taps, and used pumps to raise water to higher levels.

Assertive women with a taste for water engineering seemed to have been drawn to this field. To prevent thievery, most lead pipes were inscribed with the name of the customer and the plumber; and the study of pipe inscriptions has revealed quite a number of plumbers with female names.

Water theft was indeed a major problem. Some thirsty customers bribed officials to let them divert water. Thieves called "puncturers" also made the plumbers' lives miserable by boring into pipes here and there. In places where puncturers had been busy, only a small amount of water arrived at the intended places of disbursement.

Romans who wanted to play by the rules could buy surplus water or legally tap into a reservoir's water supply by asking the emperor for a rental license. If granted, the license applied to the owner and couldn't be inherited or sold with the property. City government made a pretty penny from these licenses—about two hundred and fifty thousand sesterces a year.

---

* Although we tsk-tsk about the Romans' overuse of lead, wiser heads, notably first-century-B.C. engineer-architect Vitruvius, had long recommended clay pipelines, both for purity and ease of repair. As Vitruvius wrote, "Water from clay pipes is much more wholesome than that which is conducted through lead pipes, because lead is found to be harmful since white lead is derived from it, and this is said to be harmful to the human system."

❖ CONTRACTOR ❖

BUILDING B.C. (BEFORE COMBUSTION ENGINES)

The to-do list of an ancient contractor sounds like that of his modern counterpart. He submitted bids, fretted over architectural plans, strove for quality control, and strained to complete contracts on schedule.

Contract work, with myriad subcontractors, was how the Parthenon temples and other great edifices in Athens were built. The main difference between then and now? Mechanization. Although Greeks did use oxen to haul materials over distances, most of the time human beings carried, lifted, and tore down building materials.

Most construction workers were free men, not slaves—although the crew mix could include freedmen and slaves leased from their owners. Another eyebrow-raiser: in the fifth century B.C., every skilled construction worker received the same wage—one drachma a day. A century later, the men were hauling in two drachmas a day.

Unlike the ancient Egyptians, who could field thousands of workers to work seasonally on the pyramids, a Greek contractor could only count on a limited number of skilled workers. Without complex machines, draft animals, or big teams of men, how did they move massive stone blocks and marble drums? How did beams get to the tops of temples and multi-story buildings?

Luckily, the bureaucrats of old wrote up detailed contracts, still extant, that reveal many of their secrets. To move a large block or drum, the Greeks built two wooden wheels around it, then hitched sixty oxen to roll the object to its home. The marble quarry might be twenty miles from the building site.

To move materials vertically, they used hoists and cranes. The hoist used wooden legs as counterbalance, along with rope ties, tent-pegged into the ground in a square around it. Over time, contractors developed ingenious ways to suspend and release blocks from the hoist. With marble, they used an iron plug, dropped into a hole cut in the block. It released when the block was dropped into place. Dressed stone had protruding "handles" called bosses so they could be lifted by slings. Besides their use in construction, simple cranes also saw action in outdoor theaters, lifting and lowering actors to the stage.

As a building was assembled, blocks were set with iron clamps and dowels, then cemented into place with molten lead, or, in later Roman times, with quick-setting concrete. Throughout the project, the contractor worked with the architect, making sure that each phase was true to the plans.

Roman contractors, called *redemptores*, employed a mix of machines and men to build. The workings of the cranes they used are delightfully preserved on the tombs of several contractors, including Lucius Peculiaris of Capua and a Roman freedman named Quintus Haterius Tychicus.

The crane utilized two to five men, slaves most likely, stationed inside a large wooden wheel of the hamster-cage variety. The treadmill action of their bodies exerted enough force on the attached ropes and pulleys to raise wooden beams and marble siding several stories high, where other workmen pulled them into place.

Contractors decorated their tombs with other work samples, from arches to temples: effective advertising, if several generations of prosperous Haterii redemptores are any clue.

❖ ❖ ❖ ❖ **ANDRONICUS** ❖ ❖ ❖ ❖
Water-thief extraordinaire

The creator of the most ingenious timepiece in Athens was an unusual man named Andronicus of Cyrrhos, a multifaceted astronomer and inventor-designer from the wilds of Macedonia. How he ended up in Athens is anyone's guess. His talent with timing also took him further afield, to the Greek island of Tenos, where he created a huge sundial for the sanctuary of Poseidon, god of the seas.

The horologium or timepiece he created in Athens was called the Tower of the Winds. About 50 B.C., Andronicus set to work building it in the new marketplace. It was a magnificent eight-sided tower, four meters high, made of milk-white Pentelic marble.

Inside it, the inventor devised a complex clepsydra or water-thief that filled a cistern from a nearby spring on the Acropolis. It showed passers-by the

The eight-sided Tower of the Winds, a showy timepiece and automated weather station, built by Andronicus.

daylight hours via a dial on the tower exterior. The tower also had sundials on each panel, along with superb bas-relief carvings of the eight gods of winds recognized by the Greeks, from Boreas the sharp northerly to Zephyrus the soft breeze of the west, from rainy Notos to Livos, the southwest wind that blew ships homeward.

As a finishing touch, on top of its conical roof Andronicus put a weather vane, a revolving bronze statue of Triton, whose wand pointed to the panel of the prevailing wind.

For centuries, the Tower of the Winds delighted the Athenians. What's more, this masterly invention continues to enchant, being one of the precious few surviving buildings of ancient Greece. How did the tower manage to stay intact? Its first stroke of luck was to be co-opted by early Christians as part of their church; they also made the area around its entrance into a cemetery.

In the 1700s, the Tower of the Winds had more good fortune. While countless Greek monuments were being destroyed by the invading Ottoman Empire, the Tower again escaped when the Sufis, a mystical Islamic sect, adopted the circular-shaped tower to use for their spiritual dance floor as whirling dervishes.

The pleasing shape of the Tower of the Winds, now tucked away in the colorful Plaka district of Athens, has inspired architectural homages to it from the British Isles to the Atlantic seaboard of the USA. Andronicus would blush with pride.

❖ MAPMAKER ❖
CARTOGRAPHY GOES HEAD TO HEAD

Once a querulous quorum of Greeks agreed on what constituted a "continent"—whopping land mass, but don't get us started on islands; and how many continents there were—Europe, Asia, and Africa—the mapmaking thing seemed like a breeze.

Greek cartographers designed round maps, the continents huddled together and surrounded by ocean. Some maps gave the center spot to the oracular shrine at Delphi, which had long prided itself on being the navel of the world. On the faraway bits, the cartographers wrote *"hic sunt leones"* or "here are lions"—the poetic Greco-Roman way of saying: "We haven't a clue."

The travels of Alexander the Great and the techies he brought along to step off distances added new knowledge and impetus to the idea of pulling together a really decent map—and one that would fold properly as well. That goal, apparently unattainable, has not yet been achieved.

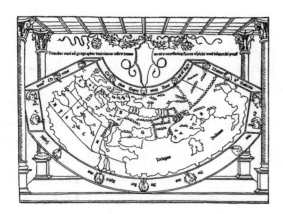

About a hundred years after Alex, a polymath librarian named Eratosthenes studied existing maps, geography accounts, and other bits and pieces of evidence. Although his data were incomplete and often shaky, he decided that indeed the earth was round, calculating its circumference as 25,200 miles, nearly spot on. A science geek before much in the way of science existed, Eratosthenes even dreamed up the notion of a world crisscrossed with meridians and parallel lines here and there. Only trouble was, neither he nor anyone else had sufficient data about the inhabited world, much less the whole enchilada.

As het-up scientists are wont to do, an irate geographer named Hipparchus arose to refute Mr E. Trembling with anger at Eratosthenes' slovenly, slapdash parallel lines, Mr H immediately dispatched a diatribe offering his own nifty world view. His map had a grid of north–south and east–west lines at equal intervals, the whole shebang divided into 360 parts or degrees.

Both these men had made giant intuitive leaps in celestial science and cartography; maps, however, still looked inadequate. Africa, then called "Libya," all floated far above the equator.

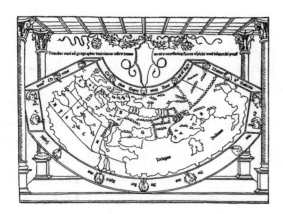

Three centuries later, around A.D. 110, another bold figure stepped forward to take a whack at mapping the world. Claudius Ptolemy used astronomical observations and two coordinates to plot locations on his map. Borrowing key points of Eratosthenes' scheme, he proclaimed (again) that the world was round, and gave his intersecting lines catchy names: longitude and latitude. But Mr P floundered terribly by forgetting the basic tenet of plagiarism: steal all the ideas, not just one or two. He neglected to pick up Mr E's circumference figures and his estimate of seventy miles for every degree. Ptolemy had some decent data (a lunar eclipse in 331 B.C. with three timed observations) with which to calculate longitude, but he mysteriously failed to capitalize on it. Instead, he proclaimed that everyone lived on a more petite earth, eighteen thousand miles around, with fifty miles to each degree of longitude.

Ah well, minor mistakes and omissions. Unfortunately, Ptolemy's work, and more especially what he left out, deeply influenced later explorers. One of them was a head-scratching Christopher Columbus, whose crew kept hearing him mutter, "According to that blankety-blank Ptolemy, I should be in India about now."

❖ HYDRAULIC ENGINEER ❖
CONCRETE SOLUTIONS

Greeks and Romans were incredibly fond of marble as a building material, and loved the variations of color and pattern found in specific quarries. While still at the quarry, stonemasons usually cut big chunks of marble into rough "drums" or slices that later became the fluted columns of a temple, leaving a heap of chips behind.

About the second century B.C., an environmentally sensitive soul who also happened to be a Roman engineering genius looked at the rubble lying around the quarry and thought: Hmm. Wonder if this stuff could be recycled into anything useful? He began fooling around with *caementa,* as quarry chips were called. He already knew that if he added sand, water, and hydrated lime to caementa, it made a useful mortar.

This unknown innovator happened to be innovating in southern Italy, where, thanks to Vesuvius and other active volcanoes, the soil contained a sand-like volcanic ash that locals called *pulvis puteolanus,* roughly translated as "that grit we've got way too much of around Puteoli."

In experimental mode, he substituted pulvis puteolanus for regular sand and made a batch. The grayish-red material took a while to harden—then got harder than stone, tougher than any other building material he'd ever mixed or poured. The guys loved it. Builders immediately set to work, throwing up high-rises in towns and cities around Italy.

This new stuff (today called hydraulic concrete—i.e. concrete that hardens under water—but then known as *opus caementicum*) had another useful quality: it would harden under water! Roman engineers tripped over their togas, getting back to the drawing boards. Now they could build bridges, aqueducts, breakwaters, lighthouses, and other structures whose footings were not on dry land.

With his breakthrough, our innovator ushered in the new career of hydraulic engineer. By the time of Emperor Augustus, these job-holders were knee-deep in work projects around the Med. If such feats seem ho-hum today, it's only because we have lost sight of the workings of the Greco-Roman world. Superb Roman roads notwithstanding, virtually all trade items and heavy cargo traveled by sea; safe harbors and coastal infra-structure, therefore, were vital to economic expansion.

Workers in allied fields benefited too. Underwater divers found new work. Crews of the huge superfreighters that hauled grain to Italy didn't need to return empty; instead, they could haul pulvis puteolanus to where it was needed. One writer, the architect Vitruvius, made his reputation on books describing concrete and the structures made from it.

Not everyone rejoiced at the concrete explosion. Those masons who'd had a lock for centuries on carving and fitting huge stone blocks for large structures found their workload greatly reduced.

Nevertheless, concrete in its hydraulic and non-hydraulic forms was here to stay. Breathtaking structures made with this wonder material, from the aqueduct at Segovia, Spain, to the Pantheon of Rome, still stand. And beneath the restless waves of the Med, archaeologists continue to find the rock-solid remains of maritime harbor structures, like the granddaddy of them all at Cosa, on the Etrurian, ninety miles north of Rome.

❖ ❖ ❖ ❖ SOSTRATOS ❖ ❖ ❖ ❖

A wondrous startup

Sostratos probably arrived in Alexandria, Egypt, as an official representative of his home town, the Greek city-state of Cnidos. An architectural enthusiast, he was welcomed by a ruler with the puffed-up name of Ptolemy I Soter (*soter* is Greek for "saviour"). In a former life, he'd been plain old Ptolemy, son of one of Alexander's trusted generals.

In the undignified scramble to divide the pizza-pie of Alex's empire after his death, Ptolemy scooped up the piece with maximum pepperoni: the province of Egypt. Clever Ptolemy also got Alex himself, whose corpse he'd kidnapped en route to its funeral in Macedonia. Citing that useful old chestnut, "Alex woulda wanted it this way," Ptolemy built a glamorous glass-fronted tomb in Alexandria, allowing crowds to goggle at the miraculous failure of the Great One's body to putrefy.

Within months of his arrival, Sostratos had ingratiated himself enough with Ptolemy to receive the prestigious post of "official friend," which in Alexandria-speak meant a sinecure.

Sostratos could tell that Ptolemy I Soter longed for more than wars and wealth. It wasn't half bad, being worshipped as a god-king, but this ruler wanted to be remembered in a more creative, Alexandrian sort of light. Official friend Sostratos had just the notion.

Alexandria being a major port, Sostratos suggested that he design and build a lighthouse at the city's entrance. Not just any old lighthouse: an instant superlative, a forty-five-story masterpiece. Ptolemy loved it, immediately claiming the idea as his own—another perk of the god-king job.

The genius of one architect: the lighthouse as killer attraction. It even made it to the Seven Wonders of the World lineup.

Sostratos slaved away for twelve years, as did countless slaves. Finally the lighthouse at Pharos stood in the harbor, its fiery beacon visible for miles out to sea. Ptolemy missed the dedication ceremonies, having died in the meantime, but the edifice had his royal name all over it.

A glory-hound at heart, Sostratos wanted to be remembered as well. To that end, he secretly carved a dedication on the lighthouse that read: "Sostratos of Cnidos, son of Dexiphanes, [dedicated] to the savior gods for sailors." Over time, the plaster wore off, revealing the true architect.

Sostratos and his ego had the pleasure of living long enough to see the Pharos become one of the Seven Wonders of the World. The eight-sided structure, topped with two smaller towers, rested on red granite blocks, their seams joined by molten lead for greater strength. A wide ramp spiraled up the interior to the third tier. This ingenious setup allowed pack animals to carry firewood up to where the beacon constantly burned.

Climbing the 450-foot tower while avoiding the dung left by the pack animals, visitors stopped at the first level for overpriced food and drink. Those undismayed by heights then ascended to a balcony at the top, there to gaze at the vista of harbor, lighthouse island, and city below.

Although his name appeared on buildings at Delphi and Delos, we don't know what else Sostratos built. We can say with confidence that he built to last. His lighthouse survived fifteen hundred years of storms, tidal waves, and earthquakes, finally falling into ruins around A.D. 1346. In the sea where it fell, archaeologists have found two thousand massive chunks of stone, each weighing fifty to seventy-five tons—the building blocks of his world wonder.

DIOSCORIDES

Seeing red

Working as a sawbones in the Roman army could be humdrum. But Pedanius Dioscorides, a Greek from Anazarbus with a talent for amputating gangrenous fingers and patching up battle wounds, had other interests. As a young man, he'd studied with a mentor who stressed the importance of medicinal herbs. Off-duty, Dioscorides spent his time studying the local fauna and flora. Among his discoveries was *kermes ilices*, a pea-sized insect that liked to feed on the leaves of a certain evergreen oak growing around the Mediterranean. After simmering a handful of these little bugs in water, he had the most luscious red dye he'd ever seen—quite unlike the orangy red hue of the madder plant.

Dioscorides knew he was on to something. He lived in an era of flamboyancy, an era when his fellow Romans, from Emperor Nero on down, were mad for color. Scarlet was in high demand for fancy homes, expensive garments, and the lips of fashionable women. Dioscorides thought that kermes might be easier (and safer) to extract than another crimson called cinnabar, a greasy mineral that came from the highly toxic mercury mines.

In short order, kermes became the color du jour of the Roman Empire. A new insect-collecting industry sprang up; kermes-ridden Roman provinces like Spain even paid some of their taxes in bags of red bugs.

But Dioscorides had bigger goals than cashing in on kermes. He stayed in the military, moving with the legions from Britain to southern France, from Asia Minor to Greece. All the while, he worked furiously, drawing the plants he'd collected and making extensive notes about their characteristics, which he often put to use in his practice.

About the time that Emperor Nero committed suicide, sniveling, "What an artist dies in me," Dioscorides finished a real work of art: his five-volume *De Materia Medica*. And what a book it was: over 4,700 entries, organized around the medical uses and preparation of drugs from plants and natural substances. His practical work stuck to empirical data instead of wandering off into the often-horrendous medical beliefs of his time. Among his entries, the author described a plant genus called *ephedra* that he used to stop hemorrhage and cure coughs—a resource overlooked by modern medicine until its "rediscovery" in the twentieth century (ephedrine, the drug derived from the plant, is now used to treat a variety of conditions).

Long before Dioscorides' time, the peoples of the eastern Mediterranean had carried out a lively trade in kermes. The young Greek doctor, however, made it an object of desire across the Roman Empire. As a dye and later a pigment for painters, kermes cost the earth—until the late 1400s, when it was upstaged by its even more vivid New World cousin, the cochineal insect.

De Materia Medica never went out of print and remained a key reference for pharmacists and doctors until modern times. We know little about the modest man who wrote it, but what he left us is worth far more than kermes.

❖ ASTRONOMER ❖
REPAIRING THE CALENDAR

In Rome, priests had long been in charge of the calendar, which was lunar; part of their job description was keeping track of religious festivals and the *fasti* or "good omen" days on which business could be conducted. Nobody carried out commercial transactions on the *nefasti,* the bad luck days—no one, that is, except slaves and poor people and a few thousand others who had to work daily to put food on the table.

Since the lunar calendar (at 354 days plus change) didn't match the number of days in a solar year, over time the months slithered around like anything. By the time Julius Caesar came into power, the calendar was three months out of whack. New year's celebrations were now happening in the fall. The harvest festivals occurred in summer. The whole thing was a mess.

No worries, the priests assured Julius. They would patch things up with an intercalation, as they'd always done. Around the temple, they always kept a spare month called Mercedonius handy; when needed, they plugged it into the calendar to approximate reality.

Julius wasn't having it. It had been eight years since the last intercalation. This makeshift business offended his sense of Roman order. Besides, he knew the truth. The priests were using the calendar as a political football, manipulating it with cunning. Officials in high office were elected for a term of a year, which began on January 1. If, however, the wrong candidate got elected, the calendar priests could easily abbreviate his "year." Conversely, when a friendly face got into office, his "year" could be fattened up with an intercalation.

Not being an astronomer or mathematician himself, Julius Caesar went to Alexandria, Egypt, where the best hung out. There he chose a brilliant numbers man named Sosigenes as his chief adviser.

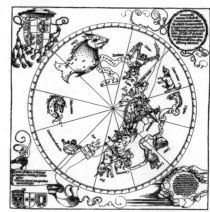

Sosigenes, a Greek geek and a genius in math and science, had spent years studying the movements of the sun relative to the dates. His flow chart said: abandon the lunar year, go to a solar year made up of 12 months and 365 days;

197

every fourth year, add a day to the month of Februarius. Ergo: 365¼ days, or close enough for Roman lifestyles.

Julius Caesar was tickled right up until Sosigenes told him the bad news. Their conversation might have gone something like this:

"Before we launch the new calendar, Caesar, we need to make a major adjustment."

"How major?"

"Well, let's just say that 46 B.C. will be kind of long."

"How long?"

"Uh, 445 days."

"Yikes." Muttering about the stink the priests would raise, Julius forged ahead.

After the "year of confusion," as 46 B.C. came to be known, things settled down and the Romans enjoyed a calendar that echoed the natural seasons.

Julius Caesar only lived fifteen months into the brand-new calendar before being assassinated on March 15, 44 B.C. The rest of the world, however, continued to use Sosigenes' innovation until A.D. 1582. Wouldn't you know it, however, those fun-loving, math-allergic Roman pontiffs had trouble with the leap-year idea. For quite some while they added a leap day every three years instead of four, until they were caught out by an emperor who could add.

❖   ❖   ❖   ❖   SERGIUS ORATA   ❖   ❖   ❖   ❖

Everything he touched turned to hot water

At beautiful Baiae in southern Italy, an entrepreneur named Gaius Sergius Orata farmed succulent species of fish, from red mullet to sea bass. (His Orata nickname came from his success at raising *aurata* or sea bass.) The only problem in paradise was the occasional cold spell, which could spell disaster for more tender fish species.

A hands-on sort, Sergius experimented, finally coming up with a heating system for his fishponds, adapted from a Greek idea. Encouraged by this, Sergius started the first oyster farm in Lago Lucrine (the name means "Money Lake"), which brought him more fame, cash, and a reputation as an oyster connoisseur.

To soak up his superfluous profits, Orata began to buy derelict properties in the country, fit them up with such mod cons as shower baths—yet another invention—and sell them.

His success got the talented engineer to pondering other sorts of liquid luxury. That's when he built his first *balneum* or bathhouse. In his day, the second century B.C., bathhouses were small, dark, and chilly; in cold weather, most folks only took a full bath once a week. To visionary Orata, this whole bathing business had promise. Could a daily dunk become a pleasurable experience instead of an ordeal?

Orata dared to dream big; in his balneum, he installed a system similar to what he'd used to keep his farmed fishes happy. Called a *hypocaust*, it was revolutionary. Against the hollow walls of the bathhouse, Orata built a furnace, which did two things. Above the flames sat two large vessels of water, heated by the fire. Through a series of flues or pipes that ran below the entire floor of the building itself, the furnace also pushed hot air, later vented by chimneys in the walls and roof. Result? Toasty toes and no shivers whatsoever for wet bathers.

Orata's hypocaust system for bathhouses spread faster than malaria in a Roman marsh. Since the subterranean part was largely hollow, yet reinforced with sturdy brick pillars, the system could be expanded to heat numerous rooms—even modified to give some rooms more heat than others. The readily accessible furnace was fueled by an even more ready supply of firewood-carrying slaves.

By A.D. 350, the city of Rome alone boasted eleven state-owned public baths called *thermae*. These glass-windowed palaces of aqueous pleasure had multiple rooms and baths; in them, air and water were heated to different temperatures so that bathers could choose the order and type of their ablutions, from red-hot sweat rooms to tepid baths to cool-down areas. The baths sat in park-like surroundings, rich with cultural amenities from libraries to gymnasia.

The smaller *balnae* were no less glorious; at least 856 public, private, and association-owned balnae dotted Rome in that era. Cities in the provinces got wet and wild too. Athens had twenty baths; North African Timgad, founded as a veterans' colony in A.D. 100, boasted fourteen baths a century later.

Rich and famous when he died, even the perceptive Sergius Orata may not have anticipated the enormous splash his inventions and adaptations would have on the health and comfort of millions.

❖ CARPENTER ❖
BINGE-WORTHY FURNITURE A SPECIALTY

In the first century B.C., Rome was hit by a virulent epidemic: table-mania. While rich women competed to buy the largest pearls, their husbands outbid each another to purchase tables carved from aromatic thyine or citron-wood. Their satiny surfaces, fragrant scent, and unusual markings brought goggle-worthy prices. A senator named Gallus Asinius slapped down over a million sesterces, the going rate for a large chunk of real estate, for one gem. People gasped even more over the sum paid for a four-foot-wide table by Nomius, a mere freedman of Emperor Tiberius.

Why were citron-wood tables so red-hot? Practicality, perhaps. Spilled wine wouldn't damage citron-wood a bit, a fact that apparently meant the world to a fashionable wine-bibbing Roman.

But rarity was the big factor. Restricted to the Atlas Mountains of North Africa, the citron-wood industry was an underground operation. Literally. The timber for tables came from burls located on the tree roots. (Moroccan wood-carvers today still dig deep to find what's left of the citron-wood supply.)

And the *fabrii tignaurii,* the talented carpenters and carvers who made them? Most were slaves or freedmen, using still-common tools: saws, axes, hammers, planes, lathes, and chisels. They bored holes with bow drills, glued dovetail, tenon, and mortice joints, and sanded their pieces with shark-skin. When not busy with tables, carpenters fashioned chairs of beech and fancy chests from cypress or oak.

Besides high-end furniture, carpenters built ships, wagons, and houses. Although the walls were made of marble, Greek and Roman temples had floors, ceilings, and moldings of carved wood. At just one temple on the Athens Acropolis, twenty-two carpenters and seven carvers were employed full-time for a year.

Despite their humble status, the fabrii fellows (origin of our word "fabricate") were some of the first working men to found guilds, called collegia. Each collegium met regularly, collected dues, and held banquets. It also functioned as a burial club, guaranteeing that even the handful of carpenters who hadn't cleaned up during the citron-wood table craze would get a proper funeral.

Greco-Roman carpenters made another important contribution to their society. Early on, they created comfortable beds that doubled as couches. No Greek dining room was worthy of a drinking party unless its walls were lined with couches. These B.C. Lazee-Boys were meant to hold one reclining male; or one drunk sleeping it off. Soon, however, astute users saw that the couch also offered lounging room for a pert slave or a toothsome call girl. Suddenly the equipment to turn a drinking bout into a lustier free-for-all was at hand.

With their taste for one-upmanship, the Romans carried things even further, paying carpenters fat sums to make higher capacity couches. Soon doubles and triples with reinforced webbing were seen in the best dining rooms.

Eating from a horizontal position wasn't especially comfortable, but even doubters had to admit: the lie-down format made couches the real ice-breakers at an orgy. The unwitting skill of carpenters had brought sex from the bedroom into the dining room, where it stayed for centuries.

❖ ❖ ❖ ❖ **FRONTINUS** ❖ ❖ ❖ ❖

Liquid legacy

During seventy years of vigorous life, Sextus Julius Frontinus was by turns magistrate, governor of Britain, highway surveyor, and author. But the most memorable feats on his CV occurred during his last post, that of *curator aquarum* (not to be confused with overseeing the wellbeing of exotic fishes).

At an age when most public servants had long since retired, Frontinus ran Rome's water system as its curator aquarum or water commissioner. He oversaw everything to do with Rome's aqueducts, a river-sized system that delivered more fresh spring water to its metropolis than New York City did nineteen hundred years later.

An engineer by training, educated in Alexandria, Frontinus was a lifelong thinker and tinkerer, always fascinated by the nuts and bolts of infrastructure. (And that's before there were nuts and bolts.)

After being elected consul, the top political office in Rome, Frontinus was tapped for the job of provincial governor. Not everyone would have been thrilled, since the place he would govern was a remote island called Britain.

While there, Frontinus manfully quelled various uprisings, including the revolt of the Silures, a warlike bunch from Wales whose hooliganisms rivaled those of twenty-first-century soccer fans.

Frontinus served several more times as consul, all the time writing copiously, although most of his books on the art of war, surveying, and farming have not survived.

But it was as curator aquarum that he achieved his finest work. Sextus was already in his sixties when he was chosen in A.D. 97 by Emperor Nerva, who chirpily suggested that the office might need municipal reform. A bit of fiscal tightening, perhaps. "Look, I'll throw in a secretary, three public slaves, and a couple of lictors to help. C'mon, whaddaya say?"

Despite the staffing, Frontinus found himself in a quagmire of a job that had been abused and mismanaged for decades, through more than one administration.

Frontinus attacked this massive task as though it were a wild Welshman. To grasp the big picture, he personally examined his watery domain, drawing up scale models and charts of everything, then began to write a little volume called *Of Aqueducts*. His handbook detailed the size, height, and history of the nine aqueducts that existed in his day and the water distributed from them, down to the number of taps from each and the laws regulating their maintenance.

Roman water usage had strict priorities; water went first to public fountains, then to the public baths. Runoff from the baths got channeled through the loos at the baths and the public lavatories before going into the sewers and out of the city. Water use for private customers came after all public uses had been satisfied.

Frontinus' book—still extant, fortunately—was a treasure-trove for his successors, as it is for modern engineers and historians, who can read precisely how the Romans built and maintained their engineering feats.

Sextus Julius Frontinus also served as head watermeister under the next emperor, who would've been crazy to let such a man retire. Frontinus recognized the importance of his task. "Remembrance will endure if the life merits it," this admirable man often said before he left this world, a maxim preserved in the writings of his pal, Pliny the Elder.

❖ SALVAGE DIVER ❖
UNDER EXTREME PRESSURE TO LEAK

At the port of Ostia could be found the large guild of salvage divers, called *urinatores* in Latin. Notice an unfortunate resemblance to the word "urine"? No coincidence. According to the historian Flavius, the more the boys went below, the more frequently they had to go, due to presssure on the abdomen. (No data as to whether excessive trips to the john continued once on dry land.)

Their diving equipment was modest; besides free-diving, the men used kettle-shaped diving bells that could be refilled with air. With lead weights, they descended as deep as thirty meters. To ascend, they used inflated bladders—of animals, not their own much-abused organs. Their main task? Salvage diving, mainly the moving of construction materials underwater.

Most freight in the ancient world moved by ship, meaning that safe harbors, docking facilities, piers, and freight warehouses were high priorities. Only a handful of harbors around the Mediterranean could accommodate the superfreighters that hauled grain.

Salvage divers were key workers in the building of jetties, bridge footings, and other structures. They also installed complex wooden forms underwater, into which hydraulic cement (a special mortar that got rock-hard below the waves) was poured for piers and the like. Divers also labored for years on such ambitious projects as the Portus harbor enlargement begun by Emperor Claudius.

These busy ports must have been the equivalent of today's most hazardous airports. Where the mouth of the Tiber River met the sea, conditions were often rotten, a combination of volatile currents, heavy silting, and unpredictable winds. In the shallow waters of the crowded port, ships often collided or sank, sending urinatores below to salvage the goods. In A.D. 62, over two hundred ships went down at Ostia alone.

Given the skill required and the risks involved, urinatores deserved decent wages and got them. Some men rose to leadership positions in their guilds—like Claudius Severus, who served three times as president. His business acumen above water made him affluent, and he became a major patron of the Tiber River guild. After upgrading the clubhouse, he gave a fund of ten thousand sesterces to his guild, the interest to be distributed yearly among the members. Who says a weak-bladdered man can't do good or get ahead?

❖ BRICK MANUFACTURER ❖
SOLIDLY BEHIND THEIR PRODUCTS

Modern contractors would be amazed at the legal guarantees that manufacturers used to provide. Roman law decreed, for example, that brickmakers could be held liable for building quality, requiring their products to be individually identified with a manufacturer's stamp.

Men like Lucanus and Tullus Domitius, brickmaking brothers in the village of Bomarzo, rose to the challenge. Their worksite had some of the best alluvial clay around, plus plenty of water and wood for the furnace. Their place was fifty miles from Rome but a mere brickbat's throw from the Tiber River, so shipping their wares didn't present a problem.

Their factory held terracotta tubs, production vats, and two large rectangular furnaces for firing materials. The Domitii brothers also owned an adjacent brick field, where newly made bricks aged for two years before use.

At their plant, these industrious siblings also manufactured roof tiles and the huge storage jars called *dolii*. Once hauled to their intended storage area, dolii containers were buried up to their necks, then filled with olive oil or wine.

In 2005, Italian archaeologists serendipitously stumbled on the brothers' place of business. There they found over one hundred Domitii bricks, each stamped with a half-moon logo displaying the owners' names, the brickfield name, and Titus Ianuarius, the man in charge of the kiln. Prior to this, their stamped bricks had been found at the Pantheon, the Baths of Caracalla, and the Colosseum, making it clear that their work played a key role in many of Rome's most important buildings.

Brickmakers from Greece to Britain also used marks or logos in circular or rectangular shapes, giving names, the place of manufacture, and, in later years, the date. The making of fired brick, a mainstay in construction, had a long and prosperous history in Greece as well, judging by the records about bricklayers' pay. As early as the fourth century B.C., most received two drachmas a day, while others were paid piecework, from twelve to seventeen drachmas per thousand bricks.

Among Roman brickmakers, the brothers Domitii enjoyed widespread success; bricks and other clay products with their logo have turned up in France, Spain, and North Africa, as well as Italy. From their beginnings around A.D. 50, their enterprise remained a family business for more than a century. In 121, a family member named Domitia Lucilla Minor gave birth to a son who became emperor. Solid as the clay his family used in business, Emperor Marcus Aurelius eventually inherited the Domitii brickworks as well as the Empire's highest office.

An ancient marvel still in one piece, the Pantheon was built with bricks from the busy brickyard of the Domitii brothers.

❖ ARCHITECT ❖
LASTING IMPRESSIONS

Roman architects achieved giddy heights with their work, but the steepest assignment ever taken on was the one accepted by Gaius Julius Lacer. The 616-foot-long bridge he built of fitted granite (Look, Ma, no mortar!) at Alcántara, Spain, immediately zoomed to the top of the superlatives chart. It rose into the clear blue sky for 233 feet, the highest bridge ever built in the Roman Empire.

People gawked at its six huge arches—and still do. Lacer knew he'd made something to last; and it has, despite two wars and various attempts to blow it up. A small Roman temple at one end of the bridge houses the architect's burial place and the words: "I leave this bridge for all times to the generations of the world."

Another reach-for-the-stars builder was Chares of Lindos, who created the Colossus of Rhodes around 275 B.C. This 107-foot bronze of Helios, the Greek sun god, roughly the size of the Statue of Liberty, only stood for fifty-six years before tumbling in an earthquake. Even in ruins, it awed the world, standing as one of the Seven Wonders of the World for centuries.

There were plenty of stars in architectural circles. Vitruvius, Roman architect and author of important works, also dreamed up the "Vitruvian

man" of Da Vinci fame. Architect Apollodorus of Damascus, commissioned by Emperor Trajan to advertise his triumph over the Dacians, built a flashy forum, including Trajan's famous column, which illustrates every last detail of the campaign.

Plenty of lesser lights did bread-and-butter work that still stands. Take the *insulae*, for instance, the multi-story apartment blocks that dominated city and town landscapes for centuries. Rome alone had forty-four thousand blocks of insulae, housing most of its population.

What did it take to sail into the harbour at Rhodes between the legs of a well-endowed sun god? Brazen courage.

The most thankless job ever taken on by an architect? That would have fallen on the aching shoulders of a whiz kid named Decrianus.

In A.D. 80, Emperor Titus had a "Must do—get cracking!" project for him. Titus had finally gotten work completed on the gargantuan Flavian amphitheater (later known as the Colosseum), begun by his father Vespasian. What with delays, the project was a nightmare. Titus had already booked the inaugural event, a series of memorial games for dear old pater, which would employ gladiators for one hundred days and end the lives of nine thousand wild beasts.

Standing in the way of progress, however, was this stupid, 115-foot-tall gold-plated statue of the late, unlamented Emperor Nero, a leftover from his equally unlamented palace, the Golden House. Titus had a magnificent brainstorm for recycling the thing. He told Decrianus, "Sheesh—it's hideous. But what a crime to waste all that metal. Just change the head!"

Once architect Decrianus dutifully oversaw the job of reworking the giant head to resemble the sun god Helios instead of Nero, he had to drag the statue from its original locale to a spot near the new Colosseum. That was a tall order. The real knicker-twister, however, was the emperor's insistence that the ten-story statue remain upright during its travels.

His ulcers screaming, Decrianus finally arrived at a solution. It took twenty-four elephants, countless pooper-scoopers, and any number of agonizing days and nights to get the statue into position. Finally, his job completed by the deadline, Decrianus had a few nanoseconds to bask in his success before learning that Emperor Titus already planned to have a companion statue erected of the moon goddess—by another architect.

❖ SURVEYOR ❖

MASTER OF ALL HE SURVEYS

All roads did lead to Rome—but before any roadwork commenced, the findings of that key person, the *agrimensor* or surveyor, were needed.

For road-building, surveyors used a unit called a pace, in fact more like a giant step of nearly five feet. One thousand paces equalled a mile. On the other hand, if a surveyor needed to mark out land, he worked with a measurement of 120 feet, called an *actus* or "driving." It represented the distance that oxen pulling a plow would go before being turned.

The surveyors who plotted out Roman roads were military specialists, an important part of the army. Their Mission Impossible assignment was to devise the most direct route between points A and B—and to do so with the minimum of bends and the maximum of straights. (Sometimes this meant gradients of ten to twenty percent in hilly country.)

The army agrimensor used a four-armed *groma,* an instrument with two plumb lines at forty-five and ninety degrees, along with bronze sighting rods and leveling posts. Helpers called *gromatici* placed the rods, running a line called the *rigor* and moving the rods as ordered by the agrimensor. For longer distances, or on terrain that wasn't level, an agrimensor sat down with geometric formulas.

Surveying was one of antiquity's first jobs of importance—and only free men could hold the job, and sometimes it took them overseas. In early Greek times, when city-states or islands grew overcrowded, settlers were invited or booted out to colonize another land—preferably one rich in resources to funnel to the motherland, yet passably far away so disgruntled pioneers wouldn't trickle back to home base.

Both the Greeks and the Romans loved to measure things. Pythagoras, that grand philosopher of the sixth century B.C., believed that numbers and relationships between them were sacred. Doodling with a stick in sand, he came up with the hypotenuse.

The Romans demanded precision even for the humblest of tasks. Each night when the army stopped to make camp by the side of the road, junior officers called *mensores* laid out the exact positions for each of the soldiers' tents. If the camp formation wasn't shipshape and military, that field commander wouldn't sleep—and neither would his hapless mensor.

❖ HIGHWAY BUILDER ❖
ROADS SCHOLAR

The bumpy, mountainous terrain of Greece was a nightmare for highway builders. Slave labor built the few roads that existed, linking marble quarries with cities like Athens and carrying streams of pilgrims to shrines like Delphi and sanctuaries like Epidaurus. Greek armies had to make do by following rivers and marching through dry river beds.

In contrast, beginning in the third century B.C., Roman highway builders ultimately created the equivalent of the US interstate system, using army specialists rather than slaves or civilians.

Highway builders, including the masons who dressed the stones, sometimes identified their work with their own marks.

The Roman legions, with their thousands of infantrymen, wheeled vehicles, chariots, siege machines, and pack animals, needed to move with ease and speed around an expanding empire. They were the heaviest users of the network of highways that eventually spider-webbed around the Mediterranean basin. Ultimately, the Romans built an all-weather, paved road system over fifty-three thousand miles long. Certain stretches, for instance in Arabia, even had divided highways, two lanes separated by a low wall of stones.

Directed by civil engineers and surveyors, the legionaries spent more time using their spades than they ever did swinging their swords. First the men dug trenches several feet deep and as wide as twenty feet across. If the soil was soft, they drove piles into the earth. At the bottom, the men smoothed a layer of dirt or sand, followed by a thick layer of stones for drainage, then a stratum of gravel set in clay or concrete. Depending on the area, weather conditions, and the importance of that stretch of highway, there might be more layers of concrete and rolled sand, topped by a pavement of stone blocks dressed on the top side and closely set in concrete.

The finished product resembled a sturdy wall laid on its side, with plenty of drainage and a cambered center so that moisture ran off. Before moving on, the road builders finished each stretch with curbstones and smoothed the unpaved shoulders for horse traffic.

In some areas, the head honcho might find that there was no good source for making concrete. If warranted, the road builders would pour molten lead to set the blocks of paving stone. Only a few scraps of these especially costly roads still exist; in the post-Roman era, locals quickly ripped up the lead to use or sell.

A road builder could be proud of his work; these babies were built to last eighty to one hundred years before needing repairs! The first superhighway, begun in 312 B.C. by Appius Claudius, the public-works commissioner at the time, still bears his name: the 112-mile, 33-foot-wide Appian Way heading south from Rome. In later centuries, it was extended to run further south, into the toe of the Italian boot. Nicknamed "the Queen of Roads," parts of it are still in use. The section at Ostia is especially atmospheric, still possessing some of its original paving, milestones, and roadside tombs— shaded by more recent generations of pine and cypress trees.

All this enormous and ingenious building was carried out with the simplest of tools—no mechanical diggers, no asphalt spreaders, not a single dump truck filled with oiled gravel. The road-building manpower was basic, too: usually a legionary equipped with a pickax, a spade, and a bountiful supply of sweat. What a legacy those long-ago soldiers left.

NINE

GLAMOROUS POSTS & UNSAVORY OCCUPATIONS

❖ LITURGIST ❖

MY PHILANTHROPY'S BIGGER THAN YOURS

Since the thought of physical labor and the notion of "trade" sent well-heeled ancient Greeks into a faint, they struggled to fill their days in a way that showed up other rich people as cheapskates.

The Athenian assembly came up with a gratifying solution. The *liturgy*, they called it. This once-yearly, soak-a-rich-person activity was only imposed on—ahem, granted to—the three hundred wealthiest citizens in Athens. Its success led to its adoption by other Greek communities who also wanted to give their distressed plutocrats something meaningful to do.

(Liturgy, or "work for the people," had a secular meaning to begin with; today the word describes the religious ritual of certain Christian denominations.)

Eager liturgists sought the glory of being thought magnificent by helping to fund the building of temples and civic structures. In addition, ninety-seven lucky benefactors per year subsidized annual drama and music festivals; still others outfitted warships and paid the annual wages of the crews. A sought-after liturgy was *gymnasiarch,* where one affluent individual would expend a fortune on the olive oil needed for daily cleansing at gymnasia and during a major festival.

Once novice benefactors had gotten a taste for community-minded liturgy, they might slide further into philanthropy. Some went as far as *anathema*—a word we don't hear much these days except in exorcism movies, where it means "devoted to evil." Back then, anathema referred to any object that was devoted or dedicated, the more dazzling the better. These high-profile gifts were often fabulous works of art, from gold statues to paintings. Presented to a god or goddess, they were then ensconced in that deity's temple, where they could be admired by the rapturous benefactor and an envious public for centuries.

The Romans developed their own benefactions to enrich the toil-free lives of their wealthy. While serving in office, patrician Romans did not dream of drawing anything as plebian as a salary. Instead, they were expected to cough up monies for a variety of needs. Emperor Trajan began a family allowance program for the poor, which flopped with later administrations. But the *alimentum,* a social program for the poor primarily subsidized by private donors, provided a reliable food supply for needy orphans or school-children.

Pliny the Younger, for instance, funded the alimenta for his home town. Instead of a lump sum, Pliny rented out some of his property, yielding the equivalent of a cool half a million dollars a year to the fund. To ensure posthumous praise, he also willed the townspeople money for a Pliny Memorial public bath and free annual dinner. Donors often specified char-

itable beanfeasts on their birth dates, giving recipients a regular anniversary on which to recall them with gratitude.

Women rolling in dough weren't forgotten, either, and held wage-free posts as magistrates from Spain to Italy. A number of Roman women bequeathed million-sesterce sums for alimenta, including a mother who underwrote the food needs for two hundred girls and boys in memory of her son Macer.

On the Greek mainland, women like Menodora of Sillyon funded huge feeding programs and took on multi-year liturgies. In Asia Minor, full of prosperous cities from Alexander the Great's time forward, countless energetic women had a yen to help and an eye to their legacies. After becoming the first female magistrate for the city of Priene, a go-getter named Phile underwrote a reservoir and an aqueduct for her water-starved home town, achieving another first.

Male or female, Roman or Greek, ancient liturgists had one thing besides wealth in common: they all agreed that there was no such animal as "an anonymous donor."

❖ GYMNASIARCH ❖

GOING WITH THE FLOW

Greeks were big on daily athletic endeavor, both for competitive events and for military preparedness through exercise. All social classes made heavy use of gymnasia, private and public, large and small. These facilities, however, would soon have ground to a halt without…olive oil. Although it might sound counterintuitive to lather yourself with extra virgin, then scrape it off your skin with a curved metal instrument, that's how every Greek (and Roman) cleansed himself two millennia ago.

High-quality olive oil wasn't cheap, either. The procurement of a steady supply became a key task for the gymnasiarch, an elected (sometimes appointed) official who ran the gymnasia in a given city.

Judging by the gleeful inscriptions left on tombstones, being a gymnasiarch was the most sought-after liturgy or philanthropic assignment any filthy-rich person could aspire to. Merely to qualify, a person between the ages of thirty and sixty had to have a net worth in the high six figures.

Athletes and gym-goers went through astounding quantities of extra virgin olive oil at their workouts. This year-long oil subsidy was underwritten by the gymnasiarch, who kept the flow going.

Wealthy women made their mark as gymnasiarchs too, although it might have been more of a greasy stain, given the properties of olive oil.

This hands-on job had interesting perks. You got to wear special white shoes and a purple cloak. You carried a special stick with which you were allowed to whack any sullen youths who were misbehaving; you could also levy fines for disorderly conduct. In essence, the gymnasiarch, as superintendent of his or her city's gyms, had jurisdiction over anyone using them.

During the twelve-month tenure of a gymnasiarch, a donor could offload quite a pile of cash. A generous officeholder might also pay for festival expenses, sacrificial animals, and dedications for the gym's victors in athletic meets. They also shelled out for more mundane items too, such as the special fine sand that the wrestlers rubbed on their bodies before working out.

Theoretically the gymnasiarch could make back a few drachmas by selling wrestlers' sand after a match; this oily, sweaty mess was believed to have medicinal value. The sale of the used sand and its revenues, however, were usually given to the keeper of the wrestling school.

At the end of the year, the gymnasiarch had to present a profit-and-loss statement of the gym's funds, justifying and reconciling accounts to the city auditors. Many affluent men and women went back for more, holding multiple tenures in their lifetimes.

Although the Greek gym began as a simple affair, with a wrestling pit, a dirt track for running and long jumping, and some shelter for exercising in bad weather, by Hellenistic times it had expanded into an elaborate complex, with bathing facilities, ball courts, covered walkways, artwork-filled rooms and corridors—even seating areas for philosophers and other effete types to converse.

The lavish public baths that would soon become the hallmark of Roman civilization were modeled on these very gymnasia. There, too, wealthy Romans would also vie for the slippery, glorious opportunity to be a gymnasiarch.

❖ SOPHIST ❖
THE SPIN-DOCTOR IS IN

Plato gave us platonic love; cynic philosophers gave us cynicism. What, pray, did the sophists bequeath? Sophistication. With sophistication came obfuscation and rhetoric, empty of course. Although *sophist* comes from *sophos* or wisdom, that perfectly good Greek term morphed into our *sophism*, a wise-guy sort of cleverness, all sound bites and specious arguments.

Genuine philosophers were seekers, trying to define their world or discover how to live a good life. Although sophists were philosophically adept, in essence they were hired guns, high-end teachers who would travel anywhere and teach anyone. Their beliefs were wide-ranging, their intellectual end-product fuzzy—a good adjective, since what these glib, highly paid men did was talk in circles, using clever tricks and high-blown rhetoric to amuse, bemuse, and confuse the listener.

To become a sophist took a good education, a knack for phrase-coining, and a well-endowed trust fund—all that travel didn't come cheap.

In the golden age of Greek sophists, men like Protagoras of Abdera and Gorgias of Sicily became household names—as long as your household cleared $100,000 a year, that is.

Protagoras kicked out some catchy maxims; it was he who said, "Of all things the measure is Man..." (Unfortunately, the rest of his quote ends with a dull thud: "...of the things that are, that they are, and of the things that are not, that they are not.")

He did a regular circuit of Greek cities; for a change of pace, he wrote the law code for the city-state of Thurii, the hometown of Herodotus. Protagoras ruled rhetorically until he was seventy—then came a cropper when a misfired aphorism got him convicted of atheism in Athens.

Selling sophism must have been a healthy occupation; Gorgias was even longer-lived than Protagoras—some claim he saw 108 birthdays. Gorgias first got noticed when he successfully pleaded for the city-state of Athens to come to the military aid of Syracuse. He specialized in teaching other sophists and rhetoricians the art of persuasion. He was of the "nothing exists—and if it did, it couldn't be known or communicated" school of thought, if you could call it that.

The career of sophist reinvented itself in Roman times, when higher education emphasized flowery Latin and Greek, artificial sentence structure, and painfully convoluted arguments.

Lucius Philostratus, a Roman general, was stationed for years in Athens, considered at that time a nowheresville post by brass in the know. For his midlife crisis he took up sophism, and soon found a congenial berth with the imperial court of Septimius Severus. The emperor's wife Julia Domna took a shine (sophisticated but apparently non-erotic) to Philostratus, and became his patron for decades. The benefits were superb: he got expense-paid trips to the Parthian empire in the east, where Julia commissioned him (oh joy!) to write a romanticized *Life of Apollonius the Philosopher*.

Before his opus was finished, Julia was. She committed suicide, driven to it by fatal sibling rivalry between her sons; and if that weren't nerve-racking enough, by a palace coup. Philostratus somehow escaped the messy aftermath, fled to Athens, wrote several more books, and lived to be another cranky old septuagenarian sophist.

❖ TATTOOER ❖
GETTING THE BLUES, LOSING THE BLUES

Although tribal warriors and more than a few women from Britain to Thrace proudly ornamented their skins with dark-blue animal designs, most Greeks and Romans thought tattoos were bad news. They called them *stigmata*, signifying skin pricked or cut with a sharp instrument.

Getting a tattoo B.C. called for cojones. After washing the skin with leek juice, the tattooer pricked it with needles, then rubbed in ink made from bark, gall, vitriol, vinegar, and corroded bronze. Germs and infections? You betcha.

The Greeks routinely used tattoos to humiliate, label, and visually imprison criminals, prisoners of war, slaves, and others who had no choice in the matter. (Prisoners usually became slaves, since ransom was rare and POW camps non-existent.)

After defeating the islanders of Samos in the fifth century B.C., the Athenians marked prisoner foreheads with an owl, their city's symbol. The Samians got the upper hand and in turn defaced the Athenians with their ship logo. But the real tattoo-fest occurred when Athens attacked Sicily in 413 B.C. In that disastrous military expedition, over seven thousand Athenians were captured, saddled with horse tattoos, symbol of the victorious city-state of Syracuse, and put to work in the rock quarries.

In later centuries, the Romans enthusiastically developed the "stigmata as ID" idea. As army legions grew and auxiliary units from subject nations were added, recruits received tattoos on hands or elsewhere, usually the name or number of their unit. These identifiers also made it easier to find deserters. The ID idea spread to municipal slaves working for the Roman government. Some callous papyrus-shufflers carried the dual-purpose tattoo to sickening lengths by inking the words "tax paid" on the foreheads of slaves exported to the eastern provinces.

Most historians believe that wide-scale branding or burning was rare. Nevertheless, gladiators sometimes got tattooed or branded. If recaptured, runaway slaves were branded "F" for fugitive. Oddly enough, at certain Syrian and Egyptian temples, a runaway slave who there acquired a sacred wrist or neck tattoo couldn't be reclaimed by his owner. He was now considered the "property" of that god or goddess.

Although widespread in the ancient world, slavery wasn't always a permanent state. In the thirty years between 80 and 50 B.C. alone, nearly five hundred thousand slaves won manumission. Once a slave became a freed person, what did he or she do to remove those brutal images on forehead, arms, or legs?

Most made an appointment with an un-tattooer special-ist. Barbers also did stigmata removal, doubling as primitive plastic surgeons. One excruciating method: apply resin for five days, dig out the design with a sharp pin, salt the area, then follow up with a caustic poultice. Twenty days later, ulceration and scar tissue should have formed, hiding the tattoo. Some un-tattooers swore by a mixture of strong vinegar and the scum from the bottom of a chamber pot. Others used a potion of sulfur, wax, oil, and cantharides or Spanish fly.

Few Greeks or Romans wore tattoos willingly. Dancers sometimes wore a tattoo of Bes, ancient dwarf-god of music, who also protected women in childbirth.

Clearly the people of long ago had stouter hearts and higher pain tolerance than twenty-first-century folks. And there were freedmen, no doubt, who simply decided to wear longer hair or longer sleeves, or to live with their stigmata.

❖ TAX FARMER ❖

DIRTY JOB, BUT SOMEONE'S GOTTA COLLECT 'EM

Taxes have been around for ages, as a browse through the New Testament will confirm. Much earlier, Greeks and Romans gave taxation an exciting new twist. Instead of making it the task of government to collect revenues, they privatized the job.

Far from being repelled, well-to-do men vied for the post of tax farmer. After the job was auctioned off, the highest bidder became the official tax farmer of a given area.

Citizens could also form legal entities, making themselves the equivalent of a tax-farming corporation. Known as *publicani*, these corporations carried out other functions and contracts too.

What sorts of things were taxed in ancient times? The usual levies: property and inheritance taxes; surcharges on mine ownership; certain foods, animals, and market goods; customs duties when passing from one province or Greek city-state to another. Perfume, for instance, got taxed per camel-load; traders paid twice as much for fancy scent in alabaster jars as for the cheap stuff in goatskins.

The ingenuity of taxation B.C. went far beyond our modest imaginings. Ships paid port, river-passage, and docking taxes. All goods sold at public auctions were subject to duties. Greeks who moved from their home city-states to live in another paid taxes as metics or resident aliens. There were taxes on salt, taxes on leather. Even urine, used to clean clothes and hides, was taxed by a succession of emperors.

Slavery brought in immense sums. Emperor Augustus slapped a two percent tax on the sale of each slave, later hoisted to four percent by Caligula. This irony was not lost on workers, since the legwork to collect said revenues was carried out by slaves working at the behest of the tax farmer.

Once countries and nations became subject to Rome, they got hit with special assessments. After the Jews were conquered in A.D. 70, they had to fork out the Fiscus Judaicus. Ten years later, when Emperor Domitian found that current revenues wouldn't cover his building projects (such as a 440,000-square-foot palace complex), he ordered tax farmers to wring more from Jews throughout the empire, practicing or not. This led to shameful abuses, such as the examination in court of males to see if they were circumcised and thus Jewish, according to an eyewitness account by the sensation-loving Suetonius.

The indemnity was a huge tax, inflicted as a lump sum on a nation once defeated. Its purpose? To repay Rome for its costs in fighting the war against them!

Poll taxes, collected annually from each Roman province, were based on census returns. Each year, all members of a household had to return to their own hearths to be officially counted—the same tax that sent Mary and Joseph to Bethlehem.

Earthy yet pragmatic, the Greeks had long taxed their sex workers. Rome followed suit. Prostitutes paid a tariff to become licensed hookers; thereafter, each pro coughed up a monthly tax equal to the sum she or he charged for one sex act.

The mechanics of tax farming were simple; the bidder paid a lump sum, gambling that he would collect more lucre than he put out. Clearly it was a magnificent way to make the rich richer, since tax farming flourished for centuries.

❖ BOOKIE ❖

A FLUTTER ON LADY LUCK

There must be a DNA sequence for the urge to gamble, as rampant among ancient cultures as it is in the world today. They too utilized gambling enablers, professionals we'd call bookies.

The Greeks found dicing and other games of chance addictive. To conquer the Greeks, King Philip of Macedon encouraged the gambling fever that was sweeping Athens at the time, realizing that it would fatally distract his enemies. It worked; he won.

Although Roman law forbade most forms of gambling—with penalties ranging from exile to fines of four times the wager—few gamblers and even fewer bookies got nailed. The latter, thick as fleas, made a fat living in Rome.

Roman emperors weren't very good role models for the anti-gambling lobby. Augustus was more of a "do what I say" sort of ruler. The man loved a flutter. Often he gave each house guest a thousand sesterces to play dice—later regaling them in detail as to how he'd let them win. Other emperors weren't so high-minded; Caligula not only cheated at dice, he confiscated many a Roman's property to pay the debts he owed to a bookie. Emperor Claudius could have started a Gamblers Anonymous chapter; he had his carriage customized, allowing him to play dice en route to wherever he was heading.

For most Romans, there were plenty of exceptions to the gambling ban. During the December festival of Saturnalia, anyone could indulge in dice, board games, or silly bar bets.

The law also permitted betting on athletic events year-round, from boxing to track meets. Cockfights and other blood-and-gore events were bread-and-butter for bookies. At the amphitheater, gladiators put on warm-up exhibitions, using wooden swords in mock battles. These matches were closely followed by bookies, who kept handicapping records on the fighters, their health, and their won/lost stats. Using an abacus, they set odds for the real matches that followed. Superstition ruled in gamblers' minds—they chose fighters on the basis of weapons or lucky crests on helmets, or even the colors worn by a gladiator.

But the real rake-it-in biz for bookies was the chariot races at the circus, the most popular and well-attended spectator sport. Bookies on and off the track placed customer bets on one of four factions or stables of racing drivers. Everyone followed the thunderous fortunes of these stables. Some betters staked six figures—or even their freedom—on the outcomes. From time to time, charioteers succumbed to bribery as well. Partisan emotions about favorite stables ran high, occasionally turning into riots. Even after the empire itself officially "fell" around A.D. 476, racetrack gambling flourished.

Although gambling dens never wanted for business, the circus kept bookies prosperous. The day-long event offered gamblers everything: excitement, noise, the chance to yell insults at the high and mighty, blandishments from prizes to food feasts, and an edgy life-and-death ambience. For Romans high and low, it was the lottery, the casino, the side bet on the home team, the numbers game, the poker tournament, the bingo parlor, all in one brutal, fashionable, deliriously cathartic package. Who wouldn't adore it?

❖ CURSE-TABLET MAKER ❖

A WAY TO WITCH YOUR TROUBLES AWAY

So you're worried about the competition at the next athletic meet, or that a business competitor is about to sue you. Cheer up, ancient person: a lead curse-tablet's your answer. That meant a visit to your neighborhood curse-tablet maker, a specialized scribe with a qualification in black magic.

The tablets themselves were small, made from thin sheets of soft lead, two to four inches long. Using a *stylus*, a bronze writing instrument with a pointed tip, the curse-tablet maker created a lip-smacking curse to your specifications, or supplied one of his generic execrations. To give the curses maximum power, the scribe often wrote them backward.

Whether plain or fancy, maledictions followed a formula: first the victim's name, then a series of what the Greeks called "curses that bind tight" and the Romans referred to as "curses to fix or fasten." One binding spell, commissioned by a defendant in an Athenian trial, included such phrases as: "Theagenes the butcher I bind his tongue, his soul and the speech he is practicing…" Clearly aimed at a witness who had been well-rehearsed by his lawyer!

Another curse-tablet from a sanctuary of the goddess Demeter named every single juror in a trial. Race drivers (and betters on them) at the Roman circus were repeat customers; one of their curse-tablets said, in part, "bind every limb and sinew of Victoricus, the charioteer for the Blue team…and the horses he is about to race…blind their eyes so they cannot see and twist their soul and heart so they cannot breathe."

Once finished, the curse-tablets were tightly rolled, then given to the customer. He or she wedged them into the outer wall or under the floors of the intended victim's house. In A.D. 19, the famous case of the sudden death of Germanicus, heir to the Roman Empire, revolved around a cache of curse-tablets, blood-smeared ashes, and other skin-crawling props found under his floorboards.

For curses to work properly, customers took their purchases to a temple dedicated to the appropriate underworld deity, then used bronze nails to attach them to the walls or the altar. Archaeologists have found masses of these curse-tablets and nails in ancient sanctuaries from England to Carthage.

As if living enemies weren't enough to cope with, at times Greek and Roman customers had quarrelsome family ghosts to placate or vampires to quell. On these dire occasions, the curse-tablet maker prepared special incantations to chant, along with figurines or tablets to dump into the family well or fountain. If the matter were dead serious—or worse yet, seriously undead—the professional often gave on-site guidance for burying the malediction in the proper place, often with the body or the ashes.

Even the most carefree person knew that vampires and ghosts were nothing to trifle with. Accordingly, each May the Romans held a ghost-placating festival called Lemuria, where heads of household spat black beans at midnight and carried out other ritual measures to appease hostile spirits.

But what if you were tormented by unrequited love, revenge pangs, or an unwanted stalker? Love charms and anti-eros solutions were handled by another occult professional—the *saga* or wise woman. In concert with the wise woman, the customer sacrificed and prayed to the correct deity, then watched her prepare a red wax image and cast magical spells over it as the customer riddled the figure with pins or burned it with fire. For a higher fee, the wise woman would concoct fancier figurines, sealed into a pot. Customers with raging obsessions paid top drachma to get custom-made lead figures in miniature coffins, since it was generally believed that the more one paid, the nastier (or the more fulfilling) the outcome.

❖ ❖ ❖ ❖ **CRASSUS** ❖ ❖ ❖ ❖

The crassest Roman of all

Shady businessman, slimy politico, sleazy military figure—these epithets don't begin to describe the career of Marcus Licinius Crassus, who may have been Rome's most inglorious overachiever.

Around 95 B.C., Crassus saw that easy money could be made in real estate. Like a hyena, he followed Sulla, the politico gangster running Rome at the time. As Sulla exiled enemies and confiscated their properties, Crassus sold them—for maximus profits.

Mr C then started another astute business venture, using a team of five hundred slaves skilled at shoddy construction. When one of Rome's fires broke out, Crassus and crew showed up, offering to buy the red-hot properties and put out the flames; if owners hesitated, Crassus lowered his offer. Unsurprisingly, he got countless buildings at fire-sale prices, then rebuilt them on the cheap.

Before long, it was official: Crassus was the richest man in his world, his net worth: two hundred million sesterces. *

Enough of these light-hearted business ventures, he decided. Time to start investing in promising political figures. Among the loans he gave was a whopping sum to young Julius Caesar, who used it in his first political post to fund the most spectacular gladiator games and races yet seen in Rome.

During that era, a time of rough-and-tumble near-lawlessness, his fortune gave Crassus the wherewithal to raise and maintain his own army. Even he knew, however, that an army's not much use unless it can fight and plunder. As a result of much wheedling, Crassus finally got a crack at glory. After other generals failed, he was sent to smite Spartacus, the Thracian gladiator-slave who led the mammoth slave revolt of 72 B.C.

Oops, right away one of his subordinates lost a big battle with Spartacus, and a peeved Crassus decided to decimate his army's survivors. In case anyone's forgotten, decimation consisted of assembling the troops, then picking every tenth man and having them killed in a humiliating fashion in front of the rest.

Now quite subdued, Crassus's remaining armed forces had a bit of luck. Left in the lurch by lying pirates, Spartacus and his army of slaves couldn't flee Italy. Crassus corralled them on a peninsula, where Spartacus died in battle. The six thousand survivors of this battle probably wished they had fallen with Spartacus, since, to make a splash, Crassus had them crucified along 350 miles of the Appian Way into Rome. (He was always good at detail work; those crucified were neatly spaced, seventeen to the mile.)

Mr C held a couple of political offices, and even got to buddy around with Pompey and Caesar in a loose coalition called the First Triumvirate. It was fun,

---

* To put that sum into context, the annual military budget of Rome during the heyday of Crassus was five hundred million sesterces annually.

bullying the Senate into passing laws favorable to his business interests—but hang it all, Crassus still longed to out-glory everyone on the battlefield. His slaughter of the Spartacus band didn't really count, since they were slaves.

Despite Roman opposition, in 54 B.C. Crassus and his forty-four-thousand-man army attacked distant Parthia. The Parthians hadn't menaced Rome; but Crassus, now getting on a bit, thought they would be glorious opponents. Well, that part was true. Skilled Parthian archers shot his army to pieces. Crassus had his head cut off by their king, who poured melted gold into the mouth of the corpse.

What was left of Crassus was returned to Rome, where relieved survivors threw a well-attended funeral, complete with gladiator matches and distributions of raw meat (a nicely vulgar touch) to the populace.

❖ ACCUSATION SPECIALIST ❖
DENOUNCING DO-BADDERS, INVENTING THE REST

Thanks to our diet of movies, television, and paperback thrillers, stool pigeons are part of the global vocabulary. Eons earlier, however, the Romans proved themselves past masters of the fine art of snitching.

In the early centuries of imperial rule, there were several types of accusation specialists, the juiciest post being *delator* or public informer. After the delator denounced a citizen, he was paid by the emperor's right-hand man. His methods were simple. As Romans had said for ages, "*Audacter calumniare semper aliquid haeret*—Slander boldly, something always sticks." Fees varied according to the importance and/or sleaziness of the information, after which the accused would be brought to trial.

Sometimes greed galvanized high-status men into becoming informers. Nero's reign was infamous for the way men of rank ratted on their peers for a crack at their assets. In Emperor Domitian's day, one noted orator regularly squealed for pay—only pausing to write a touching memoir (self-published, of course) when his young son died.

At the Roman Senate, the delator was a familiar face. According to satire-writer Juvenal, whenever a delator sniffed out a miscreant who'd disobeyed a senatorial decree, he received half the amount the wrongdoer was fined.

Accusers called *quadruplatores* operated on a similar fee schedule; they either received twenty-five percent of the assets of whomever they successfully denounced, or four times the fine slapped onto the culprit. (The latter usually applied to illicit goings-on, like gambling or loan-sharking.)

A delator or quadruplator could earn extra coinage by working as a bounty hunter. For instance, if a murder occurred in a prominent family, and any of the house slaves fled before the inquest, the delator took action. He received a reward of five gold coins for each slave he nabbed, payable from the estate of the deceased.

Who could blame an emperor for hiring informers? After all, big spenders like Caligula often ran into budget crunches—and had an urgent need to empty the pockets of the newly dead. If no wealthy person had the courtesy to die on cue, the delator would sometimes bring charges against the living, often causing such havoc that the accused would commit suicide. Since the rich were warmly encouraged to will a big chunk of their estates to the emperor, that paved the way for an easy flow of assets into the imperial treasury—with a percentage for the delator.

Professional accusers found life delightful, relishing their power to frighten friends and subdue enemies. As a result, this career field became extremely crowded, forcing later emperors to punish a few. In the course of his duties, however, any halfway-competent informer could amass enough compromising details about his own emperor to serve as "insurance."

There must have been some good apples in the bunch, as author Lindsey Davis's wonderfully wry novels about private informer Marcus Didius Falco lead us to believe. Thanks to her vivid portrayals, we can envision a myriad Falcos, busy with investigation assignments, undercover work, and what amounted to law enforcement in an era without a professional cadre of police.

But rotten apples, together with corrupt leaders willing to pay them for infamous deeds, were more likely the informer norm in ancient Rome.

❖ ❖ ❖ ❖ JULIA BALBILLA ❖ ❖ ❖ ❖
Poetic justice—or irony?

Before she got out of bed each morning, Julia Balbilla reviewed her dazzling family tree, starting with grandpa Claudius Balbillus, who'd been the prefect of Egypt. He didn't just sit on his sinecure, either; he'd served honorably as president of the Museum and Great Library of Alexandria. Grandpa Claudius was a real antiquities buff. He was the first person in ages to sweep away the sand around the Sphinx. Partially uncovered it, too.

Great-granddad Antiochus added more luster to her reputation, being the last king of Commagne (not that anyone knew where Commagne was, but social climbers were easily impressed). Thrasyllus, her other grandfather, had likewise run the Museum and been a top-notch astrologer—not just any old horoscope jock but the personal sky reader to Emperor Tiberius. He'd even managed to survive the querulous Tiberius. Then there was daddy, known as Balbillus the Wise, and her late brother Philopappus, a king in exile who'd made tight friends with Hadrian, the current emperor.

She hadn't done badly herself. Fabulous education, knew all the Sappho lyrics by heart, hung out with the imperial inner circle—and best friend of the empress! The Empress Sabina needed friends—anyone could see that her husband Hadrian was a waste of time, emotionally. Poor naïve Sabina; Julia

didn't have the heart to tell her that Hadrian's heart, and other parts, were smitten by the smooth young men he was seen with from time to time.

She, Julia B., was the court poet in residence. And oh, the perks, from dining daily at the palace to getting first claim on Sabina's silk castoffs. The travel benefits were unreal. As Rome's roving diplomat, the emperor traveled incessantly, with a huge entourage. And he almost always brought his wife, which meant Julia as well.

They'd already spent two years touring Greece, Asia Minor, and Syria. Now in the fall of A.D. 130 they were in Egypt—one of her favorite places to remind everyone about her aristocratic kin.

She and Sabina were on cloud nine. From their luxury ship on the Nile they'd already gone twice to the Colossi of Memnon, the great statues that sometimes "sang" as the dawn sun hit them. Julia had composed several poems about herself (including lines about the imperials, of course) in Aeolic verse, which were being hacked into the foot of the statues by a stone mason.

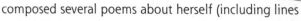

The only gloomy note was the emperor; depressed, still sulking because his erotic favorite, Antinoos, had somehow drowned in the Nile. When he finished mourning, maybe Sabina would stand a chance of having a real marriage.

Even with astrologers in her family, it's doubtful Julia B. could have foreseen Hadrian's future—or her own legacy. The possible murder of the vanished Antinoos would remain one of history's juiciest unsolved mysteries. The subsequent deification of the boy by the distraught emperor would become one of history's absurdities. The disappearance of untold works of great literature and poetry from the ancient world would remain one of history's ironies—especially since the four insipid poems of Julia Balbilla would survive into the twenty-first century, clearly visible amid the "I was here" graffiti on the famed statues of Memnon.

❖ FULLER ❖

NO TREAT TO BEAT HIS FEET

Who had the ancient world's nastiest, smelliest jobs? Some would nominate the tanner, who routinely used quantities of urine and dung to prepare hides for leather.

But the occupation that got everyone's vote for rankest was the fuller, the drycleaner and laundryman of ancient Rome and Greece. Romans had the fanciest baths ever known to man, but darn it, they'd forgotten to invent soap. To make matters worse, for centuries they refused to acknowledge that German barbarians produced soap and found it very handy.

Instead, fullers had to make do with stale urine combined with potash to clean wool cloth and garments. For more delicate fibers, such as cotton and linen, workers mixed urine and fuller's earth (an absorbent clay) to degrease the fabric.

Recycling urine was a familiar concept to the Romans and Greeks. Passers-by (one might well call them pissers-by) stopped to discharge their bladders into large clay pots, conveniently located on street corners, at urinals, and near the fullers' operation. The one place you wouldn't whiff such a pot? At taverns. Fullers, being connoisseurs of urine, knew that what came out of a drinker was poor-quality pee—too low in nitrogen to clean properly.

In the fulling process, barefoot workers wearing short tunics first soaked the cloth in the ammoniac mixture of the first tub, then stomped the garments or yardage clean with their feet. (The stomach quakes at what fullers' feet smelled like at the end of the day.) Vats were narrow to allow the fullers to lean onto the sides while they jumped. Their vigorous motions were called *saltus fullonicus*—the fuller's dance—and it's thought that they often "danced" to live music provided by the management.

After cleaning, garments were wrung out by hand. It took several men to wring one wool toga for drying, since they measured up to ten by twenty feet.

Citizens of lower rank wore togas made of natural wool; candidates for office traditionally arrayed themselves in *candidus* or snowy-white togas. To get those bright whites, the fullers bleached the wool further by hanging the toga over a wicker hemisphere. Under it they placed a fuming pot of burning sulfur for several hours, then rescrubbed the wool in fuller's earth. After drying, garments got carded to raise the nap, then smoothed in a screw press to give the customer an unwrinkled article.

As if they didn't have enough workplace hazards, fullers had to watch out for fires. If mishandled, garments treated with lime and sulfur could burst into flame, especially if stored in sealed containers. On more than one occasion, cargo ships carrying quantities of clean cloaks met a spectacular end after bursting into flame at sea.

Few Greeks or Romans had the fortitude to wash or clean clothes at home; we can readily see why.

❖ ❖ ❖ ❖ FELICISSIMUS ❖ ❖ ❖ ❖

Destined to make money

His mom knew he'd do well; after all, she'd named him Felicissimus ("the most fortunate"). And here he was, chief of the state treasury, the go-to guy in charge of every imperial mint worker in Rome.

He'd been fortunate in his bosses. Big turnover in emperors: plague, assassination, you name it. Aurelian, his latest, was an absentee ruler, busy fighting Vandals, Goths, and that outlandish Zenobia, the Palmyran queen who'd told Rome to shove it.

Felicissimus loved his work. He loved his office in the temple of Juno Moneta, the mint on Caelian Hill. He loved putting his own name on certain coin issues. His idea of a great evening was to go and gaze at the newest batch of money.

His mint produced millions of coins, so many that it had been child's play to dilute the mix, debase the silver with a dab of copper, a soupçon of lead. A quick bath in acid, and the coin blanks looked like pure silver again. And who did it hurt? The slightly debased coins were readily accepted. His workers—the die engravers, the furnace stokers, the hammermen—were content; he'd made sure of that by letting them pocket a bit of bullion now and then. A happy crew was a hard-working crew, he always said.

All the while, his own honors and personal wealth grew, befitting his elevated status. He hung out with senators; he was on a first-name basis with the head Vestal.

Life was as perfect as a newly minted sesterce. But what's this? A rumor of house-cleaning at the mint? A threat to his status quo? Ye gods, Aurelian's back in town.

The imperial reprimand hit Felicissimus like a lightning bolt. Time to show this upstart of an emperor who really ran Rome! By Juno, he'd lead an uprising of his fraudulent fellow coinmakers.

The men responded to his rallying speech in the most heartening way. In a flash, they closed the mint and hit the streets. Before long, they'd taken the Caelian Hill district for their own.

When the first wave of soldiers stormed them, Felicissimus shuddered. His fear soon turned to amazement: why, his mint workers were natural-born killers! Blood ran in the streets, and the monetary resources of the Empire were theirs. Their triumph widened further after a couple of Roman senators joined in.

Emperor Aurelian ordered in more troops, but the marvelously murderous money men went through them like butter. After the victory, Felicissimus got to count the bodies of seven thousand soldiers, which made a nice change from coin-counting.

Felicissimus had several weeks of sheer happiness before a Roman officer managed to slay him. With him gone, the rebellion died also.

His stunning gesture and the unprecedented mutiny of his workers forced the Roman mint to shut down in amazement for several years. Not until A.D. 274 did an exasperated Emperor Aurelian begin monetary reform—or find enough skilled workers to turn out coinage that would ring true at the proper weight and purity.

❖ AUCTIONEER ❖
GOING ONCE, GOING TWICE—
THE ROMAN EMPIRE

E-bayers, eat your hearts out—the most colossal auction ever held already took place a while ago. Eighteen centuries, to be precise.

That's when two crazed Romans with more money than brains started outbidding each other for a prize that almost no one else coveted: the job of Roman Emperor. One of these dumbos was Flavius Sulpicianus, the father-in-law of barely cold Emperor Pertinax, who'd been axed (literally) after eighty-seven days in office by his own mutinous troops. The other dimwit was a senator and former governor with the moniker of Marcus Severus Didius Julianus.

The ad-hoc auction began when the two hopefuls presented themselves at the camp of the Praetorian Guards, where the real power lay in the second century A.D. Because they weren't allowed inside, the thwarted rivals started shouting out numbers to the troops. The numbers in question? How much each was willing to pay as a "donative" (read: a windfall bribe often given by incoming emperors to ensure Praetorian "loyalty").

Sulpicianus hollered out a figure in the low ten thousands; Julianus raised him. Before long, the ante was up to twenty thousand sesterces per soldier, offered by Sulpicianus. Then came a long ominous silence as Julianus frantically worked his abacus. Finally he countered with a shriek: "My final offer—twenty-five thousand per man!" (The annual salary for a typical soldier in that era was about twelve hundred sesterces.)

Auction concluded: the Roman Empire, a stretch of real estate the size of the United States, was sold to the highest bidder on March 28, A.D. 193—all without the help of a professional auctioneer!

Except for rare occasions like this one, professionals normally ran auctions. The *argentarius* or money man organized the event, which began when his assistant, the *magister auctionarium*, drove a spear into the ground—a tradition recalling the centuries when auctions were held immediately after a battle on the field of war.

The man doing the vocals was the *praeco* or town crier. Announcing the conditions of sale beforehand, he called out the bids, jollied the crowd, and engaged in that double-time patter so beloved of auctioneers and attendees.

Public sales of goods were held for estates of those who died, or to satisfy debts, with auctioneers taking a reasonable one to two percent of the gross. Auctions also became a popular way to dispose of sticky items like war booty. Because they dealt in various levels of sleaze with sometimes-dubious clients, including slavers, the occupation was considered disreputable. Auctioneers couldn't hold public office, but shady dealings didn't bother most.

Then there were eager beavers like Caecilius Jucundus of Pompeii. Thanks to short-term loans that he extended to dozens of auction buyers, he metamorphosed into a small-time banker. His transactions, from a modest spot of slave-dealing to some thirty-thousand-sesterce deals on wheat, allowed him to buy his way into politer society. The vagaries of chance let his working files, hundreds of documents, survive the A.D. 79 destruction of his home town.

Oh, yes, about the biggest auction ever held: it cost the senator-made-Roman-Emperor a mere 175 million sesterces. Julianus held the imperial office for sixty-six days, after which he was executed by order of the new improved emperor Septimus Septimius Severus—a man clever enough to get himself proclaimed Caesar without a bidding war.

❖ ❖ ❖ ❖ **ROSCIUS** ❖ ❖ ❖ ❖

Like Clint Eastwood, only shorter

Among the Romans, acting was an infamous career. One beloved exception? Quintus Roscius Gallus, Rome's most adored thespian and first superstar.

To study his craft, as a youth Roscius hung around the courtrooms where orators and lawyers tried cases. He copied their most eloquent gestures, imitated their smoothest segues, and stole their best jokes. Hortentius, a distinguished advocate, was his role model.

On stage, Roscius became known for pert grace and nimble, loose-limbed movements, used to hilarious effect in the comedies he made famous. He had a natural squint, which probably helped. His voice was melodious and carried well, important because dramas and comedies alike were declaimed to a musical background. Acting parts were also singing roles, and this man was one of the best.

By age thirty, Roscius had it made, bringing in star-spangled fees and running things as the manager of his own troupe. Although teaching wasn't his favorite offstage activity, he gave elocution lessons to a favored few. One was a gifted teen named Cicero, who became his friend, his entrée into aristocratic society, and, in 66 B.C., his legal defender.

Roscius took on another pupil, a slave called Panurgus whose owner had approached him and said, "Teach this youngster the art of acting, and we'll share his future earnings." Roscius groomed him for acting success, and the slave showed promise—but then the kid got killed somehow. Actor Roscius immediately sued the killer (slave deaths weren't capital cases) on the grounds that he had increased his pupil's value 150-fold. His eloquent patter won the case; he was awarded a farm worth a mint. Then, however, the legal fur really began to fly. The boy's owner sued the actor for not splitting the farm award, at which point orator-advocate Cicero came to the rescue.

Cicero won the case for Roscius, partly because it became apparent that the plaintiff had already sued the killer himself and gotten damages—and you think modern court trials are a zoo!

232

The friendship between Roscius and the orator grew; Cicero attended his performances and quoted him in letters to friends. At chichi parties, the actor mingled with the likes of Catullus the poet and the top man himself, the dictator Sulla.

This led to greater things: in 81 B.C. Sulla gave Roscius a gold ring. An erotic declaration from a dictator fan, perhaps? Way better: this ring was the symbol of the actor's new status as an *equite* or knight—the equivalent of Paul McCartney getting dubbed Sir by Queen Elizabeth.

As well-heeled as McCartney in buying power, Roscius in his mature years continued to act on occasion, but preferred less strenuous roles with more leisurely singing. In his long career, Roscius gave memorable performances as both comic and tragic leads. His favorite parts, however, were portrayals of the common man—or in drag, the common woman—especially fishermen, slaves, maidservants, parasites, and pimps. When asked why, he said impishly, "Lots of scope for innuendo."

❖ TEN ❖

DOOMED CAREERS & DEATHLESS PURSUITS

❖ ORGY PLANNER ❖
MUST HAVE PEOPLE SKILLS, HANDS-ON STYLE

Although ad-hoc offers like "Hot chicks want to party" covered tavern walls from Corinth to Capri, insider posts like orgy planner were rarely advertised.

Ad-lib chaos and sexual free-for-all weren't the hallmarks of an orgy; these events were meticulously planned—by religious figures, no less. The word "orgy" originally meant secret rites or mysteries.

The events calendar for the goddess Cybele, for example, was put together by its priests. This cult sprang to life in Phrygia, later spreading throughout Greece and Italy. Uninhibited dancing to jazzy double-pipes, coupled with wine consumption and coupling, let everyone reach that sweet state called mania.

The Greeks also invented the Dionysiac mysteries, later co-opted by the Romans and called the Bacchanalia. Bacchantes had to surrender to frenzy, which often got out of hand—a result spelling success to an orgy planner, but frowned on by Romans who weren't invited.

234

In 186 B.C., the Senate banned the drunken, come-as-your-favorite-satyr Bacchanalia from Italy and put hundreds of members to death. Undeterred, the cult went underground. Some archaeologists believe that Bacchantes used Pompeii's famous Villa of the Mysteries for their blowouts.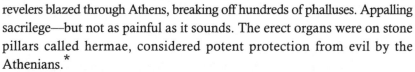

Private orgies sometimes ended badly. At the height of one free-for-all, the bisexual general and turncoat Alcibiades and his drunken revelers blazed through Athens, breaking off hundreds of phalluses. Appalling sacrilege—but not as painful as it sounds. The erect organs were on stone pillars called hermae, considered potent protection from evil by the Athenians.*

Dionysus the Younger, who'd inherited the top tyrant job on Sicily, loved a good orgy with himself as centerpiece. Whenever he headed home to Locris, he ordered up masses of wild thyme, roses, and stark-naked virgins, piled onto the beds of the biggest house in the city. Once there and in the buff, he worked his way through the alphabet of girls and positions, causing maddened fathers in due course to abduct the tyrant's wife and kids for orgy payback time. Not satisfied with pedophilia and spousal humiliation, the vengeful dads drove needles under the innocent victims' fingernails before putting them to death.

Once Romans got into orgy planning, Greek mischief paled by comparison. Messalina, wife of Emperor Claudius, once carried out a four-day orgy that got great reviews—until she lost her head and married a fellow orgiast, shortly thereafter losing her head again—this time to the ax (Claudius not being best pleased with her carryings-on). Your average Roman citizen couldn't hope to be invited to such goings-on, but they got plenty of vicarious orgy thrills. As they went about their daily lives, they were entertained, appalled, and/or stimulated by the wealth of porn and explicit sex acts painted on public walls and buildings.

---

* Herm statues, much reverenced by locals, sat everywhere in Athens; at doors of private houses, in gardens, at crossroads, near temples, libraries, and gymnasia. Usually bearing the head of the god Hermes (Roman Mercury) with an erect phallus below it, the stone or marble pillars were thought to be fertility-givers and luck-bringers. Some sculptors specialized in hermae; in fact, the nickname for sculptors in general was "herm carver."

Rome's star orgy planner was Gaius Petronius Arbiter, whose panache and wit made him adored by Emperor Nero. Petronius even threw orgies while writing the *Satyricon,* his satire about Roman debauchery. More than most, he understood his decadent countrymen's biggest fear: the death of desire. To Nero and his crowd, sex was like cocaine—each time requiring a stronger, kinkier dose.

Pandering to Nero's growing habit while expressing his own creativity was a tricky balancing act. Eventually, Petronius fell from favor and was ordered to commit suicide. Ever the party boy, he pulled together what might be called a death orgy. First he did a mass mailing of Nero's most despicable deeds. Paperwork attended to, Petronius then luxuriated in a hot bath, surrounded by friends, and drank wine, prolonging his exit by opening his own veins, then binding them.

He was soon replaced on the job by a gifted sadist named Tigellinus, a man with a towering talent for abominations. At the December Saturnalia and in July of A.D. 64, he threw a series of talked-about orgies in the Basin of Agrippa, complete with daisy-chain sex, maidenhead plucking by gladiators, extreme degradation of the high-ranking by Nero himself, plus the morbid bonus of accidental deaths by rose-petal smothering.

After that success, Tigellinus had to top himself with some new insult to humanity. A few days later, when the Great Fire of 64 burned down most of Rome, he (and, secondarily, Nero) became a prime suspect, especially when the blaze came to life again in Mr T's gardens! Nevertheless, Tigellinus remained the emperor's prime producer of perversity until A.D. 68, when he abandoned Nero to his fate as swiftly as ditching a wallflower at an orgy.

❖ PARASITE ❖

LIKE A LOUSE, ONLY BIGGER

When Greeks held a symposium or drinking party, everyone chipped in. Everyone, that is, except the professional parasites. Like frequent flyers, only a certain number of parasites could be accommodated on each occasion.

Parasiting was no job for sissies. You had to possess at least one clean robe or toga, along with a generous store of quips, one-liners, and salacious gossip. A talent for extemporaneous verse was very desirable. A parasite

couldn't gobble his food, drink too much, or fondle the prettier dinner slaves. He had to keep his eyes and ears open, ready to deliver a perfect thrust or a jocular sally to make the company laugh or nod approvingly.

In Greek times, the most sought-after parasites were male poets and philosophers. Witty female philosophers were also in demand—women like Hipparchia, who never kicked in a dime at symposia and thus could be considered both a parasite and a cynic, since she and her husband Crates were leaders of that philosophical school.

Rome was rife with parasites too. Marcus Martial, the slyest wit in first-century-A.D. Rome, was well-educated, a would-be lawyer from northern Spain who came to the capital to devote his life to poetry and sucking up. Cultivating wealthy patrons who each paid him a lousy "retainer fee," Martial regaled guests at their dinners with his signature epigrams: short, candid, often naughty and/or surprising verses. This man, who called himself and others "toga'd little parasites," became celebrated enough that publisher-booksellers sometimes paid to be the first to copy his newest book. Although given privileges and goodies by two emperors, his decades on the parasitic circuit took their toll. Martial returned to his boyhood home, only to find its idyllic country life a dead bore.

Most but not all poets massaged egos to stay solvent. The towering exception? Sappho, born in the seventh century B.C. and idolized as "the Tenth Muse" for millennia. Her poetic talents were formidable; moreover, she could have chosen to live off her well-to-do family on Lesbos. Instead, she had the get-up-and-go to establish her own sort of school, accepting female students from all around the Med and charging them top-whack fees for mentoring them in music, poetry, composition, and other arts. She also got commissions to write wedding songs and had protégées like Damophila, who traveled five hundred miles from Asia Minor to study with Sappho.

Imitation being the easiest form of flattery, several of Rome's famed poet-parasites, notably Catullus, saw fit to pay homage to Sappho's work by stealing it. The twelve lines of Catullus's most famous poem, "That man seems to me to be equal to a god," are blatant but sadly clunky copies of fragment 31 of Sappho's love poetry.

This particular parasite paid for his hubris in other ways. Although his often-obscene verse was the toast of 50 B.C. Rome, his personal life was Hades, caught for years in the harpy's embrace of a charismatic, sleep-around lover named Clodia.

❖ CRYPTOLOGIST ❖

INSTANT MESSAGING, BETA VERSION

A staple of thrillers and spy movies, code-breaking had its origins long before the Da Vinci era.

The Greeks adored secret messages, cryptic oracles, and ambiguous notes. Sparta in particular was charmed by them. You remember Sparta, the totalitarian and militaristic little city-state known for appalling cuisine and its quaint use of iron rods instead of coinage. The city-state had sixty thousand serfs, called *helots*, to work the land so that the real Spartans could turn their attention to more important things. Like secret messages.

If you were a sixth-century puzzle-meister, you might very well get hired as a cryptologist, since the military was very keen. Along with hot water and other basic comforts, the Spartans lacked computers. Nevertheless, their cryptologists kept busy, dreaming up non-electronic ways to send code.

One concocted a cunning method of transmitting top-secret updates in the field using a transposition cipher. To make his device, the cryptologist rounded up a wooden baton plus a few strips of leather left over from making the last batch of cat o'nine tails. Attaching the leather to one end of the wood, he rolled it tightly at an angle to cover the baton.

The device, called a *skytale,* could now be loaded with data. All a general had to do was dictate "Help! I'm getting killed here!" and the cryptologist quickly wrote each word in a series of rows on the leather. Message written, the leather was taken off the baton and belted around the waist of some hapless field messenger, who shot off to deliver it at top speed.

At the other end, provided the messenger survived, another eager general grabbed the fellow, removed his belt, rewound the leather around his own identical baton, read the secret cipher, then launched a rescue mission or laughed heartily, depending on his relationship with the other general.

Sometimes the cryptologist used strips of papyrus to make the cipher; its appearance, however, was a dead giveaway if the Spartan messenger got caught—in which case the unfortunate would be forced to eat the message. Given the food the Spartans regularly consumed, including their infamous black broth, made from pig's blood and vinegar, chewing a hunk of papyrus might have been viewed as an exotic low-cal treat.

❖ TOWN CRIER ❖

THE CRYING GAME

The Greeks liked their news updates to be audible, so town criers found steady employment everywhere, from Crete to Corfu. As Plato once wrote, "The ideal polis or city-state should be no bigger than the distance a crier's voice can carry." Most of the hundred or more Greek city-states were towns rather than sprawling urban centers. Athens itself, including its slaves, may have exceeded one hundred thousand, but as a city it was compact, only fifteen minutes' walk from any quarter to the central agora.

Besides iron lungs, a town crier needed the ability to shout it out in all kinds of weather. On a crier's typical round, his sound-bites included births, deaths, and misdemeanors. He also shouted out the lost-and-found items, which are fun to imagine. "Mrs Socrates says that a wheelbarrow of feta and her husband have gone missing—again." As part of his job, the crier had to help search for lost items, husbands included.

At public assemblies and trials, both frequent in quarrelsome Athens, the crier acted as bailiff, summoning plaintiffs and defendants and growling for silence. He also took the announcer's role in auctions.

To enhance his verbal communication in those unamplified times, the crier drew on *chironomia,* the laws of gesticulation also used by actors, orators, and demagogues. His rich vocabulary of gestures were as readable to his audience as sign language is to the hearing-impaired. (Greek and Italian cultures have preserved many of these eloquent hand signals, head tilts, and eye-rolls, which can be seen on TV series like *Rome, The Sopranos,* or almost any film about the Mafia.)

In later Roman times, the job of *praeco* gained more responsibilities. Criers circled neighborhoods, inviting the public to upcoming games and races; at their conclusion, they announced the victors. They quieted theater crowds at the beginnings of performances. During Roman elections, they called out the groups of citizens, called centuries, for their votes; later they gave the election results—and no exit-poll guesses, either.

While Senate laws and decrees were being voted on, the praeco recited them aloud. At the demise of a bigwig, he rattled off details about the funeral procession. This always drew a good crowd; no one, especially pickpockets and beggars, wanted to miss a really impressive parade and pyre.

At the end of a criminal trial, the praeco solemnly announced the punishment ordered by the magistrate to the lictors, the strong-arm chaps who would escort the guilty party to his fate.

Once a humble, somewhat marginal job, during the imperial centuries the crying game grew in stature. And remuneration. Criers collected their fees from the courts and official bodies. They also charged gladiatorial promoters, who hired them to bellow out the names of upcoming headliners.

Criers began to see sideline money, such as tips from grateful citizens united with missing husbands and other objects. And somewhere along the line, lovesick suitors discovered that if slipped something extra, criers would "announce" flowery messages to adored ones amid their usual patter.

In this fashion, well-networked criers rose to businessman status. A famous example was praeco Sextus Naevius, who got rich with his partner, then wrangled with his partner's heir over land sales; eventually his case was taken on by name-brand orator Cicero, who somehow managed to lose the verdict. Cicero's tediously lengthy argument survived to become an obligatory object of study by today's put-upon students of rhetoric.

Surprisingly, despite the advent of mass media and modern communications technology, the job of town crier still exists in many places in England. Usually dressed in a red topcoat and a quaint tricorn hat, these guys are wheeled out every now and again to keep the tourists happy, ringing their handbell and beginning their pronouncements with the words "Oyez, Oyez!"

❖ SYCOPHANT ❖
THE SECRET WORLD OF GREEK DATING

The tasty position of *sycophant* owed its origins to the thin rocky soil of Attica, the region surrounding Athens. Here nothing much grew well except olives and figs. The latter were a cherished crop, being sweet as well as nutritious. From the time of the lawgiver and reformer Solon, locals were forbidden to export figs, fresh or dried, from Attica—yet Greek islanders and even dullards like the Spartans would pay top drachma for them.

Who immediately sprang up to satisfy the foreign hunger for Attic figs? Fig smugglers, of course—and where there was smuggling, there was always going to be a job opportunity for informants.

They were called sycophants or "fig detectives." Sycophants were familiar figures in Greek courts, where they frequently gave testimony on the whereabouts of clandestine dried fruit. Cheered by their success, the sycophants expanded operations; by the fourth century B.C., they were stool-pigeoning and flinging false accusations on other matters.

Eventually the specialty of fig informer disappeared, and sycophant came to mean (as it does now) an everyday toady.

The pro informer industry grew exponentially, however, with none of the altruistic overtones of today's whistleblowers. Rewards to informers for successful convictions were in the order of two-thirds to three-quarters of the accused's property. With that kind of incentive, Athenian informers stood in line to squeal and deal.

❖ ❖ ❖ ❖ DEMOCEDES & MILO ❖ ❖ ❖ ❖
Meat-eaters & miracle men

As heavy events like wrestling gained favor in the ancient Olympics, more athletes turned to protein-rich diets, not to mention trainers to train them, and doctors to patch them up.

In the sixth century B.C., sports doctors like Democedes were rare. He came from Crotona, a Greek colony in southern Italy, where a philosophy founded by

241

Pythagoras of Samos held sway. Pythagoreanism was a way of life, whose followers practiced communal living and wellbeing through diet, meditation, and the healing powers of music and dance.

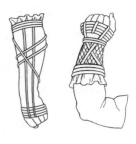

Dr D seemed to have it all: medical education, enthusiasm for athletes, and a deft touch at setting dislocated joints. His father was another story. To escape his ungovernable temper, Democedes fled to the Greek island of Aegina and worked as a doctor for a year. That city-state, delighted with his work, offered him six thousand drachmas for another contract. To capitalize on his newfound desirability, Democedes anticipated twentieth-century tactics and turned free agent. The following year, he squeezed ten thousand drachmas out of the Athenians. In year three, the tyrant who ruled the roost on the island of Samos paid twelve grand for Democedes' services.

Dr D had barely had time to savor his new tax bracket when Persian troops captured Samos, taking him captive as a slave in the court of King Darius. Things looked black until the Persian king took a fall and screwed up his ankle something rotten. After working his magic on the injury, Democedes went from slave to hero—still captive, though.

Call it physician's luck: one of the king's wives fell ill with an abscess in her breast. Before curing her, a harder hearted Democedes extracted a promise from his patient to help him escape. After numerous adventures, Democedes made it back to Crotona (dear old psychotic dad had gone to Hades by now)

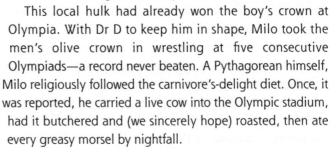

and married the daughter of a superstar wrestler named Milo.

This local hulk had already won the boy's crown at Olympia. With Dr D to keep him in shape, Milo took the men's olive crown in wrestling at five consecutive Olympiads—a record never beaten. A Pythagorean himself, Milo religiously followed the carnivore's-delight diet. Once, it was reported, he carried a live cow into the Olympic stadium, had it butchered and (we sincerely hope) roasted, then ate every greasy morsel by nightfall.

Like other top athletes, Milo competed at the other three Great Games, called the circuit. He won thirty-one circuit victories, the first to do so. "I was never brought to my knees," he boasted, since that counted as a fall in wrestling.

After retiring, Milo showed that he was more than just an aging mountain of muscle. In 510 B.C., the Crotonian led his home city's army to victory over rival city-state Sybaris.

Then he could relax and enjoy old age with his daughter and son-in-law Democedes, petting the grandkids, drinking wine, and knocking back a fatted calf or two.

Or maybe not. As legend has it, after Milo tried to split a tree trunk with his bare hands and feet, it trapped him—and he became the carnivore's delight for a pack of wolves.

❖ OLYMPIC JUDGE ❖

SECOND & THIRD DIDN'T EVEN COUNT

The ground rules of the ancient Olympics were drawn up by a committee of law-codifiers, but the professionals who really ran things were ten stalwarts called *Hellanodikai,* or "judges of the Greeks." For this honorary, unpaid post, they were selected by lottery from the prominent men of Elis, the city-state home of the Olympic Games. For three months, they worked their tails off.

To begin with, they sent out heralds announcing the ninety-day sacred truce; if a city-state broke the peace, its athletes were banned and their home city fined. Spartans got hit by a fine in 420 B.C. for fighting, and the money they were forced to cough up was enough to purchase six thousand oxen.

For thirty days prior to the Games, the judges oversaw the competitors in Elis, organizing trial heats and dictating how they trained and what they ate. Latecomers were disqualified unless their excuse was superb. (Most excuses weren't.) With the athletes properly cowed, the judges led them on a fifty-eight-kilometer hike to Olympia, at midway point doing a ritual cleansing and pig sacrifice.

Once at Olympia, the judges wiped off the pork grease, put on lush purple togs, divided up the events, had the official discuses and javelins brought out, and began to referee. Most of the time, they eyeballed it from the judges' stand. For five days, they called the shots, settled the rare disputes over ties, and declared the first-place winners. Second and third got no recognition at all.

On day five, they presented the olive-branch crowns. Occasionally they had erring athletes whipped for fouls, training violations, or bribery attempts. (Illegal substances? No culprits recorded; if there had been, those judges would have scourged the dickens out of them.)

During the Olympics' thousand-year history few judges were ever accused of corruption. But when they took a dive, they did it Olympic-sized. Take that horrible year when a certain ghastly Roman, loaded with wishful thinking but minimal talent, sashayed over to Greece to compete. For starters, he changed the 111th Olympiad from the year A.D. 65 to 67. Why? Because, as Emperor Nero, he could. With dread, the judges watched as he drove his ten-horse chariot, fell off midway through, was helped to remount, but failed to finish. Having already received their plump 250,000-coin bribe, the judges wearily declared him winner anyway. They were quite thankful when Nero ended up dead a year later and they could declare that Olympiad invalid, striking the monster's name from the victors' list. Only one dark cloud: Galba, new skinflint emperor of Rome, demanded repayment.

With the exception of the almost-forgivable Nero incident, Olympic judges were public-spirited individuals. Besides donating their judging labors, these men were expected to help subsidize their particular Olympic Games. Judges picked up the tab for slave staff, incidentals for the processions, and a vast amount of oil for the athletes, plus those all-important fees for the whipping staff.

Olympic Games spectators paid nothing to attend. With no gate receipts, costs were shouldered instead by well-to-do families in Olympia's home territory, the Elis public treasury, and the ten Hellanodikai themselves. Millennia later, such philanthropy sounds unheard-of, doesn't it?

❖ FAST-FOOD ENTREPRENEUR ❖

WANNA SUPERSIZE THAT PORRIDGE?

Fast food is everywhere nowadays, but we're just aping a business model used with success by the Greeks and Romans of long ago.

Purveyors of takeaway got their start at early festivals like the week-long Olympic Games, where thousands of hungry, thirsty competitors and spectators camped out during the events.

More permanent emporia soon flourished in population centers like Athens and Corinth. These ramshackle establishments, nicknamed "eyelids" because their doors opened and closed with such frequency, were usually run by freedmen or resident aliens.

Although ancient writers spent an inordinate amount of time raving about symposia, the dinner-and-drinks parties held by high-status males, most Greeks lived on simpler fare, spruced up with fresh herbs or sauces: leek soup, barley porridge, beans, seafood, bread, honey, olives, plus figs, grapes, and other fruit.

Throughout the Roman world, hot spots served a mix of mulled wine, water, and spices in vessels like this one. Inside, it has a heat source.

Many homes lacked cooking facilities (a state of affairs still true in twentieth-century Athens, where housewives carried one-dish stews to neighborhood bakeries for cooking each morning). As a consequence, the eyelid shop selections provided real value. Even a frugal philosopher could afford a cheap, cheese-filled octopus on a skewer.

Rome, and later its subject cities and towns around the empire, took to fast food with enthusiasm. For some it was necessity. By the era of Emperor Augustus, Roman neighborhoods were crowded with *insulae,* high-rise apartment blocks made possible by the invention of concrete and occupied by families from all walks of life. Developers, citing fire danger but focused on profit, built insulae without kitchens or running water. Consequently, most Romans had to rely on food shops. These small businesses spread everywhere, including around the public baths, where walk-about hawkers shouted their wares, from lettuce wraps to lizard-fish.

Fast food also caught on in towns without high-rises. Processed snacks and greasy takeaway became addictive conveniences from Ephesus to Roman Britain.

The fast-food joints called *popinae* were simple table-and-stool affairs, with terracotta pots embedded in their countertops. Here the proprietors served up sturdy dishes, from lentils to barley porridge. Manual laborers needing cheap, calorie-rich meals frequented the popinae. One favorite was libum bread, enriched with cheese and eggs.

Many owners of the *thermopolii* (the slightly classier "hot spots") had started their careers as bakers, the most complex form of cooking, before opening shop as entrepreneurs. Thermopolii also served hot drinks and attracted all social classes. Hot-spot menus, sometimes carved in marble and posted outside, offered items like grilled sausages, roasted chicken, fish, ham, and *ofellae,* a cheesy forerunner of pizza. One optimistic entrepreneur even posted peacock on his "for dinner" suggestions.

Like the Greeks, Romans craved a tang of spice on their food—and got it in *garum,* the granddaddy of Worcestershire sauce, which they splashed on everything.

Ultimately, the places run by the pioneers of fast-food takeaway became social centers. In their ruins, archaeologists have found poignant clues of daily life: tables with permanent gaming boards; names of wait-persons; political adverts; and, on some walls, the scrawled payment records of a local loan shark. In Pompeii, researchers even found the till of a hot spot, holding over a thousand coins. They're believed to be the day's receipts for August 23, A.D. 79, left behind by those desperate to escape the volcanic eruption that buried the city.

❖ LIBRARIAN ❖

BOOK BROWSING, YES. CHECKOUT? NO WAY.

Librarians of long ago had street cred. Their scholarship and expertise were sought after—and the pay, thanks to generous stipends, was great.

By today's collection standards, outlawry reigned. Acquisition librarians at larger libraries had the guilt-free thrill of winnowing through mountains of literary plunder, taken from the defeated. Stolen goods and a few new purchases: that's how the great libraries of Antioch, Pergamum, Athens, and Rhodes built their collections.

Ptolemy, ruler of the ultra-busy port city of Alexandria and founder of its Museum and Great Library, had an even edgier philosophy. On his orders,

Demetrios, the first head librarian, confiscated books arriving by ship. All ships, and every single scroll and tome. After each new title had been copied, Demetrios took the copy to the ship's captain, gleefully whisking the original into its new home.

Each book, composed of one or more scrolls, was housed in one of ten library halls. A nonstop acquirer and noted scholar, Demetrios amassed about a quarter of a million scrolls during his twenty-two-year tenure; he also seems to have set up the first gift shop, where he had copies of popular works made and sold to visitors.

Julius Caesar, an avid reader and writer, had an "oops" moment in Alexandria; in 47 B.C., during a street battle between his troops and locals, he set fire to the library's warehouses. To make amends for turning forty thousand volumes into ash, Caesar planned a library for Rome; but his plans were cut short, so to speak. Still, after his assassination, up went the edifice. Not to be outdone, Emperor Augustus built two. Later emperors installed them inside the great public bath complexes, naming the whole works after themselves.

This whole notion of keeping librarians employed became a sine qua non for any legacy-hungry emperor. Luxurious libraries arose from Timgad, North Africa, to Halicarnassus on Turkey's coast. Even after the Romans ground Carthage into pebbles, they apologetically built a fine library in the flattened city. Smaller places, like the island of Cos, also set up libraries. Affluent citizens chipped in to build it and start a book-purchase fund.

Librarians of long ago didn't have to do checkout. Books didn't circulate—in-library use was it. That was why the Museum and Great Library of Alexandria also housed and fed a corps of scholars and scientists in adjacent quarters.

The wealthy had swanky private libraries, some of which are still turning up in Italy and elsewhere. Private collections had separate wings for Greek and Latin books, the scrolls making up each book organized in leather boxes called *capsae*.

One bookwormish fellow picked a grandiose library project to honor his dead father, who'd had a prominent career as governor of Asia Minor. Celsus just brimmed with character and good judgment—at least that's what his admiring son said.

City officials at Ephesus must have agreed. In the year 110, they let the adoring son begin to build the library—then bury his dad right on-site! Bodies or ashes weren't usually planted in such places, being both a sacrilege and a sanitation no-no. The twelve-thousand-book edifice turned out splendidly and is still called the Library of Celsus. Although over-fastidious tour guides at Ephesus rarely mention Celsus or his presence underfoot, the gigantic statues personifying the dead man's virtues can still be seen.

❖ ❖ ❖ ❖ CALLIMACHUS ❖ ❖ ❖ ❖

Ancient librarian action figure

Early librarians were full of derring-do. When the Romans over-ran Greece in 168 B.C., the head librarian of neutral Pergamum led a diplomatic embassy to Rome to keep his library from destruction—and sow the seeds of literacy while he was at it.

It worked—with unintended consequences. Literacy, even if it was in Greek, became cool. After five hundred years without a library, Rome now encouraged its generals to bring back libraries as booty. (The most despicable book-thief? Dictator-General Sulla, who ripped off Aristotle's library after capturing Athens, along with thousands of art pieces and other glitter.)

But the man voted super-librarian was Callimachus, second director of the Museum and Great Library of Alexandria. The Museum (literally, home of the Muses), a grand edifice housing scholars and research facilities, possessed two libraries. The annex, created when the larger building ran out of room, was inside the Serapeum, Alexandria's most famous temple.

Poet and native son of the Greek colony of Cyrene, Callimachus gravitated early to the cultural ferment of Alexandria, ruled by culture-loving rulers Ptolemy I through III. Between stints as a teacher, Callimachus socialized with the palace crowd and in time was offered the post of head librarian.

Challenges for modern librarians today tend to be fiscal. Not so Callimachus; the ghastly task he took on was organizational. Card catalog? None. Filing system, shelving categories? Forget it. All those thousands of books were written on identical papyrus scrolls; most books took up more than one scroll. No titles, just a label

Callimachus had half a million of these papyrus puppies to count—and organize—at the Great Library in Alexandria, Egypt.

tag attached with the first few words of the book. The place must have looked like the blueprint storage area for a dynasty of neatness-phobic architects.

Clearly the party was over; Callimachus set to work. After spending years and a ruinous amount of eyesight, this prince among librarians produced a document called the *Tables of the Outstanding Works in the Whole of Greek Culture and Their Authors,* thankfully called *Pinakes* for short. His opus filled 120 scrolls and divided the collection into eight groups. It didn't approach Dewey-decimal sophistication, but it fitted the bill, allowing researchers to locate books before they died of starvation in the stacks.

His catalog registered each book's title, the number of lines it held, the first words of the book, an author bio, a summary of the contents, and more. These painstaking labors won Callimachus the title of "father of the bibliography"—and the everlasting gratitude of writers and researchers ever since.

Thanks to this steadfast librarian and his labor of love (let's hope he had re-shelving help!), the eggheads at the Museum and Great Library finally learned how many books they had—42,800 at the annex and just under half a million at the big library, not including duplicates.

Posterity, however, had the last guffaw. When Callimachus died around 235 B.C., he left his catalog and the numerous books he'd written to the library. After the accidental burning of the annex in 47 B.C., and the deliberate firing of the Great Library by a Christian mob in the fifth century A.D., the librarian's own books went up in smoke. Tragically, so did his life's work, the *Pinakes.*

❖ POSTAL WORKER ❖

SADDLING UP TO GO POSTAL

"Deliver the letter, the sooner the better" was no big deal in ancient times—as long as you had "emperor" or "government official" after your name. The *cursus publicus,* established by Roman Emperor Augustus early in his reign (27 B.C.–A.D. 14), was the first Pony Express, a way to get mail, messages, and packages around a huge and growing empire.

In the emperor's initial scheme, postal carriers on foot ran in relays. Blisters proliferated, the supply of marathoners turned out to be finite, and runners were quickly replaced by a system of riders on horseback, moving from one posting station to the next, twenty or thirty miles away. Some were overnight stops, where sweaty postmen and their mounts could get watered and fed in relative comfort. Slower mail and heavier packages also traveled by the oxen-load.

A carrier made forty to fifty miles a day, on average. Augustus had even thought of Priority Mail service, called *cursus velax* or "speedy run." For urgent deliveries, the rider expended all energies to cover 125 miles or more a day. On some routes, the carrier drove a small cart carrying up to 1,500 pounds of mail, pulled by a pair of horses which could increase mileage to a blistering 170 miles a day. Regular road maintenance, by the army and by private benefactors whose names and deeds appeared on milestones, made the carrier's job easier. So did the point-to-point distance lists, which served as maps.

Although various government bureaucrats had the privilege of using the cursus publicus, this was by no means a postal service for the masses. Potentates, tyrants, and the wealthy didn't have to worry. They'd always had their own couriers, using slaves with high confidentiality ratings.

By and large, however, if the average Cassandra wanted to send a "Dear John" to someone, she'd go to the nearest port where ships were departing and ask around until she found someone headed in the direction of her letter.

This slow, sometimes indirect system worked surprisingly well. After all, the person delivering the letter would often have occasion to ask the same favor. Archaeologists have found stacks of delightful evidence: letters sent and received from angry housewives, lonely soldiers, homesick schoolboys, anxious businessmen, and girls dumping their boyfriends. (Back then, "can't we just be friends" letters and other Greek correspondence opened with "rejoice" and signed off by saying "be strong.")

The letters sent by this informal route, written on papyrus, rolled up and sealed with wax, had no need for stamps, envelopes, or even addresses, since the delivering party would be told which street and house to go to, e.g. "to Lucius who lives in Cyrene near the temple of Hera—you can't miss it. Oh, and mind the dog!"

By late imperial times, the grand system put into place by Augustus had weakened. As the number of government officials grew, the percentage using postal carriers for personal business also rose. Even worse was the growth of that newfangled Christian church. Its energetic clergymen were constantly on the move and even more constantly firing off letters and instructions, all of which brought the cursus publicus almost to its knees.

Despite abuse and misuse, postal carriers carried out their jobs until the empire crumbled around A.D. 476. In postal scope and efficiency, its like would not be seen again for a thousand years or more.

❖ TOPIARIUS ❖

MASTER OF PLANT DISGUISE

Any Roman who owned a country villa had a garden; whatever the size, their patch of green had to be filled with something—animal, vegetable, or mineral—that the neighbors would gnash their teeth over. A nice eel pond with a bronze statue of Saturn devouring his children, perhaps. Or one could dream big: a verdant zoo of a garden, filled with topiary beasts.

Although elegant homeowners lacked inspirational materials like *Homes and Gardens* magazine, it was easy for them to come up with grandiose ideas, since the groundwork would be carried out by their personal legions of gardening slaves.

Gardening posts had a hierarchy, however, with more specialists than weeds. The top of the tree? The prestigious *topiarius,* an artiste with the iron shears and the creator of such masterpieces as the box-hedge elephant. The art of topiary was introduced during the reign of Emperor Augustus by a certain Gaius Matius, said to have been the man to do the first clip job. Since he was a patrician and a buddy of the emperor, it's more likely that he directed rather than acted on the greenery.

Creating and maintaining a Roman pleasure garden took advanced skills. More than mere hedge-clippers, the topiarii served apprenticeships, learning the art of grafting, the secrets of root pruning to create dwarf trees, and other esoteric plant knowledge. As ancient inscriptions prove, many if not most topiary landscapers were freedmen.

The tools of the trade were simple implements that would look at home in modern tool sheds: pitchforks, hoes, rakes, shears, and wooden shovels with iron lips.

Then as now, any topiarius worth his pruning hook had his favorite plants, which he would insist upon using despite owner protests. Date palms and silver-leafed Jupiter's-beard bushes were a must. Ditto myrtle and bay trees, whose sweet-smelling foliage also provided garland material for dinner-party guests. Cypress? A must for making stiff green corridors and walkways.

All of this served to show off the *opus topiarium,* the art for which so many coins flowed into the expert's grubby hand. As master manipulator of limbs large and small, he could torture pine foliage into pyramids, roaring lions, or even the letters of the Latin alphabet. Some giants of topiary even managed to convert cypress groves into fleets of ships and hunting scenes. Contrived to the max; but that was the point. Plants and trees running amok, au naturel—ugh! that wasn't the Roman idea of a nice garden.

Good gardeners were a rare commodity about whom villa owners intent on topiary magnificence were tight-lipped. As a result, the elite topiarius had negotiating clout. He might even achieve a certain evergreen immortality, being allowed on occasion to sign his name in shrubbery. More permanent proof of horticultural success came post-mortem: the dignified bragging on numerous tombs left by topiarii and the members of their very own family trees.

❖ ANOINTER ❖

PROUD TO HAVE SLIPPERY CUSTOMERS

Unctuous employees? Look no further than the thermae, the Roman public baths. At them, male and female *unctores* or anointers operated on a walk-in basis. For nearly five squeaky-clean centuries, everyone from slave to senior official took a daily plunge with a sponge at the thermae (or at smaller establishments called balnae), located in every self-respecting town and city of the Roman Empire.

Many baths were free, subsidized by philanthropists. Even the ones that charged for entry cost about one quarter of the smallest Roman coin; entrance for slaves was sometimes paid for by their owners.

Rome had more creature comforts than many a modern nation. What it didn't have was soap or shampoo. Instead, bathers had a cleansing routine that sounds a bit gritty but clearly did the job. At its heart was virgin olive oil, lots of it, sometimes scented with jasmine or saffron, other times rubbed on straight.

Besides giving oil rubdowns, anointers did body massage with other unguents, applied cosmetics and potions thought to heal (which the baths charged for), offered advice on nutrition, and even suggested light exercises. Greeks had always believed in preventive medicine; Romans followed suit. This was wise, because Greco-Roman pharmaceuticals and physicians left a lot to be desired.

Although physicians from Celsus to Antonius Musa (top doc to Emperor Augustus) argued about the healing powers of hot baths versus cold, no one quibbled about the role played by the unctores. They were often called upon to anoint the sick as well as the healthy.

It had been traditional since earliest Greek times to rub athletes with oil before they went to the *palaestra* to wrestle. With the oil, the anointer mixed fine-grained sand (African was best) to close the pores and prevent excess sweat. After wrestling, the athlete got rubbed down again (oil now mixed with sand, wrestling dirt, and sweat—ouch), followed by a bath and a scrape-off with a curved tool called the *strigil*, which followed the lines of the body.

As daily bathing became mainstream for Roman citizens from Britain to Syria, these more athletic routines were modified. Most bath-goers first did some light exercise (a walk, a run, maybe a little handball to break a sweat), got massaged with oil in the *unctuarium* then bathed. The order could vary according to whim. Each facility held a series of rooms heated from warm to red-hot, and a series of baths and pools at temperatures from warm to cold. Sometimes the bather would get another oil massage after his last dip— meaning another tip for the anointer, most of whom were slaves or freedmen of both genders.

Bits and pieces of Roman public baths still stand, offering hints about the marvelous institutions they must have been. Mysteries still remain, however, about the enormous workforce they required—the third largest in the Empire. Further irksome questions about the army of anointers who oiled all those slippery customers await elucidation. How many gallons of oil did the anointers go through in a day? How much of it ended up in the waters of the baths? And the sixty-four-million-sesterce question: how did workers clean the waters—or did they?

❖ UNDERWEAR MAKER ❖
THE BOTTOM LINE

The study of Greco-Roman underwear and its underwear makers has been shamefully neglected, and the subject is still riddled with quaint nineteenth-century terms that create the wrong impression about the undergarments of yore.

Take the word *zona*, invariably translated as "girdle." You can't read a page of Homer without hearing about one goddess or another flinging off her girdle or being torn out of it.

In modern English, "girdle" summons up those rubbery pink foundation garments that grandmas half a century ago used to wear. In actuality, the zona was a wide belt, tied outside the tunic or long gown, a handy device in which to tuck the ends of your flowing garments while working or attending a call of nature. The only sexy thing about them occurred on a bride's wedding day, when she wore a zona tied in a complicated Hercules knot—an intimacy "road test" for her new husband to unravel.

So what did folks of long ago wear under their togas, tunics, and cloaks?

Female underpinnings were the most complex. Topside, they used various sorts of breast supporters. A richly endowed woman who wanted to minimize cleavage put on one of two kinds of bosom binder. Then came an under-tunic of wool, sometimes topped with a leather *strophium* over the breasts. Outside their clothing, younger gals often tied a *cingulum* sash below their boobs. It had the same goals as a modern bra: to uplift and draw attention to their shape.

Undergarment specialists had little to work with when it came to women's panties. They were disappointingly slapdash, more of a wrap-around loincloth affair. In cold weather, women sometimes donned thigh-length woolen knickers. Cheeky, they weren't.

Although the average lingerie worker limped along, whipping up bosom binders and the occasional silk chemise, concepts like peekaboo styles and fun colors were completely missing from intimate wear for gals.

The situation was even more sobering for men's briefs. Roman males swore by decency, believing it could only be achieved by layering and complete body coverage except for the hands and head. Under the toga, they threw on several long shirts or tunics and a sturdy pair of knee-length linen drawers.

There were exceptions: workers in low-status jobs sweated away in skimpy loincloths, cinched up with belts. Entertainers like acrobats and jugglers wore tight-fitting briefs that kept them from displaying more than their skills.

Greek males, at least before Roman rule came along, were more into body display. Most men spent their days clad in a *himation*, or what amounted to a bedsheet. Conservative fellows often wore nothing under it, if we are to believe the accuracy of those Greek vases. On dressier occasions, men might wear tunic undershirts and loincloths too.

Athletes competing or working out at the gymnasium did so naked. Elsewhere, to be *nudus* or completely naked was contemptible—and very low-class. Greeks and Romans both used the word as a synonym for common laborer.

Clearly, underwear makers and their modest wares were aimed at the upwardly mobile—and the already-arrived.

❖ CENSUS TAKER ❖
WHOLE LOTTA COUNTING
& CACKLING GOIN' ON

Some positions involved the weirdest array of duties. That's what happened to the well-respected post of Roman censor, which began back in 440 B.C.

At first, the job wasn't that bizarre. As elected officials, the censors pretty much stuck to counting and cleansing. Every fifth year, they took the census. Even without computerized data-swapping, the census was pretty nosy. The censor took down names, ages, household members, real-estate holdings, and other assets (he was especially interested in agricultural implements). He also demanded a person's net worth. All this let him determine your social class and your voting status. The census also revealed your tax liability, a foretaste of what you would soon owe.

After the censors finished, they couldn't relax with a goblet of wine. They had to stay on their feet to organize the *lustrum*, a ritual cleansing of Rome. At the ceremony, regular citizens milled around in the middle of

Mars Field, while a group of people with auspicious names, like Rich or Lucky, solemnly led the procession of priests, slaughtering assistants, and sacrificial victims. The animals about to get the ax were a boar, a bull, and a ram.

Once everyone had completed a circuit of the area, the beasts got sacrificed to Mars. Unlike other sacrifices, where a chunk of newly dead meat was offered to the gods and hungry humans got the rest of the barbecue, the lustrum combo had to be burnt to a crisp, a result officially called a *holocaust*. The censors then promised the gods an identical holocaust up the road, provided Rome got heavenly protection for the next five years.

These counting and cleansing tasks didn't seem burdensome enough, so additional duties were cooked up for those who loved wearing that adorable purple-trimmed toga. Censors began to monitor morals and public behavior; one by-the-book anal retentive expelled a man from the Roman Senate for kissing his wife in public—a terrible lapse.

In addition, censors had to put state-financed projects, like aqueducts and road repairs, out to tender. Then they were asked to work overtime, checking the account books of financial institutions. What was once a breeze of a job was turning into a real headache.

But the final straw that snapped the dromedary's back was when word came down about Juno's sacred geese. In 390 B.C., while Roman sentries and watchdogs slept, a flock of stalwart geese had cackled an alarm when barbarian Gauls attacked the citadel of Rome. Alerting the citizens, they had saved the city's goose, so to speak. Ever since that date, a flock had been kept in style at Juno's temple. They enjoyed a lovely view and nice digs atop one of Rome's hills. Someone, however, had to feed and care for the sacred birds. This being Rome, there had to be an overseer to supervise that someone. Who got the job? You guessed it.

❖ UNDERTAKER ❖

DYING TO DESIGNATE

Death being as reliable and as lucrative as taxes, the Greco-Roman funeral industry employed a large workforce of specialists, each shop run by a chief undertaker called the *designator*.

It didn't matter which cult you followed—or didn't. With the exception of mystery religions like Isis worship and that newcomer, Christianity, most put emphasis on doing right by the gods in this life. Even the poorest person longed to be properly disposed of, so his post-mortem spirit wouldn't bother the neighbors or haunt his survivors.

Greek and Roman cultures went through periods where burial, with or without coffins, was popular, alternating with periods where cremation was the only way to travel. The designator oversaw it all, including the funeral feast of broad beans, the send-off sacrifices of various animals, the grand procession, and the burial or cremation.

Cremation had the most elaborate packaging. The unembalmed body was first dressed in finery, then posed in a lifelike position on a fancy litter carried as the main float. The procession itself was a multi-media event, with musicians who played woodwind instruments as tall as themselves and professional mourners who expertly tore their hair and clawed their cheeks, all the while wailing. With them marched mime actors wearing wax death masks of the family ancestors, wisecracks being provided by the head impersonator of the dead man. Some parades also displayed the choicer possessions of the deceased to the avid crowd.

The procession eventually arrived at the funeral pyre, a sturdy structure of stacked logs. Rearranging the corpse and firing up the pyre were in the capable hands of the *ustor,* an undertaker underling. The next act was distressing from a twenty-first-century point of view. A fit young man, having led the deceased's favorite animals in the procession, systematically killed Old Shep and any other pets and threw them on the pyre to barbecue with their master or mistress.

257

Even the poorest Roman or Greek strove for a decent burial. The columbarium or dovecote communal tomb pigeon-holed a person for all eternity.

When everything had burned away, the fire was quenched with wine and the designator designated someone to place the ashes in an urn or directly into a tomb.

During the golden centuries of Athenian artistry, tombstones called *stelae* were carved or painted with some of the finest art ever made. Roman tombs were more self-aggrandizing. Multi-story tombs lined every road into the city, built in shapes and themes modern advertisers would envy. Many of the fascinating and beautiful details about the working lives of ordinary people in this book come from these tombs, put up at considerable expense by bakers, contractors, charioteers, and a myriad others.

Given the money thrown by the wealthy at their own funerals, the designator clearly made a bundle. But how did people fare at the other end of the economic spectrum? Even slaves and down-and-out folks belonged to burial clubs. They bought space in common sepulchers called *columbaria* or "dovecote graves," getting pigeonholed in death as well as in life.

Some had a philosophical, even jubilant attitude about their passing. One tomb inscription read: "Bones sweetly reposing, I'm not worried about starving, I don't suffer from arthritis, I'm not behind in the rent and in debt. In fact my lodgings are not only permanent—they're free as well!"

❖ FUNERAL CLOWN ❖

PAID TO MAKE MOURNERS MERRY

Think about it: who needs cheering up more than a crowd of mourners? That's what the Romans realized—and devised a job to fit the bill: funeral clown. The part of the dead man was played by an *archimimus*, the head of a mime troupe. (In Roman times, only the pantomime artists played silent roles, whereas mimes, male and female, had speaking parts.)

As troupe leader, the archimimus was usually its manager and often its lead actor. Mime companies performed for audiences at theatrical venues and in private homes. The best troupes had plenty of jobs that didn't involve cadavers. Traditionally, however, actors have always hated to turn down paying gigs.

Funerals for the highborn were amply rewarded, showy affairs. The most fortunate of clowns got coveted roles, such as playing a Roman emperor.

At the death in A.D. 79 of Emperor Vespasian, a well-liked but notoriously stingy ruler, an archimimus named Favor got the part of playing the deceased. During the funeral procession, Favor/Vespasian anxiously asked what "his" funeral rites were going to cost. Told that the bill would reach ten million sesterces, Favor shrieked and said, "Just give me a hundred thousand and throw me into the Tiber River!"[*]

The mime's whole task was to create an eerily accurate impersonation of the corpse. No one's completely sure why, but possibly the idea was to placate ancestral spirits as well as lighten the funerary gloom. To do his job, the funeral clown wore the newly deceased's clothing along with his insignia of high office. He also donned a death mask of the man's likeness.

As the procession, corpse included, moved from the house along a parade route to the funeral pyre, the funeral clown was surrounded by other mimes, who did jigs and slapstick along the route. All the while, the funeral clown did his best shtick of the deceased's mannerisms, speech idiosyncrasies, and gait. Gives a whole different feel to the phrase "dead man walking," doesn't it?

---

[*] The funeral clown's remark is funnier when you know, as every Roman did, that patricides and certain other criminals got thrown into the Tiber River, first tied inside a leather sack with a cat, snake, dog, or other live animals.

BIBLIOGRAPHY

Much of the real juice for this book comes from my thirty-year prowl through the works of ancient writers, Greek and Roman. Most are available in one of three series: the Harvard Loeb Classical Library, the Penguin Classics, and the Modern Library.

Regarding jobs and the people who held them, the most useful ancient authors are: Aristophanes, Athenaeus, Aristides, Cicero, Dio Cassius, Diogenes Laertius, Herodotus, Josephus, Julius Caesar, Juvenal, Martial, Pausanias, Petronius, Plato, Pliny the Elder, Pliny the Younger, Plutarch, Seneca, Strabo, Suetonius, Tacitus, Vitruvius, and Xenophon.

Other core material comes from non-literary sources, including ancient coins, tomb inscriptions, and artwork; letters of the period; and archaeological finds, reports, and periodicals. The volumes called *Select Papyri* from the Loeb Classical Library offer great source materials on workers, wages, and jobs.

Although the two books mentioned with this paragraph are out of print, these grand old treasures are available from online sources. In addition, much of the Smith volume—and many ancient works from Augustus to Vitruvius—appear on Bill Thayer's Lacus Curtius website, a marvelous public service and labor of love at: http://penelope.uchicago.edu/Thayer

Rich, Anthony. *A Dictionary of Roman and Greek Antiquities.* (Longmans, Green, 1890.) 756 pp.

Smith, William. *Dictionary of Greek and Roman Antiquities.* 2nd edition. (Little, Brown, 1859.) 1,294 pp.

In addition, there are many praiseworthy secondary sources that focus on a specific area of the working world, from the making of mosaics to the mind-boggling array of ancient deities and workers who served them, including the following:

Adkins, Lesley and Roy. *Dictionary of Roman Religion*. (Oxford University Press, 1996.)

Balsdon, J.P.V.D. *Life and Leisure in Ancient Rome*. (Phoenix Press, 2002.)

Brumbaugh, Robert. *Ancient Greek Gadgets and Machines*. (Thomas Crowell, 1966.)

Casson, Lionel. *Travel in the Ancient World*. (Johns Hopkins University Press, 1994.)

Champlin, Edward. *Final Judgments*. (University of California Press, 1991.)

Connolly, Peter. *The Ancient City*. (Oxford University Press, 1998.)

Dalby, Andrew. *Siren Feasts, a History of Food and Gastronomy in Greece*. (Routledge, 1996.)

de Camp, L. Sprague. *The Ancient Engineers*. (Ballantine Books, 1974.)

Dupont, Florence. *Daily Life in Ancient Rome*. (Blackwell, 1992.)

Finley, M. I. *The Ancient Economy*. (University of California Press, 1973.)

Grant, Michael. *Greek & Roman Historians: Information and Misinformation*. (Routledge, 1995.)

Greene, Kevin. *The Archaeology of the Roman Economy*. (University of California Press, 1990.)

Hooper, Finley, and Schwartz, Matthew. *Roman Letters*. (Wayne State University Press, 1991.)

James, Peter, and Thorpe, Nick. *Ancient Inventions*. (Ballantine, 1994.)

Jennison, George. *Animals for Show and Pleasure in Ancient Rome*. (University of Pennsylvania Press, 2005.)

Keuls, Eva. *The Reign of the Phallus*. (Harper & Row, 1985.)

Majno, Guido, M.D. *The Healing Hand*. (Harvard University Press, 1975.)

Meltzer, Milton. *Slavery, a World History*. (Da Capo Press, 1993.)

Ormerod, H.A. *Piracy in the Ancient World*. (Liverpool University Press, 1978.)

Potter, D.S., and Mattingly, D.J., eds. *Life, Death, and Entertainment in the Roman Empire*. (University of Michigan Press, 1999.)

Roebuck, Carl, ed. *The Muses at Work*. (MIT Press, 1969.)

Shelton, Jo-Ann. *As the Romans Did: A Source Book*. (Oxford University Press, 1988.)

Strong, Donald, and Brown, David. *Roman Crafts*. (Duckworth, 1976.)

Young, David C. *The Olympic Myth of Greek Amateur Athletics*. (Ares, 1984.)

INDEX